TERRAPSYCHOLOGICAL INQUIRY

Terrapsychological Inquiry is a path of storied, imaginative research that takes seriously our intense inner responses to the state of the natural world. This place-rooted approach studies, from the standpoint of lived experience, how the world gets into the heart. Oceans and skies, trees and hills, rivers and soils, and even built things like houses, cities, ports, and planes: How do they show up for us inwardly? How do our moods, feelings, and dreams reflect what happens in the world?

Terrapsychological Inquiry evolved over a decade of exploration by graduate students, instructors, ceremonialists, workshop leaders and presenters, and other practitioners of embodied creativity to offer an Earth-honoring mode of storied qualitative inquiry, one that transforms all involved from passive spectators of the doings of the world into active, sensitive participants. Learn how to use this methodology of earthly reenchantment in a variety of settings inside and outside academia and by doing so reenter an animate world. This new edition has been revised throughout and offers fresh insights into how Terrapsychological Inquiry, a field with roots in depth psychology, ecopsychology, and Hermetic philosophy, can also be used as an ecospiritual path.

Thoroughly updated with a new chapter and added discussion questions and exercises at the end of each chapter, this introduction to an evolving research methodology will be of great interest to students and scholars of environmental psychology, ecotherapy, and environment and sustainability studies more generally.

Craig Chalquist, PhD, is a professor, administrator, consultant, and lecturer, who teaches and writes at the intersection of consciousness, place, story, and imagination. He is program director of Consciousness, Psychology, and Transformation at National University, USA. Visit his website, Chalquist.com.

Praise from the First Edition

"While psychology has taught us how to understand the ways our family has shaped us psychologically, it has neglected how the places we inhabit also profoundly create our psychic space. How are we to get to know – *really know* – the places our lives unfold in and that are inextricably woven into our memories, thoughts, and images? How do we develop our relationship with a place so that its unconscious layers begin to reveal themselves to us? Let Craig Chalquist be your guide. He has devoted himself to these tasks over several decades. In this insightful book he crystallizes what he has learned so that others can launch their own inquiries into the places that matter to them. As you explore terrapsychological inquiry, stand on his shoulders and tell us what you come to understand!"

Mary Watkins, *PhD Chair, Depth Psychology MA/PhD Depth Psychology Program, Pacifica Graduate Institute. Author of* Mutual Accompaniment and the Creation of the Commons. *Co-author of* Toward Psychologies of Liberation

"An important new guide for all who struggle to find original, creative ways of understanding and addressing this critical moment in human-nature relations. The denial of subjective experience – in humans and other Earthly beings – by conventional psychology has been the ultimate modern absurdity, aptly described by Craig Chalquist as the delusion that 'jumping off a bridge to go swimming [is] no different from jumping off a bridge to commit suicide.' This narrowly limiting, Procrustean approach is part of the reason we now find ourselves tone deaf to Earth's warnings and cries. Chalquist's beautifully written *Terrapsychological Inquiry* offers us a creative way forward as we relearn deep listening and resonance with all that is."

Linda Buzzell, *co-editor,* Ecotherapy: Healing with Nature in Mind

TERRAPSYCHOLOGICAL INQUIRY

Restorying Our Relationship with Nature, Place, and Planet

Second edition

Craig Chalquist

Routledge
Taylor & Francis Group
LONDON AND NEW YORK

earthscan
from Routledge

Designed cover image: © Getty Images

Second edition published 2024
by Routledge
4 Park Square, Milton Park, Abingdon, Oxon, OX14 4RN

and by Routledge
605 Third Avenue, New York, NY 10158

Routledge is an imprint of the Taylor & Francis Group, an informa business

First edition published by Routledge 2020

British Library Cataloguing-in-Publication Data
A catalogue record for this book is available from the British Library

Library of Congress Cataloging-in-Publication Data
Names: Chalquist, Craig, author.
Title: Terrapsychological inquiry : restorying our relationship with nature, place and planet / Craig Chalquist.
Description: Second edition. | Abingdon, Oxon ; New York, NY : Routledge, 2024. | "First edition published by Routledge 2020"—Title page verso. | Includes bibliographical references and index.
Identifiers: LCCN 2023035762 (print) | LCCN 2023035763 (ebook) | ISBN 9781032612959 (hardback) | ISBN 9781032612942 (paperback) | ISBN 9781003462965 (ebook)
Subjects: LCSH: Environmental psychology.
Classification: LCC BF353 .C49 2024 (print) | LCC BF353 (ebook) | DDC 155.9/1—dc23/eng/20230824
LC record available at https://lccn.loc.gov/2023035762
LC ebook record available at https://lccn.loc.gov/2023035763

ISBN: 978-1-032-61295-9 (hbk)
ISBN: 978-1-032-61294-2 (pbk)
ISBN: 978-1-003-46296-5 (ebk)

DOI: 10.4324/9781003462965

Typeset in Sabon
by codeMantra

CONTENTS

FIGURES

FOREWORD

Elizabeth Nelson

It is fitting that a book describing an Earth-focused method of narrative research should begin with a story. Procrustes, an exacting archetypal figure, would delight in chopping the legs from under complex qualitative approaches for the sake of *scientism*: the narrow and misguided belief that anything worthy of attention can be measured, weighed, quantified. The book in your hands puts Procrustes in his place or, rather, like the wily Theseus, exposes Procrustes to his own method. In doing so, it illustrates what any competent research methodology must remember about itself: it is a tool that reveals some things while concealing others. Worthwhile research is both thorough in its process and humble in its claims.

Terrapsychological Inquiry (TI) is a growing field of studies, ideas, and practices for reimagining and narrating how deeply and intimately psychological life is involved with one's surroundings, whether human or other than human. It reveals the importance of something that numerous qualitative researchers who work in naturalistic settings easily forget. All inquiry is permeated by its place, the idiosyncratic *where* and *when* of the study. *Place* matters. It grounds the questions of *who, what*, and *how*. TI not only reminds researchers of where and when but also draws on ancient animistic traditions, reinvigorated in contemporary depth psychology and ecospirituality, to listen closely and respectfully to the voice of place and interweave its story with the human story. Place, Craig Chalquist tells us, includes climate, geology, plants, and animals, who are "full partners whose influences we learn to sense and work with, dance with, appreciate, be challenged by, and love" (p. 3). In conducting TI, researchers are obligated to pay attention to all of the elements of place with their entire being, living the central question of the study in an integrated, embodied, and holistic manner. In the process, they discover that place and person have much to say to one another.

Place and person not only speak to one another but also shape one another. Depth psychological research, one of the intellectual streams feeding TI, explicitly acknowledges such mutuality: what we study studies us. In one of Jung's many references to the creative process, he asserts, "It is not Goethe who creates *Faust*, but *Faust* who creates Goethe" (Jung, 1966, p. 103). Take this as a reminder, a warning, or an inspiration – or all three. In rigorous psychological inquiry, it is an inescapable fact. The challenge for researchers is to commit to the dynamic, living relationship between themselves and the participants in the study, which crucially includes the living voice of place.

Researchers who have engaged in TI have discovered that it is an initiatory journey, not transforming the person so much as performing the alchemical operation of *transmutation*. The relationship of researcher and place manifests during the life of the study and well beyond it, just as the adept, his *soror mystica*, and the *prima materia* worked on one another in the alchemical opus. The relationship between researcher and place is also a microcosm, a portrait in miniature, of the participatory cosmos valued by Jungian and archetypal depth psychologies, transpersonal psychologies, and ecopsychology. "What feels personal often links to what is collective, earthly, and even planetary and cosmic," says Chalquist (p. 000). TI at its best discovers this link, and expresses it, in a capacious narrative context. Moreover, it reminds those touched by the study – researcher, participants, readers, witnesses – to cherish the Earth and all beings that it sustains.

Although this book seldom uses the words *eros* or *erotics*, the method can only succeed when researchers are willing to strip their masks, particularly the mask of scientism that valorizes remote objectivity, and instead follow their animal noses. Thus, the reader can sniff out the influence of James Hillman's emphasis on *aesthesis*, the thought of the heart, "which ties the individual soul immediately with the world soul" and in which "I am animated by its anima, like an animal" (1992, p. 105). TI also recalls Robert Romanyshyn's *cardiognosis*, a term borrowed from Christian mysticism, which describes an intimate and mournful knowing that "gives presence and voice to what is otherwise silent or forgotten" (1992, p. xxii). Finally, the method is inspired by *The Art of Inquiry: A Depth Psychological Perspective* first published in 2004, in which Coppin and Nelson liken the researcher to the lover whose exploration leads to "close kinship bonds with other humans, with animals, and with forests, rivers, and mountains" (2017, p. 19). Terry Tempest Williams poetically expresses the imperative to become lovers of our place on the Earth, and the Earth itself, in her 1995 work *An Unspoken Hunger: Stories from the Field*:

It is time for us to take off our masks, to step out from behind our personas – whatever they might be: educators, activists, biologists, geologists, writers, farmers, ranchers, and bureaucrats – and admit we are lovers, engaged in erotics of place. Loving the land. Honoring its mysteries. Acknowledging, embracing the spirit of place – there is nothing more legitimate and there is nothing more true.

She adds a simple declaration, "That is why we are here. That is why we do what we do" (Williams, 1995, p. 84). TI shows us a robust, systematic, and sensitive way of engaging the erotics of place.

There are many things to admire in this book. Among others, Chalquist stays true to his methodological emphasis on place by doing a masterful job of placing TI in the tradition of qualitative methodology. He also places TI ontologically and epistemologically, tracing its philosophical commitments in detail and revealing the breadth of disciplines it draws from. He places readers deeply in the process, drawing on examples from those who have followed the method to describe the steps of TI, fully aware of the intricate and complex life of scholarly research. He places in front of them two crucial questions: What emerges when one listens, imagines, and nurtures the felt sense of the rich intersections of setting, psyche, story, symbol, body, and mood? What emerges when the presence of world occupies the center of psychology? Finally, and perhaps most importantly, Chalquist asserts the many creative ways, beyond a formal thesis or dissertation, that the results of TI can find its place in the world.

Elizabeth Nelson, Ph.D.

References

Coppin, J., & Nelson, E. (2017). The art of inquiry: A depth psychological perspective (3rd edn). Thompson, CT: Spring Publications.

Hillman, J. (1992). The thought of the heart and the soul of the world. Dallas, TX: Spring Publications.

Jung, C. G. (1966). The spirit in man, art, and literature. Princeton, NJ: Princeton University Press.

Romanyshyn, R. (1992). Ways of the heart: Essays toward an imaginal psychology. Pittsburg, PA: Trivium Publications.

Williams, T. T. (1995). An unspoken hunger: Stories from the field. New York, NY: Vintage.

ACKNOWLEDGMENTS

My thanks to Rosie Anderson and Matthew Shobbrook at Routledge for their wise guidance with the second edition.

I would also like to thank Elizabeth Nelson for her fine foreword and for years of stimulating research collaboration; Mary Watkins, who as chair of my dissertation committee of so long ago gave me permission to explore what I needed; Ed Casey for his work and encouragement; the memory of James Hillman, whose comments were invaluable during my work on my dissertation; my terrapsychology colleagues Matt Cochran, Laura Mitchell, Maggie Hippman, C. K. Olivieri, Kevin Filocamo, Garrett Barnwell, Phoenix Smith, Annabelle Berrios, Kaeti Humphrey, Sarah Rankin, Michael Haber, Lola McCrary, and Amanda Leetch; and, most of all, my students, whose work continues to advance the inquiry beyond anything I could have envisioned.

Preface to the Second Edition

The publisher's invitation to prepare a second edition of *Terrapsychological Inquiry* gives me a welcome opportunity to outline this edition's changes, reflect briefly on how the field has changed over time, and speculate about where it might go.

This new edition features an added final chapter on the uses of terrapsychology for activism and for developing a life-path of wisdom and reenchantment. This is partly at the request of enthusiastic readers and partly because of a shift in my own interests toward the uses of terrapsychology for practical philosophy and ecospirituality. I have also explained in more detail how terrapsychology is different from ecopsychology, one of its parent fields, despite similar premises and concerns.

Although I wrote this book mainly as an introduction to our Earth-honoring qualitative research methodology, the work won't stay in the classroom. New material throughout the book assists the non-academic explorer of the presences of place, nature, and the things of the world as they intertwine so intimately with our moods, dreams, complexes, and sense of self. Terrapsychology could be summed up thus: we are always in the discourse of *here*.

Terrapsychology began as an inquiry back in 2000 about how the presence of place – not only the soil, flora, fauna, geology, and region but also the built environment – shows up as human psychology. Although I named the field, Lali Mitchell and Matt Cochran and I were all doing similar deep-place work at the time. Since then, the work has spread to over forty academic studies (master's and Ph.D.), various workshops and festivals, and a series of books, another of which comes out soon: the edited volume *Terrapsychology: Further Inquiry into Self, Place, and Planet*, a follow-up to the 2010 volume *Rebearths*. All the contributors, including co-editor Garret Barnwell, have used TI in a variety of settings.

Although I and others have suggested wider terrapsychological explorations into areas such as ancestry and family dynamics, activism, and applied mythology, the field as its own kind of psychical entity has persistently tied itself to places, whether they be one's home, a street, a neighborhood, a valley, a watershed, or even Earth as a whole. The field itself has taught me that this remains core to its identity.

I'm not sure going mainstream ever will be. As explained in the first part of the book, terrapsychology remains rooted in qualitative inquiry, which means focused on experience, metaphor, story, and other interior and relational realms explored by the humanities.

When TI does work quantitatively, it looks for symbols in the statistics and nuances in the numbers. It will never be an exact science because the physical science paradigm that entrances mainstream psychology was designed to lessen, bypass, or diminish subjectivity, whereas subjective perception is one of our primary tools. Terrapsychological work is certainly not anti-science, but it definitely opposes scientism, the ideology that knowledge of reality comes only from what can be studied with physical science. This bias provides academic job security for Procrustes.

Whither terrapsychology, then? That depends on how you and other readers resonate with and apply its methods and ideas. Overall, perhaps the future of place-based research belongs not to methods out to prove how separate parts interact but to forms of inquiry that delight in the world's unpredictable aliveness.

At the end of the book, I indulge my speculations about the uses of terrapsychology as a gnosis of imagination: a way of knowing the enspirited world through the gifts of storytelling, inspiration, and even fantasy. Many of us terrapsychologize every day, so why not consider it a part of our spiritual path?

While driving home pondering this course of action – too speculative? Not secular enough for research? – someone threw a small green ball out a car window. It bounced across the highway and landed near my home. In the Jungian view, this might constitute a synchronicity: a meaningful coincidence which Jung framed as a kind of undiscovered natural law. But I have come to wonder – fantasize – that such are nods or gestures from the place where we mull our concerns. Either way, I accept this playful symbol as a green light to proceed.

Fillmore, CA
Summer 2023

INTRODUCTION

Inquiry as Response to the Animate World

A tricky old blacksmith-turned-innkeeper indulged in a lethal hobby. When guests stayed at his inn for the night, he measured their legs. If longer than his beds, he chopped off the offending members so they fit. If shorter, he stretched them to make them fit. One day, he tried this routine with the wrong wayfarer. The man strapped the innkeeper to his own bed and applied the house amenities. This traveller was Theseus, slayer of monsters, and his would-be right-sizer was a villain whose name was Procrustes ("Stretcher"). He also went by Damastes ("Restrainer") and Polypemon ("Many-Hurting").

Mythic motifs never die, and neither has the innkeeper. He reappears inwardly as the inner critic ready to chop up "impractical" imaginative musings. He trolls online science articles for not exhibiting his mythically high standards of rigor. He haunts academia, ready to subdue creative research ideas by subordinating them to the very methods and methodologies first devised to serve them. You might have met him in the shape of a ruthless inner critic who tears down your best ideas and tries to convince you they are worthless.

At its most metallic, the shrill Procrustean voice declares all inquiry not built out of numbers and scales unfit to be called exploration, let alone research. In 1830, Auguste Comte, French thinker and Procrustes follower, argued three years after jumping off the Pont des Arts and surviving that only what is verifiable is worth knowing. Mainstream psychology instructors still fly his flag, especially in the United States, land of flagolatry. Addiction to certainty: ever the unreachable leap of the terminally anxious. Like all addictions, it can never be satisfied.

Despite occasional plunges into the chilly waters of Procrustean perfectionism, genuine science has taught us that sustained inquiry into what fascinates us must be rigorous to compensate for our blind spots. Among these

DOI: 10.4324/9781003462965-1

must be included the failure to notice how natural science methods cling to the surface of things: witness behaviorism, for which, in the absence of a bathing suit, jumping off a bridge to go swimming was no different from jumping off a bridge to commit suicide. Jumping is what the behaviorist should study, not motives. But turning what we inquire about into objects narrows our view of them.

The problem is not the narrow view but that we forget it is narrow. We then succumb not to science, but to *scientism*, the ideology that objective physical science is the best and only way to know reality.

> One of the great sleights of hand that scientism has pulled off is to convince the unthinking public that the thin, bare, poor world that it abstracts from – i.e. "pulls out of" – our thick, luxuriant, rich world is the "really real" world, the one that "objectively exists," while the one we encounter and love and struggle with is a kind of subjective illusion, housed within our individual island consciousness. It manages this trick solely because of the practical effectiveness it provides.
>
> *(Lachmann, 2018, pp. 23–24)*

How can we widen our view and get alongside things? How might we explore with some degree of rigor the depths of lived experience in the world that continually shows up for us and within us?

Qualitative research evolved to seek in-depth understanding, in natural settings, of how we relate to ourselves and each other. This kind of research welcomes questions of meaning and experience, subjectivity and value, *why* rather than merely what or how. Instead of being treated as passive objects of study, participants work with the researcher, and thereby keep their legs.

Unfortunately, even in qualitative research, the screech of Procrustes persists. There it is, demanding imperiously that all our exploratory labors *must* end up as a case study, a Grounded Theory, a phenomenological analysis, a theoretical study, an ethnography, or a narrative analysis. But what if these methodologies, even when collaged together, do not fit a topic?

Furthermore, they and others like them were designed to study human interactions. Around us, however, breathes and moves the natural world where we evolved and with which we stay in unconscious conversation all our lives. A world, alas, in sharp ecological decline thanks largely to the scientific might of our species, a might uncoupled from the kind of disparaged conversational sensitivities that would let us love where we live.

More than a decade ago, I began teaching and writing (2007) about Terrapsychological Inquiry (TI), an approach for graduate students of psychology, ecopsychology, and the humanities seeking an Earth-honoring set of tools for studying how we interact with the places where we live, including with their geology and climate, plant and animal life, infrastructure and history: the rich, busy complexity of our profound but disregarded embodiment in locale. *Terra* is an ancient name for Earth, and, for us, it means "here." *Psychology* once referred to the study, account, or narrative (*-logy*) of soul, mind, spirit, life (*psyche*). Might it once again, renewed by being reconnected to what lives beyond the human skull?

From the start, terrapsychological research into the complexities of place, psychology, and inner life moved both outside and inside of the academic world, carried out by both students and nonstudents. On the outside, in Boulder, Utah, Matthew Cochran led public terrapsychological education groups and exercises for locals seeking more sensitivity to the presence or "soul" of that place (2018). In San Diego County, Lali Mitchell studied Indigenous petroglyph techniques and taught artists to partner with natural settings to create art together; examples of this work appeared in her dissertation (2005). Katrina Davenport taught online participants in the TerraPlaces project how to record and reflect on the flora, fauna, geology, and local stories of the places where they lived (2010). Annabelle Berrios taught the public "embodied terrapsychology" at New York Open Center; "the goal of the practices was to transform habitual relationship patterns between people and places – from neglectful to attentive, and from competitive to collaborative – to reveal interdependent perspectives" (Berrios, personal communication, October 2, 2019). At Lake Fundudzi in South Africa, Garret Barnwell has used interviewing, art, ecotherapy, dream work, local folklore (including myth), conversation, and storytelling to work terrapsychologically with the wounds of first people whose lands were ravaged by apartheid-era deforestation (Barnwell, personal communication, September 10, 2019; published paper forthcoming). I am told that a Native Californian tribe in the northern part of the state employs a version of TI to tend dreams about their colonized ancestral lands in order to reassemble forgotten ecospiritual practices. Former holy places are "telling" the dreamers how to pray.

On the academic side, a student interested in the safety and kinship felt by LGBTQ citizens finding sanctuary in San Francisco used TI for her dissertation work at the California Institute of Integral Studies (Olivieri, 2017). Before her, a student in Utah noticed odd parallels between her changes of mood and the shifting ecological integrity of the Great Salt Lake and drew on TI for her academic project on this topic (Hippman, 2017). A master's project traced the growth and evolution of the Phoenix motif in Petaluma, California (Rankin, 2007). Yet another explored the embodied erotics of consciously and sensitively tuning into a park (Filocamo, 2008). A doctoral student wrote a dissertation on themes shared by the damaged San Lorenzo River in Santa Cruz and the life stories of drug addicts who live near it (Haber, 2019).

Those who practiced and played with the methodology gradually evolved it beyond an exclusive focus on place to add the felt presence of other aspects of the material world: how weather and climate patterns, insect and animal movements, plants and stones, elements and mountains and bodies of water, and even cities, bridges, neighborhoods, and everyday objects get into us psychologically as shifting moods, body states, relationship struggles, sudden joys, and revelations. We move, feel, and breathe to their contours, their textures, and their cycles without knowing it. But we can know it.

Nature, place, element, climate, geology, plants, animals, and biology are not mere backdrops to human concerns. No: they are full partners whose influences we learn to sense and work with, dance with, appreciate, be challenged by, and love. The key that opens the door to these human-and-more-than-human relationships is our dawning understanding of the stories we share with the living natural world, whether from a mountaintop, the middle of a river, a neighbor's backyard, Earth's orbit, or the heart of a glass and asphalt metropolis.

As we will see, the depth of knowledge we gain about what we inquire into depends on the kinds of stories we tell, and retell, about what we study – and about what studies us, what shapes us and has us in mind. Some of these stories are private. Others are shared, and still others look like ancient myths and folktales charged with new relevance for how they inform our inquiries.

Stories by which we understand our place in the world and how the world speaks to us carry a neglected dimension of our ecopsychological understanding: the symbolic. Symbols bridge the dimensions of outer and inner. Quantitative, outer-oriented research can indicate how rapidly our industries overheat the planet, for example, but the data have nothing to say about the metaphor of *internal combustion* as a psychosocial force in the friction between groups of angry people, let alone combusting within them. Biological science finds that certain soil bacteria enhance human health, but what about the symbolically meaningful etymological link between "human" and "humus"? "Tree" and "truth"? "Wind" and "spirit"?

As depth psychology – the field that studies how conscious and unconscious interact – has demonstrated for more than two centuries, our most objective plans and abstract concepts spring forth from our symbol-producing imagination. In this view, research is not just about the numbers but about our fantasy of what magical powers the numbers possess. Symbolization continually relates our consciousness to what we assume is outside us while keeping an inward root: mountain peaks of insight, rivers of flowing emotion, deserts of aridity, moody shadows, and oceanic depths. Thanks to symbols, what is outside is also, always, inside. Thanks to symbols, what feels personal often links to what is collective, earthly, and even planetary and cosmic.

This observed resonance between inner and outer parallels the core insight of ecopsychology, the discipline that puts psychology and ecology back together: *Human health depends on planetary health* (Roszak, Gomes, & Kanner, 1995, and since confirmed by an abundance of research). Deteriorating ecosystems make us crazy. Flourishing biodiversity awakens our senses, elevates mood, and harmonizes how we get along with each other. Human psychological life cannot be understood apart from where and how it is situated.

As my students and I study this, we find ourselves engaged in the work as whole persons, not just as brains on legs. Indeed, before our fantasies of objectivity cut self and body and world apart, in some sense *all* perception is enfleshed in a unity of observer and observed, and touch and being touched (Merleau-Ponty, 1968), a unity of embodied experience that Mitchell refers to as an eco-imaginal (2005, p. 6) "Earthmind" (2014, p. 109) of shared relationship. The presence of our planet participates deeply in the very act of perceiving it.

Instead of assuming that a disembodied intellect or the conscious mind alone can inquire or conduct research with any real adequacy, we monitor our moods, check in with our values, listen for informative dreams, watch not only what we write but how, explore our emotional defenses and rigid attitudes, probe how body states arise and shift in the field, meditate at length on what we learn. From each other we receive support and new ideas, fact and reality checks, directions to explore, insight into how personal complexes pop up, and advice on how to manage them.

We also remember to "play attention" (Leetch, 2017, p. 50) with our tasks, with the data, with our ideas about what is going on. Research without play succumbs to superegoic stiffness, to pretentious seriousness: to Procrustes, generous with his blade but miserly in spontaneity. He has mistaken the exploratory nose of inquiry for its verification backside – an olfactory-rectal inversion – and passed judgment on the former by imposing the standards of the latter. But at this stage of what we know, most terrapsychological work is exploratory. We follow our noses without the excessive and premature worry about exactly what can be quantified.

Inquiry with Earth in mind asks: *How shall I respond deeply, reflectively, creatively, and with integrity to how the world gets into my heart?* Heart not only as blood pump in the chest but also as ear in the breast, repository of felt images, resonator to being called forth, and rhythmic chamber in which introversion and extraversion, seeking and finding, knowing and wondering can alternate in a heartbeat. In research that calls us to participate fully and respond, we find ourselves moving from ego to eco, outgrowing the anxious need to freeze life into abstract facticity. We would rather listen to its pulse.

Inquiry then opens out into an initiatory journey for the researcher, whether academic or otherwise, as perceptions and perspectives shift. "Transformation" tends to be the preferred word in those inquiries and methodologies that emphasize it, but one can transform simply by putting on or taking off a hat. We refer instead to *transmutation*, an alchemical operation in which researcher and topic undergo lasting mutual change, in effect becoming an alloy brighter and more enduring than its constituting elements.

Terrapsychological inquirers often compare this metamorphosis to acquiring a set of extra senses attuned to the world's speech.

This book describes how to prepare for, design, carry out, reflect upon, write up, and present Earth-honoring qualitative research, whether formal or informal, through TI. Its ideas and practices can be used for academic research or the less strict sort outside the classroom. Instructors will find the book useful for courses that highlight the psychological side of ecology. Research classes can offer it as an alternative or supplement to the usual qualitative methodologies. Master's-project and dissertation-committee members will find guidance here when students decide to explore the intricately storied complexities of our deep relations with nature, place, and Earth. Examples of these explorations appear throughout the book. Activists and advocates should find "Managing Ecological Complexes" in Chapter 4 of interest for handling the stressful emotional undercurrents stirred by advocacy of injured ecosystems.

Chapter 1 answers the question of "What Is Terrapsychology?" by discussing its origins in depth-psychological and ecopsychological graduate work. We will see how a set of tools for clarifying the presence of place as a psychological dynamic evolved into a broader psychology of how we use story, myth, reflection, and dream for consciously reconnecting with the natural world.

Chapter 2, "Philosophy of the Methodology," discusses TI's ontology (theory of being), values, and commitments. This chapter places the methodology in its philosophical context and argues for a fresh consideration of animism, the sense of everything being alive and interactive, a disparaged perspective in the West but ancient and vital long before either urban civilization or the scientific method.

Chapter 3, "Preparing for the Work," examines the kinds of research projects suitable for TI, compares it to other qualitative methodologies, and assists with formulating the research question around which the entire study pivots. The chapter includes suggestions for bringing oneself to readiness for the research and describes tending symbol, dream, archetype, and myth as ways into deeper inquiry.

Chapter 4, "TI in Practice," outlines the key phases and methods and discusses how to start the study. Terrapsychological research emphasizes working consciously with what in psychotherapy is known as a *transference*: the strong emotional reactions that arise when we conduct deep work. We will also consider how to wrap up the study.

Chapter 5, "Analyzing the Data," offers a palette of tools, methods, and ideas for organizing and sifting the data collected during the study. The discussion introduces TI-style thematic analysis and the role of coding for sorting the harvest. This chapter is primarily for academic work; readers using TI for less formal inquiry can skim or skip it.

Chapter 6, "What the Findings Mean," provides guidance for making sense of what we have harvested. As we link themes into an overall interpretation, we ponder questions of reliability, validity, and relevance to understanding the deeper story within what our sources of research have yielded.

Chapter 7, "Sharing the Results – and Onward!" treats of bringing ourselves and our topic's story fully to voice. This storytelling phase may include rich imagery and offers an array of creative possibilities. We will also reflect on the importance of sharing the transmutative effects of our research results.

Chapter 8, "Terrapsychologizing for Life," explores the uses of terrapsychology for assembling one's own wisdom path. How might we move through life in a reanimated world, place by place? This chapter also looks at the implications of this for crafting an ecospiritual wisdom path.

The Glossary defines terrapsychological terms used throughout the text. Appendix I lists some of the common pitfalls of conducting research and how to avoid them. Appendix II provides a checklist for place assessment ("locianalysis"). Appendix III gives suggestions for creating a *heartstead*: an inquiry study and support group organized around a central inquiry question. Appendix IV offers a look at exploring deep ancestry for recurring issues and themes.

In working terrapsychologically, we remain open throughout to spontaneously arising mythic and archetypal motifs of collective fantasy; motifs that recur unbidden not only in our research but in our lives. These motifs are not so much things to factually pin down as fluid perspectives waiting in the wings for recognition. They haunt our endeavors like the presences of place haunt our lives and loves and dreams. Held with discernment, even Procrustes may prove useful in separating out what no longer serves, but only if we keep an eye on him. He does better in the watchful presence of Hermes, alchemical god of hermeneutics, the ancient art of interpretation.

To explore the depths of our ties to nature and place across threads of psyche and story uncovers unexpected riches woven into the thickening tapestries of our inquiries. The weave includes far more of our interior life than we could ever have known otherwise. Disturbing insights sometimes surface, as do many joyful surprises. All take their places in the tale as what seemed lost, exiled, or dead returns to life and animation, a wondrous new design held in a frame of reenchantment.

References

Chalquist, C. (2007). *Terrapsychology: Reengaging the soul of place*. New Orleans, LA: Spring Journal Books.

Cochran, M. (2018). Boulder is dreaming too: A mythic look at place. Presented to the Boulder Harvest Festival, Boulder, UT.

Davenport, K. (2010). TerraPlaces. Powers of Place Initiative. Retrieved from www.powersofplace.com

Filocamo, K. (2008). The alluring universe: Exploring an erotic relationship with the world (unpublished master's thesis). John F. Kennedy University, Pleasant Hill, CA.

Haber, M. (2019). Unattended trauma of the San Lorenzo River: A terrapsychological inquiry (unpublished dissertation). California Institute of Integral Studies, San Francisco, CA.

Hippman, M. (2017). The psychology of salt (unpublished master's thesis). Environmental Humanities Program, University of Utah, Salt Lake City, UT.

Lachmann, G. (2018). *Lost knowledge of the imagination*. Edinburgh: Floris.

Leetch, A. (2017). Weaving meaning: Terrapsychological inquiry and the historic industrial placefield of Lowell, Massachusetts (unpublished master's thesis). Prescott College, Prescott, AZ.

Merleau-Ponty, M. (1968). *The visible and the invisible*. Evanston, IL: Northwestern University Press.

Mitchell, L. (2005). The eco-imaginal underpinnings of community identity in Harmony Grove Valley: Unbinding the ecological imagination (unpublished dissertation). Pacifica Graduate Institute, Carpinteria, CA.

Mitchell, L. (2014). Nomadic dimensions of education with the earth-in-mind. In D. A. Vakoch & F. Castrillón (Eds.), *Ecopsychology, phenomenology, and the environment: The experience of nature* (pp. 109–126). New York, NY: Springer.

Olivieri, C. (2017). Your church, my bar! A terrapsychological inquiry of the relationship between queerspace and queer spirituality in San Francisco, California (unpublished dissertation). California Institute of Integral Studies, San Francisco, CA.

Rankin, S. (2007). A terrapsychological study of the psyche of Petaluma as found in the stories of the land and as mirrored by my own psyche (unpublished master's thesis). Sonoma State University, Rohnert Park, CA.

Roszak, T., Gomes, M., & Kanner, A. (Eds.) (1995). *Ecopsychology: Restoring the earth, healing the mind*. San Francisco, CA: Sierra Club Books.

1

WHAT IS TERRAPSYCHOLOGY?

"My Name Is San Diego"

When I informed my doctoral fieldwork adviser that I did not know what to study, she advised me to get to know the underside of San Diego, the city of my birth. I had been away for eighteen years and only recently returned to the county. As a student in a depth psychology program, I was required to do some kind of psychological work in the community. Teaming up with a local attorney, I volunteered to teach assertiveness and communication skills to parents on welfare. Although I believed in the value of this work, I felt I was missing something important.

As I worked that summer of the year 2000, I felt unaccountably defended and depressed. This mood infected a relationship that cracked under the strain and fell apart. The more I tried to ignore how militarized and overbuilt San Diego had grown in my absence – jets overhead, combat ships crowding the bay, soldiers in the streets, traffic everywhere – the deeper I fell into melancholy and guardedness. I failed to connect any of these outer events to my inner states until an unexpected dream linked these parallel dynamics.

In the dream, a feminine figure I took to be my ex-partner stood before me. Happy to see her, I called her by name, but she shook her head in disappointment. As I stared, her form altered: tougher, grimmer, and with a macabre frown running down her chin like a gash. I felt depressed and defensive just looking at her. No, this was not my former partner at all. When I asked for her name, she replied, "San Diego. My name is San Diego."

Upon awakening in astonishment, I began connecting the dots. This mood of gloomy defense, for example, reflected the militarization of the city since its founding, when its first building rose as a fort to fight off Native Californians

DOI: 10.4324/9781003462965-2

now oppressed in their own homeland. Down the decades, as army, navy, marines, and other armed forces moved in, the resulting dredging of San Diego Bay made it look from high above like a deepening frown. Seen from orbit, San Diego possesses a crone-like face, with Mission Bay eyes, Point Loma nose, and the bay for a grimacing mouth. My mood could not be mine alone, I realized with astonishment. It symbolically reflected the altered lay of the land. Trying to repress my sense of it had only strengthened the mood of frowning defense until it ricocheted throughout my life.

My next move was to call up Dr. Chellis Glendinning to ask for ecopsychology resources for understanding how the environmental trauma of a physical location could translate into metaphorically similar states of mind and mood. Since its formation in the mid-1990s, ecopsychology had studied how psychological and ecological health support one another. What kind of ecopsychology might illuminate these uncanny parallels of dream and depression, relationship and defense, ecology of place, and its fierce image addressing me from within?

None, she said. Indigenous animism, perhaps, of the kind I did not grow up with: that was about it. And even then animism tended not to link inner with outer; psychology was a Western discipline. If I wanted some kind of theory for researching what was resonating between me and San Diego, I would have to come up with one.

Not just for one city. After graduation, I realized that I wanted to explore and understand the presence or soul of California. I explored the state for eleven years, making tools as I went, and talking to people about their reactions to Californian places, then branched out to other locales.

Hearing the Soul of Place

By the time I published *Terrapsychology: Re-engaging the Soul of Place* (2007), I had collected many examples of how qualities of geographical sites reappeared within us as pieces of "our" psychology. By 2010, which saw publication of the anthology *Rebearths: Conversations with a World Ensouled*, there were more:

- A graduate student realizing that the writing style of her master's thesis – half-concentrated and anecdotal and half-linear and expansive – closely paralleled civic history and development in the city she was studying.
- A yoga instructor dreaming of her mother being stalked and violated in Flint, Michigan, where the water supply would be poisoned one day.
- San Diego, Paris, Moscow, New York City, Hong Kong, and other places showing up in dreams as characters who spoke accurately about themselves; a dream sign stating "POLLUTED" held over San Luis Obispo County, for example, site of broken sewers, invasive species, and underground oil spills at Avila Beach.

- The Garden of Eden imagery playing out in Sebastopol, California, where a dream figure named Evie (Eve) gently addressed me, a gardener, as Cain.
- The numbers "911" decanted from the New York Lottery on September 11, 2001.
- Spring Street, originally named "Primavera" (First View), site of these and many other Los Angeles firsts: first multistory building, first public school, first tall hotel housing the first mechanical elevator, first nightclub, first place motion picture contracts were signed, first city hall, first city jail, first brewery, first beer garden ... as though the street itself contained some invisible but persistent personality trait of "firstness."
- Kings" in Memphis, Tennessee, a city named after Egypt's royal capital: B. B. King, Martin Luther King Jr. (who died there), Elvis "the King" Presley, the Royal Court of Carnival, Johnny Cash ("King of Country"), King Curtis ...
- Matthew Cochran's discovery of petroglyphs resembling jets and bombs inscribed long ago at what was now a gunnery range in Three Rivers, New Mexico. Local tales describe Three Rivers as the house of the mythic Thunderbird.
- The presence of a vibrant gay community at the foot of Mount San Jacinto, whose name recalls Hyacinth, the athletic boy loved by the god Apollo.
- Inadvertent "continuities" in London, where the Public Cleansing Department was unknowingly built on the site of an old public privy, where Whittington Hospital stands over the former healing wells at Barnet, and where a sauna on Endell Street echoes an ancient bath. Road courses and curves often correspond to ancient Roman counterparts unmapped, invisible, and discovered only later (Ackroyd, 2009).

A graduate student who grew up in Wuhan wrote the following after thinking about the place's association with the COVID-19 pandemic:

The meeting of rivers means change and exchange. Humans who chose to settle down at the crossing of rivers thrive on water and wane on water. Rivers bring harvest and birth; rivers also bring flood and death. Rivers bring people, and people bring commerce and prosperity, but rivers also bring away people, for there will be just as many departures as there will be encounters. Of all the poetry that is produced on this land, the number of poems on the theme of departure and farewell is significant (Xuan Wen, 2020).

In Wuhan stands the Yellow Crane Tower, named after a red-crowned crane that left this world for another. Over 2,000 years, the tower has been destroyed by natural calamities and then rebuilt twelve times. These images of convergence, transition, death, departure, and rebirth seem thematically – not causally – relevant to the pandemic outbreak there.

Might animals "speak" an unconscious symbolic language, as when a grizzly bear enters a hospital emergency room at the moment a conservationist describes our species as entering the "emergency room" phase of its existence? How might we story it when gangs of rodents immobilize smog-spewing automobiles by chewing up their wiring? What about jelly fish who jam industrial plant intakes? Squirrels who short out power grids?

Another question: When imaginatively interpreted, do even storms and earthquakes seem to gesture or parody, like Hurricane Katrina invading one oil-rich gulf while American troops invaded another? Is it random or meaningful that the name of refinery-threatening Hurricane Wilma meant "Determined Protector"? That a big tornado touched down one year later on the same spot as a previous one – on World Environment Day? That Bay Area earthquakes frequently rattle through on anniversaries of prior earthquakes?

What allows us to read symbols like this? The nature lore and poetry of every land. Chinese and Indian thematic interpretations of land forms and the elements. The Book of Nature tradition in Christianity. American Transcendentalism. The Romantics, who blended the imagery of myth with that of the natural world. Pronouncements by Indigenous elders in cultures like that of the Yurok of California, who understood a whale stuck in the Klamath River in 2011 as a symbolic signal of accelerating ecological imbalance.

Depth psychologists knew long ago from examining symptoms, fantasies, mistakes, and dreams that conscious mental life rests on a foundation of unconscious fantasy, image, metaphor, and theme. Long before depth psychology, this imaginal dimension received abundant description by Plato and Neoplatonism, Suhrawardi, Ibn Arabi, Boehme, Blake, Avicenna, Ficino, Vico, Paracelsus, Goethe, Yeats, Coleridge, Gaston Bachelard, Kathleen Raine, Gilbert Durand, J. R. R. Tolkien, Owen Barfield, Hermann Hesse, Henri Corbin, and C. G. Jung, among so many others throughout history and across many cultures. *The mind is in the imagination rather than the imagination being in the mind.* This perennial insight allows novelists, dramatists, artists, naturalists, and poets to reveal richer wisdom about human nature than is available in academic textbooks on empirical psychology. Imagistic life is what makes cognition and its theories possible to begin with.

As for place: We have always gravitated intuitively toward locations that symbolize what we seek, whether mountaintops for peak experiences and higher views, deserts for clear skies and contemplative austerity, valleys for settling down and soul-searching, open plains for spacious thoughts, estuaries, bays, and river mouths for opening the mind to the rest of the world.

It is not that the features of such places *cause* our states of mind. The simple logic of cause and effect cannot serve the complexity of the relationship – or its nonduality; rather, geology, geography, and materiality also live as forms or styles of psychology. *Where* is where *we* begin. Mount Fuji is not only a basalt and andesite height but a psychospiritual height too, as those who built temples on its flanks understood. California is geologically new compared to the mainland and, as a site of major fault lines, restless and edgy like so many who live here. Its Bay Area opens on a vast estuary: an ecological *and* cultural gathering site characterized by diversity, productivity, and innovation.

Below we will consider terrapsychology's evolution from a deep study of place presence exclusively to a psychology of reenchantment of our relations not only to place but also to many aspects of the material world. First, we will position the approach as a field of study and practice in relation to like-minded fields.

A Widening and Deepening Inquiry

Terrapsychology represents an evolution of early psychologies and, later, ecopsychologies, that initially concentrated their researches and practices on individuals before eventually expanding attention to families and then ecosystems.

Early Nature-Honoring Psychologists

Although appreciation for our deep psychological ties to the natural world that birthed us has never been absent from psychology, that knowledge has had to live underground until recently, when the polar ice caps began to melt and allowed what was buried to surface. Repression of the nature dimension has been particularly stout in the United States, where the only social science data that have counted were those we could measure, a limitation reminiscent of the old Middle Eastern joke about the drunk searching for his wallet not where he dropped it but under a street lamp because the light was better there.

As a result, Gustav Fechner is known in textbooks as the father of physiological psychology, but not as a nature spiritualist who wrote under a pseudonym so his scientific colleagues would not deprive him of his livelihood. Fechner's eco work was partially resurrected by William James, an avid hiker who left psychology and its behavioral obsessions in disgust for philosophy, where he could publish all he wanted about consciousness and human nature. Wilhelm Wundt achieved acclaim for building the world's first psychological laboratory but not for insisting that psychology study the unity of inner and outer experience, embody emotion, and promote humanitarian community. Christine Ladd-Franklin was also a botanist and feminist. Margaret Floy Washburn studied animal consciousness and, scandalously, compared it to that of humans.

Through erasures and revisions, the science of soul flattened out into the science of surface. But Earth-honoring sensibilities persisted underground.

Deep Psychologies

Pierre Janet was a founder of depth psychology. A gardener, he favored metaphors of growth in his writings, most of which – like Fechner's – have never been translated into English. C. G. Jung, long considered too mystical to be taught in mainstream psychology programs, wrote about what we now call ecopsychology (Jung & Sabini, 2002), as did his one-time pupil Jane Hollister Wheelwright (1988). Widely disparaged Freud (1990) regarded the id, the instinctual base of the unconscious mind, as our primal mental link to the natural world. He was also the first animal-assisted therapist, with his dog often sitting in while he analyzed patients. He was known to take long walks outside with some of them. Although psychoanalysis after Freud largely ignored our inner connection to the natural world until recently, exceptions occurred – like Harold Searles (1960) warning about the psychologically disastrous impact of unregulated urbanization.

Expanding beyond depth psychology's emphasis on the shadowy and pathological, the organismic psychologies – humanistic, existential, and transpersonal – rose in the 1960s to study and strengthen consciousness-based capabilities like creativity, responsibility, love, and the unfolding of human potential.

Family Systems

Starting in the 1950s, psychotherapists and social workers began to see the family as an organism that resisted unexpected change even while doing its best to adapt to shifting circumstances and new developmental phases. Many of the family dynamics studied – feedback loops, boundary adjustments, repetitive interactions, legacies of wounding, regulations of emotional intensity, most of this unconscious – resembled ecosystem dynamics. Sense of self as understood by psychology continued to include ego, pathology, and individuality but had now broadened to relationships between people: families, then larger groups. See Appendix IV for more about how Family Systems informs Terrapsychological Inquiry (TI).

Ecopsychology and Ecotherapy

In the early 1990s, a group of San Francisco Bay Area psychologists, educators, and environmentalists met to inquire into why psychology and ecology had remained separate from one another. This group knew of the work of Professor Robert Greenway, a former Maslow student who took his own students out into the wilderness for extended exploratory trips, and of Indigenous societies that refused the madness of trying to split nature and culture.

From these conversations grew *ecopsychology*, the study of how to understand, heal, and enrich the psychological dimensions of our relations with the natural world from which we evolved (Roszak, Gomes, & Kanner, 1995). All ecopsychologists agree that the well-being of ecosystems is inseparable from that of human beings, and that "we too are part of nature" (Fisher, 2013).

Here are some of the premises of ecopsychology:

- The flourishing of human and nonhuman life is of intrinsic value.
- Human health and the health of nature go together. To be fully well and human, we need to live on a healthy world.
- Current industrial forces in society distract us from the organic roots of our nature even while selling us technological distractions manufactured by destroying nature.
- Although we usually misattribute it as purely personal, all of us now feel, if only through numbing, anxiety, nightmares, depressions, or symptoms, the pain of the Earth.
- One result of patriarchy is a delusional sense of independence from the natural world, as though we were masters of it instead of members of it.
- Ecopsychology seeks to heal the alienation of our relations with the natural world while calling for kinds of industrial and political reorganization that foster healthy interdependency and humane and just community.
- Part of this task of healing includes ensuring security and basic resources for people hit hardest by pollution, displacement from global warming, and other forms of environmental injustice.
- Alienation decreases when we face the task of grieving (Macy & Brown, 1998) all that we are losing to unnaturally high rates of extinction and habitat destruction while we strive to preserve what remains.
- New forms of Earth-honoring community experimented with around the world offer lessons for how to live with ourselves, each other, and nature in circles of mutual healing and appreciation.
- Most psychologies are psychologies of departure, of the lone ego moving through the world without attachment to tribe or place. To fully embody our lives here on Earth, we need psychologies of how to come home to our home world (Chalquist, 2013b).

The original ecopsychology anthology (Roszak et al., 1995) was long on ideas but short on practices. This changed with the publication of Howard Clinebell's book *Ecotherapy: Healing Ourselves, Healing the Earth* (1996).

Clinebell was a pastoral counselor and former Civil Rights activist who had marched with Martin Luther King Jr. Having grown up on a farm, he decided one day to take his clients outside for their counseling sessions. This had good results. In his book, he defined ecotherapy (which he also called "green therapy" and "Earth-centered therapy") as an approach for establishing healing relations with the Earth. He offered a number of methods for doing this, one of which was the telling of "Earth stories" about times when nature became real and influential. I have used this exercise with circles of students in many locations, including outdoors, and it can go deep quickly.

At the time Clinebell published his book, research on the beneficial effects of enhanced nature exposure – especially to plants and animals – was accumulating rapidly. Clinebell mentions healing modalities like horticultural therapy and animal-assisted therapy, but he is careful to emphasize the mutuality of healing between humans and other-than-humans. Ralph Metzner (1999, p. 8) coined "green psychology" to include Indigenous herbal and natural medicine, bioregionalism, ecofeminism, social ecology, ecopsychology, ecotheology, the neo-pagan revival, and other aspects of an increasingly ecological worldview.

In 2009, Linda Buzzell and I published *Ecotherapy: Healing with Nature in Mind*, a follow-up to both Clinebell and the first ecopsychology anthology. In the introduction, we defined ecotherapy as an umbrella term for nature-based methods of physical and psychological healing; ecotherapy includes reinvention of psychotherapy as if nature and the human-nature relationship mattered (Buzzell & Chalquist, 2009). Perceiving how what happens to nature for good or ill impacts people, and vice versa, leads to new methods of individual and community healing. We need not vision-quest, hike Everest, or camp in the backcountry to change our relationship with nature. Direct nature contact is so powerful that just the presence of a window in a patient's room can help them recover faster from surgery. Combat veterans, sexual-abuse survivors, people depressed or anxious (or both), dementia patients, combative teens, obese children, recovering addicts, and many others of us below our mental or physical best have moved toward greater calmness and health, heightened happiness, and increased vitality. How, then, to live together?

Ecocommunities

Ecosystems and their inhabitants are dying on every side as habitat destruction and climate change accelerate. Reconnecting consciously with the natural world, with insects, plants, animals, elements, and beloved landscapes, raises our relationship with it from unconscious, dissociated, and symptomatic to consciously responsible. What we love we cannot stand by and watch being ravaged.

Very often, oppressed communities bear the environmental brunt, as the work of Robert Bullard (2005) and others has underlined. Colonizers turn nature against the colonized; healers do the reverse, as my friend and colleague Phoenix Smith demonstrates when she goes outdoors with groups of Black excursionists born into a legacy of ecological trauma and works with them on what surfaces emotionally in them in need of healing. This also deeply changes how they perceive and live with the natural world.

Both ecopsychology and its application in ecotherapy must remain mindful of the deep shadow of the Western habit of splitting nature and the social, with the first offered as an antidote to the second. For too many people, "nature" does not mean scenic national parks but slave shacks, poor wages, or being sprayed with pesticides. As Pramod Parajuli (2001) of Nepal expresses it,

> Creating wilderness preserves designed to save the tigers or the rhinos will simply be cosmetic dressing and museum displays unless these projects also save the fisherfolk, forest dwellers, and peasants with whom they have shared these habitats for centuries.

Relevant here are ecovillages and other communal experiments that strive to tend social justice and equity, participatory democracy, local environments, and ecological integrity together: Plum Village, Auroville, Navdanya, Earthhaven, Dancing Rabbit, and many others. Beyond serving as experiments, they are blueprints and challenges, raising the question of what humans might create for justice, peace, and sustainability by connecting all around the world.

Meanwhile, aging psychology paradigms creak. Mainstream psychology has chained itself to Procrustean positivism, and, as a result, the American brand has involved itself with political oppression, influence-peddling, world-eating consumerism, and eugenics (Chalquist, 2019a). Depth psychology tends to psychologize ecological experience by relegating it to the human interior on the one hand and the collective unconscious on the other; a hill to be bulldozed becomes a breast of the Great Mother, to be analyzed psychologically but not to be physically preserved. Family Systems includes the inner life in theory but pays most attention to external interactional cybernetics in practice. Neither depth psychology nor ecopsychology is particularly diverse culturally.

Terrapsychology finds its place as a continuation of psychology's gradual tending of larger and more complex circles in which we find ourselves embedded. As Thomas Berry wrote,

> Our challenge is to create a new language, even a new sense of what it is to be human. It is to transcend not only national limitations, but even our species isolation, to enter into the larger community of living species. This brings about a completely new sense of reality and value.
>
> *(Berry, 2015, p. 42)*

Students sometimes ask: Could terrapsychology be of use on other planets? Wherever we tend psyche, story, place, element, and even matter as it "speaks" within us, we are doing terrapsychology. Perhaps it means something symbolically, for example, that our solar system floats in the Arm of Orion not all that far from a stellar nursery. Or that a planet-wide dust storm covered the face of Mars just as the first Gulf War broke out. Be that as it may, we have much to do on Earth, as the field's lineage can show.

Terrapsychology's Ancestors and Allies

No field grows alone. Indigenous animism and lore, Hermeticism, Romanticism and *Naturphilosophie*, Goethean science, Black ecological practices, ecofeminism, deep ecology, depth psychology, mythology, ecopsychology, ecotherapy, ecophenomenology, somatic studies, Family Systems theory, and aspects of complexity theory all inform our projects. Rather than simply relying upon – or appropriating – either past knowledges or present ones from various cultures, terrapsychology appreciates them while casting its explorations in terms useful to people not born into Earth-honoring or place-honoring social systems.

Indigenous Animism

The Indigenous perception of the entirety of nature, from soil particles to stars, as enspirited or ensouled is attested to around the world and is a feature of many cultural traditions with deep roots, including Taoism, Shintoism, Hinduism, some forms of Buddhism, and Orisha. Probably all our ancestors held this "pagan" sensibility. Some cultural groups still do (Basso, 1996).

To select a single case from countless examples of Native American nature appreciation: Before Emerson or Thoreau, George Copway (Ojibwa name Kah-ge-ga-gah-bowh) published these words in 1847: "On the mountaintop, or along the valley, or the water brook, I searched for some kind intimation from the spirits who made their residence in the noise of the waterfalls." "Nature," which was not thought of as apart from the human realm, he described in terms of "her robes, and the wreath about her brow – the seasons – her stately oaks, and the evergreen – her hair – ringlets over the earth" (Copway, 2004, p. 354). All of it animated, spiritual, and inviting.

Sherry Gobaleza names *kalikasan* as a Filipino word similar to "nature" or "mother Earth" but without the split between nature and humans: "Filipino wisdom of kalikasan acknowledges that nature is more than just a place that you can enjoy. Kalikasan is a life source. Without this relationship a person is not human" (2016, p. 5). She also writes that the core Filipino value of *kapwa* ("shared self") includes not only humans but animals, rocks, plants, bodies of water, and other aspects of the natural world.

Here is one more example, from traditional Hawaiian culture:

> In ancient Hawai'i, humans, gods, and nature formed a consciously interacting and interrelating cosmic community. All the species were thought

> to be sentient ... Hawaiians lived in a community in which humans, gods, and nature cared for one another and watched over and protected one another as family.
>
> *(Dudley, 1996, pp. 125–126)*

Some of the complexities of animism will resurface in Chapter 2.

"World Soul" Image in Platonism, Neoplatonism, and Later

In the *Timaeus*, Plato (2008, p. 96) refers to the world as "a living creature truly endowed with a soul." This *anima mundi*, or world soul, reappears in Neoplatonic thought and Stoic philosophy. Johannes Kepler, the astronomer and mathematician who described the orbits of planets around the sun, regarded Earth as ensouled (*anima terrae*), with grass and trees for hair, sulfur for excrement, and rainwater and springs for sweat and urine; flooding meant that the planetary soul was ill (Pauli, 1955). From this vantage, what might it mean that flooding increases as the seas rise?

Folk Traditions of Nature Spirits

The Greeks and Romans experienced each stream, field, grove, village, and mountain as inhabited by its resident spirit, its *genius loci*. In rural areas, people still do: the hearth does not stand for Hestia, its goddess; it *is* Hestia. Every preindustrial society knows such nature spirits. Examples from Europe include the Hyter Sprites, Black Shucks, and Yarthings of the British countryside, the Doire well guardians of Celtic folklore, and these spirit-nature pairings: naiads with springs, dryads with trees, Oreads with hills and rocks, mermaids, Nereids, Oceanids, and sirens with the sea, and trolls and gnomes with caves, crevices, and the undersides of bridges.

Hermeticism and Alchemy

Hermeticism is a wisdom path that began in Alexandria in the third century CE. Taking up the ancient teaching of Egyptian religion that all things are interconnected as well as a sensitivity to symbolism as a gateway to higher knowing, Hermeticism regarded deep knowledge of nature and the cosmos as necessary for self-cultivation. A key tool of this was *nous*, usually translated "mind" or "intellect" but in a Hermetic understanding more akin to knowledge through imagination. One of the deities of Hermeticism, Agathos Daimon, was among other things a god of the presence of place. Although Hermeticism bears the name of the Greek god Hermes, it is actually named after Hermes Trismegistos, or "Thrice-Great," an evolution of Thoth and more a magus and knowledge god than a trickster. As time went on, Hermeticism developed various branches of practice, one of which was alchemy.

Rationalists tend to dismiss alchemy as a long-fruitless attempt to make gold out of base metals like lead, but the serious among these experimenters searched for the "divine power in matter" (Von Franz, 1997). The roots of this quest reach back 5,000 years to Egypt and to India and China as well. Although many of the most notable alchemists in this long tradition were also scientists by our present definitions (e.g., Jabir al-Hayyan the chemist and polymath, Abu Bakr al-Razi the physician and philosopher, Sir Isaac Newton the physicist), they sought the wisdom of nature as symbolized by the Philosopher's Stone of knowledge and healing. Paracelsus the philosopher-physician wrote about looking into nature the way sunlight shines through glass (Hartmann, 2010).

Margaret Cavendish

The Duchess of Newcastle wrote poetry, essays, plays, an early science fiction novel (*The Blazing World*, 1668), and five books on natural philosophy. Anticipating the likes of Leibniz and Spinoza, she argued from her earliest work, *Philosophical Fancies*, published in 1653, against the mechanistic worldview popularized by Hobbes and Descartes. She did not dispute the material reality of nature; rather, she saw all things, whether considered animate or inanimate, as having their own interlocking self-movement. Matter not only thinks (Cunning, 2006), it dances harmoniously with itself. (See Chapter 2 for more on panpsychism, the philosophical position that matter is animated and even conscious in its own way.) It would not have surprised her if a chair suddenly blocked a doorway leading to an unlucky meeting, or, in our day, that a computer hard drive dumped a badly written paper: in their own way, things speak.

Black Nature Spirituality

From since the days of slavery, Black singers, poets, storytellers, and agriculturalists left vivid accounts – including those in blues songs – of how intimately ensouled the land was for them (Ruffin, 2010). This was often so in spite of the agricultural activities they were forced to carry out. Hunted by dogs and White captors, Solomon Bayley searched for his wife, his son having died in slavery, in western Virginia, where he halted in the forest to hide from those who sought him. Noting that sudden thunder, lightning, and rain helped him evade them, he found himself cornered again later on his way to Dover: "When I awoke, there had come two birds near to me; and seeing the little strange-looking birds, it roused up all my senses" (Bayley, 2004, p. 245). Seized by a feeling that he must remain still to avoid capture, he looked around and saw himself surrounded by a circle of birds. This, he believed, reinforced the message not to leave cover. The searchers checked one side of a fallen tree while he hid on the other. One White man looked directly at him but did not see him and passed by.

Gardens which slaves created to feed themselves took on the aspect of a lost Eden; territory to the north was a Promised Land of liberation. This wedding of story to place continued decades later; for example, as W. E. B. Du Bois mused:

> Perhaps Atlanta was not christened for the winged maiden of dull Boeotia; you know the tale, – how swarthy Atalanta, tall and wild, would marry only him who out-raced her; and how the wily Hippomenes laid three apples of gold in the way. She fled like a shadow, paused, startled over the first apple, but even as he stretched his hand, fled again; hovered over the second, then, slipping from his hot grasp, flew over river, vale, and hill; but as she lingered over the third, his arms fell round her, and looking on each other, the blazing passion of their love profaned the sanctuary of Love, and they were cursed. If Atlanta be not named for Atalanta, she ought to have been.
>
> *(Du Bois, 2012, p. 37)*

Later still, Alice Walker wrote of her awareness of reciprocity through appreciation of nature:

> What I have noticed in my small world is that if I praise the wild flowers growing on the hill in front of my house, the following year they double in profusion and brilliance. If I admire the squirrel that swings from branch to branch outside my window, pretty soon I have three or four squirrels to admire.
>
> *(Walker, 1989, p. 189)*

Transcendentalism

In 1836, Ralph Waldo Emerson published the essay "Nature" and inaugurated Transcendentalism, which saw the natural world as an expression of the divine: "From the earth, as a shore, I look out into that silent sea. I seem to partake its rapid transformations: the active enchantment reaches my dust, and I dilate and conspire with the morning wind" (Emerson, 2003, p. 43). For Henry David Thoreau (2012, p. 30), the natural world held stories and sacred symbols: "The morning wind forever blows, the poem of creation is uninterrupted; but few are the ears that hear it. Olympus is but the outside of the earth everywhere."

Romanticism and Naturphilosophie

In the late eighteenth century in Europe, artists, musicians, and poets revolted against the flat materialism of the Industrial Revolution backed by supposedly value-neutral science (which always equips the highest bidder, with morals to the back of the line) by celebrating creative passion and emotion, the wisdom found in folklore, subjective truth, and natural beauty. The movement spread its love of the natural world's sensual intelligence and its emphasis on the primacy of imagination culminating in the likes of Coleridge, Shelley, Keats, and Yeats. In Germany, *Naturphilosophie* sprang up in 1790 from a similar discontent with modernity's shadowy gifts of smoke and steel. Pushing back against the growing mechanistic and reductionistic separation of self from nature atomized and objectified, Schelling sought to show that mind and matter were one and that human creativity was founded in that of the enspirited natural world. In "The Eolian Harp," Coleridge asked:

And what if all of animated nature
Be but organic harps, diversely framed,
That tremble into thought, as o'er them sweeps
Plastic and vast, one intellectual breeze,
At once the Soul of each, and God of All?

(Coleridge, 1997, p. 88)

Goethean Science

Although Johann Wolfgang von Goethe opposed mechanism as a worldview, he also grew weary of the more self-absorbed expressions of Romanticist emotionality. For balance, he wondered whether a poetic science joining inner and outer might be possible. Even as a law student he noticed the Gothic cathedral in Strasbourg, sketching it and telling friends it felt incomplete. His sketch of what would have resulted from following the original design, which he had never seen, turned out to be accurate. About this Goethe remarked, "I observed it so long and so attentively and I bestowed on it so much affection that it decided at the end to reveal to me its manifest secret" (Lachmann, 2018, p. 60).

Applying this kind of deep seeing to plants, Goethe, having shown in 1784 that humans possessed the intermaxillary bone found in other animals, sought, saw, and wrote about what he called the Ur-plant, the primal image of Plant. Through what Henri Bortoft (1996, p. 22) translates as "exact sensorial imagination," Goethe, having studied a plant carefully, could see with his interior vision this dynamism or archetypal becoming at work in the plant's sprouting, growing, and bringing to seed: one example of the Ur-phenomena that infuse and power nature from *between* the realms of abstract label and hard matter. Here, he believed, was nature at work alive and whole rather than cut up and killed, and perceptible not through distant observation but in active participation. For Goethe, nature was not a collection of things to be proven related to one another, but an interconnective flow, a constant state of becoming.

Henri Corbin

From this French scholar, terrapsychology takes an appreciation for the imaginal as a realm or way of being as inspired by Islamic gnosticism, particularly that of the seer-philosophers Suhrawardi and Ibn Arabi. The "location" of this realm is "between" those of pure ideas and physical reality, and it can be accessed by heart-based, imaginative contemplation. Also, the Qur'an mentions signs (*ayah*) of the divine embedded in the natural world, signs that can be read. Reading this may have inspired Corbin's reflective "Theology by the Lakeside," written in 1932, which declares in part,

> For it is not necessary to strut about like a conqueror and want to give a name to things, to everything; it is they who will tell you who they are, if you listen, yielding like a lover; for suddenly for you, in the untroubled peace of this forest of the North, the Earth has come to Thou ... and in this apparition, this greatly green and thronging solitude, yes, the Angel [Earth] too is robed in green, the green of dusk, of silence and of truth.
>
> *(Cheetham, 2004, pp. 63–64)*

Corbin also referred to the Arabic term *ta'wil*, mentioned in Qur'an 3:7 as a practice of interpreting. By the eighth century, this meant spiritual interpretation of the text in contrast to *tafsir*, the conventional or literal reading of it. Corbin took *ta'wil* to mean moving beyond surface signs and meanings to the originary depths: from symbol to symbolized. In some ways, this is akin to Goethe's imaginative seeing and to interpreting psychological symptoms in the traditions of depth psychology.

Depth Psychology

Part of the psychological work of terrapsychology derives from practices within depth psychology, including the "seeing through" surfaces to underlying fantasies and archetypal structures as first developed by Jung and further elaborated by James Hillman (1992). Depth psychology imagines consciousness as situated upon a primary process or substrate of fantasy, image, and myth that informs every realm of human experience (e.g., the computer as a return of the mythic figure of the robotic Golem; Artificial Intelligence as the dazzling and dangerous alchemical homunculus). Irreducible to neurochemistry and resistant to literalization or centralized ego control, this polycentric language or layer of being must be approached through its own mythopoetic movements – movements that exist *prior* to thought and reflection, with a shimmer of myth already at work under everything we perceive and categorize.

Terrapsychology also leans on psychoanalytic understandings of defense, internalization, identification, and the intersubjective or relational field (Atwood & Stolorow, 2014). However, terrapsychological work moves *through* complexes and fantasies, impulses, and dreams, and on out into the world they refract. We understand archetypes – Birth, Life, Death, Resurrection, and Initiation – as styles or qualities or basic patterns of existence found in abundance in the natural world.

Pierre Teilhard de Chardin

For this Jesuit scientist and scholar, everything possessed an outer dimension and an inner "within of things" (Teilhard de Chardin, 1976, p. 53). The more developed the nervous system, the more conscious this subjectivity or interiority can be of itself. A bird has a more complex inner life than a stone, but both have one as a layer or quality inherent in matter. Everything has an inside. Nothing is truly unalive.

Gestalt Psychology

Not to be confused with the Gestalt Therapy of Fritz Perls, the Gestaltists (Wertheimer, Koffka, and Kohler) replaced an atomistic approach to consciousness, thought of previously as an assemblage of sense impressions one at a time, with a field theory of interactive impressions and possibilities, paralleling depth psychology's view of psyche as a kind of interior democracy. Social scientist Kurt Lewin, coiner of the term "action research," extended Gestaltist work by describing how the features found in one's immediate environment held psychological values. Psychology, then, could not confine itself to the study of the insides of people's heads. Lewin's topological approach has largely been ignored within psychology, which instead has invested itself in hydraulic, mechanistic, and cybernetic models of mind.

Ecofeminism

Named in 1974 by French feminist writer Françoise d'Eaubonne, ecofeminism views the systematic industrialized destruction of nature as a direct result of patriarchy, which categorizes both women and nature as dispensable property and seeks to dominate them. According to d'Eaubonne, patriarchy likewise oppresses people of color as well as the poor. Ecofeminists call instead for egalitarian and just forms of community and power-sharing and an end to the split between nature and culture.

Ecofeminist Animism

Subjectivity, for ecofeminist Stephanie Lahar (1996), is found throughout the natural world, not just in humans, who possess our own variety of it. Val Plumwood (2002, p. 177) calls for an "intentional panpsychism" that avoids the living/nonliving duality in our thought by recognizing kinds of life:

> The rich intentionality the reductive stance would deny to the world is the ground of the enchantment it retains in many Indigenous cultures and in some of the past of our own, the butterfly wing-dust of wonder that modernity stole from us and replaced with the drive for power.

A guide here is how our sense of wonder speaks to the apparent aliveness of the things around us.

Deep Ecology

In the early 1970s, philosopher Arne Næss criticized mainstream ecology and conservation for focusing on surface issues of land and resource management while ignoring the materialist attitudes that enabled the wholesale destruction of entire ecosystems. He coined "deep ecology" as a call for a philosophy and set of practices focused on *biocentrism*: the idea that everything has inherent worth (Devall & Sessions, 2001). The resulting platform linked human self-realization to biocentric equality and health.

Ecopsychology

As Theodore Roszak explained, all psychologies were once ecopsychologies (Roszak et al., 1995) that considered human and more-than-human health together. The industrialized decline of ecosystems inevitably degraded health all around. Efforts at healing must include environmental justice and restoration.

Ecopsychology-Influenced Jungians

Although Jung himself spoke and wrote repeatedly about the need to stay consciously connected to the natural world (Jung & Sabini, 2002), the Jungians he personally trained seem not to have taken this to heart – with one exception. Analyst Jane Hollister Wheelwright grew up on a ranch west of Santa Barbara. With a vivid sense of place, she described the living presence of the Hollister Ranch before it was divided and parceled by real-estate developers. She also referred to Earth as a deity in need of recognition (Wheelwright, 1988). She went into even more depth in her private and undated Tepitates Journals (unpublished). She should probably be considered the first ecopsychologist.

Depth-psychology instructor, psychotherapist, and vision-quest guide Betsy Perluss (2005, p. 236) writes about landscape perception as deeply psychological and full of symbolic meaning: "To observe the world through the lens of soul reveals the psychic material that is hidden in the landscape, and conversely, it reveals aspects of the landscape that are hidden within the psyche."

Ecotherapy

Since the publication of Howard Clinebell's book on ecotherapy (1996), a wave of studies has confirmed the beneficial effects of being in the presence of plants, animals, natural settings, and other aspects of nature (see also Buzzell & Chalquist, 2009). Clinebell (1996) cautioned, however, against merely using nature for healing, insisting that ecotherapy must observe an ecological circle of mutual giving between humans and the nonhuman world. He would not have supported the distinction now made between Level 1 "Ecotherapy" (taking health from nature without giving back) and Level 2 (recognizing the need for mutuality of relations); for him, only the second constitutes real ecotherapy.

Somatic Studies

Terrapsychological research emanates from that center of perceptions we know as the human body. Rae Johnson's Elemental Movement is a practice for heightening subjective awareness of the flesh through engaging as metaphors the five elements (earth, air, fire, water, ether) of traditional alchemy (Johnson, 2001). This moving meditation also includes an emphasis on social justice (Johnson, 2017): not only how oppression shapes the body, but how resistance to injustice can be embodied effectively.

Somatic psychology hones sensitivity to the meanings in how our body feels and presents itself, its sensations and movements an enfleshed language of the psyche and its responses to "outer" events. The "embodied realism" of George Lakoff and Mark Johnson (1999) offers evidence that "higher" faculties like human reason are built out of basic metaphors rooted in the body and its continual sensing and tracking of its surroundings.

Landscape Art and Design

The ancient Chinese design art of feng shui, the harmonious and beneficial alignment of built structures with the natural features of their geographical locations, finds an echo in contemporary artists who take the presence of place seriously. Landscape designer Lawrence Halprin camps out at future building sites to study and get a feel for them. Sculptor Andy Goldsworthy fashions art from driftwood, root, stone, leaf, and ice as gifts to the place where he creates and shows them. Muralists, musicians, dancers, writers, and dramatists have incorporated the border between Mexico and the United States into their performances to show the absurdity of severing families, nations, and natural regions. The Sustainable Singapore Movement experiments with new homes built not only to be ecologically wise but beautiful as well.

Evolutions of Terrapsychology

Beginning as the deep study of the presence of place, terrapsychology evolved over the years and much use by my students and me into *the deep study of our largely ignored and unconscious interdependencies with the multileveled presence of our living Earth*, including that of specific places and their creatures and materials. "Deep" because what links us to places and animals and the elements travels along bridges of symbol, metaphor, image, and dream. We explore how the patterns, shapes, features, and motifs at play in the nonhuman world sculpt our ideas, habits, relationships, culture, and sense of self: freeway congestion in congested conversations, lake toxins in our darker moods, salt-choked fields and bitter relations, healing landscapes, and regenerating hearts.

We also study the reverse, looking for how what we perceive as personal or inner reflects events abroad and around us. This includes a focus shared by ecopsychology and environmental justice: the impacts of colonialism, nationalism, and other dissociative cultural pathologies on the increasingly paved and gridded world around us.

As terrapsychology evolved, it kept its place-based emphasis but broadened its inquiry. Its expanding sphere of interest is reflected in this partial chronology of terrapsychological works and areas of study:

- "Locianalysis": investigation of the presence of place via moods, dreams, and somatic states (Chalquist, 2003). Lali Mitchell (2005) studied hieroglyphs in San Diego County as artistic collaborations between people and place. Matthew Cochran's Archetypal Geology translates psychological terms like "defense" into geological events like "weathering" (Cochran, personal communication, 2004). "Locianalysis" refers to when a specific place is the primary focus of inquiry.
- Terrestry (2007b): assembling a coherent life map from the study of recurring images and motifs in one's birth story and ancestry, especially when linked to geographical sites and travel routes. Deep ancestry.
- *Terrapsychology: Reengaging the Soul of Place* (Chalquist, 2007b); "locianalysis" now meant a place-based version of TI. This book has been superseded by decades of later work and is now out of print.

- Sarah Rankin (2007) studied the past and presence of Petaluma, CA, in the psyche and actions of its inhabitants.
- Chalquist reviewed Howard Clinebell's *Ecotherapy: Healing Ourselves, Healing the Earth* in *Santa Barbara Therapy News*. Ecotherapy establishes mutually healing relations with the Earth via plants, animals, soil, and other characteristics of the natural world.
- Kevin Filocamo's (2008) master's thesis examined the erotic and embodied nature of our relations with the natural world in general and with trees in particular.
- *Ecotherapy: Healing with Nature in Mind*, edited by Linda Buzzell and C. Chalquist (2009), is an anthology that brought together many theorists and practitioners of ecotherapy and provided some current research evidence for its efficacy in psychological and physical healing.
- Chalquist published the Animate California Trilogy, a terrapsychological study of California (2009, 2011, 2012a). "Mythocartography" introduced to delineate relationships between places and the mythic motifs inhabiting them (Chalquist, 2012b).
- The paper "Tracking the City's Psyche: Terrapsychologizing in San Francisco" (Chalquist 2012b) grew from a class exercise at the California Institute of Integral Studies, where my Planetary Psychology course invited students outside for an afternoon tour to hunt mythic images around South of Market.
- Intersubjective animism: interpretive work with matter and objects and elements, storying them as always in conversation with us (Chalquist, 2007a). "Intersubjective" because we fantasize the conversation as between subjectivities rather than a human subjectivity encountering inanimate things. See also *In the Thick of Things: Brief Musings on Living in an Animate World* (Chalquist, 2013b).
- *Rebearths: Conversations with a World Ensouled* (Chalquist, 2010). This anthology included an article on validity and reliability in TI.
- Eradigmatics (Chalquist, 2018): a call for examining large worldview shifts by tracking how their underlying archetypes rise and subside in collective consciousness. These shifts also characterize how we relate to the natural world: as maternal goddess (Eradigm Mother Nature); as backdrop to heavenly drama (Heavenly City); as machinery (Big Machine); as a site of homecoming and global community (Earthrise).
- TerraPlaces project (Davenport, 2010) to invite the public to get to know their locales and neighborhoods – major land forms, soils, geology, flora, fauna, history, ecological health, etc. – and post online what they find out about.
- Anima Loci, Greening Self: Reconnecting with Place by Meeting the Mythic Soul of Orange County," a master's thesis by Katherine Humphrey (2012) drawing on insights from terrapsychology.

- Hunukul: Archetypal Reflections on the Soul of Place," a dissertation by George Kohn (2012), with terrapsychology one of the methodologies employed.
- Name, Place, and Emotional Space: Themed Semantics in Literary Onomastic Research," a dissertation by James Butler (2013) drawing on terrapsychology.
- On Ecological Identity and Terrapsychology" (Chalquist, 2013a). From its inception, terrapsychology has remained alert to the trauma of colonized people displaced from or turned against their own ancestral lands.
- Nomadic Dimensions of Education with the Earth-in-Mind" by Mitchell (2014) in Vakoch and Castrillon (Eds.), *Ecopsychology, Phenomenology, and the Environment: The Experience of Nature*. This chapter explores education based on deepening awareness of our primal locatedness in the Earth.
- Chalquist, "Lorecasting the Weather: Unhumanizing Phenomenology for Decoding the Language of Earth" (2014), also in Vakoch and Castrillon (Eds.), *Ecopsychology, Phenomenology, and the Environment: The Experience of Nature*. A playful combination of depth psychology and Goethean phenomenology for recasting natural events like storms as gestures, signals, or bids for attention. This is an example of lorecasting (Chalquist, 2007a).
- *Immanence Journal* launched in 2015 to promote applied folklore studies and writings. One edition featured retellings of wisdom stories about nature, place, and the Earth (Chalquist et al., 2019b).
- C. K. Olivieri (2015) revisioned queer lifespan development as an example of a heroic quest.
- C. Chalquist (2015) examined the importance of the image of Earthrise for collective education.
- In 2016, A. Berrios taught embodied terrapsychology as part of the New York Open Center Certificate in Holistic Psychology.
- Lola McCrary (2016) wrote about "Deep Genealogy" in a blog at the website of *Immanence Journal*. The author examined the intersection of psychology, symbol, ancestry, and place.
- Applied Ecobricolage: Mountain Being(s)/Mountain Becoming(s)," a dissertation by Tanya Miller (2016) drawing on Gaian methodology, terrapsychology, and the visual arts.
- The dissertation "Your Church, My Bar!" by C. K. Olivieri (2017) relied on TI for its main methodology. The study explored the uses of "queer-space" as sanctuary and community in San Francisco, a city filled with images and themes from the mythology of the genderqueer god Dionysus.
- A Psychology of Salt," a terrapsychological master's thesis submitted by Maggie Hippman (2017) to the University of Utah Environmental Humanities Program. The thesis tied together the presence, shape, and

composition of the Great Salt Lake with the history unfolding around it once the Mormons arrived in search of holy ground.

- Terrapsychological Inquiry and the Historic Industrial Placefield of Lowell Massachusetts," a master's thesis by Amanda Leetch (2017).
- The same year, 2017, a certificate in ecopsychology launched at Pacifica, with Linda Buzzell, Andy Fisher, and Craig Chalquist as instructors. The certificate covered Earthdreaming, the embodied practice arm of terrapsychology.
- A Folklore of Hope: Storytelling for a Reenchanted World" was given by C. Chalquist as a keynote presentation to *The Anthropocene and Beyond* conference at Hong Kong Shue Yan University, 2018.
- Nature myths and commentary on them were included in *Myths among Us: When Timeless Tales Return to Life* (Chalquist, 2018).
- At the 2019 conference "Emergent Truth in Soulful Times: How Do We Face, Speak and Act in Truth in a World of Falsehood and Fear," psychologist G. Barnwell presented "Thathe Vondo Forest: A Terrapsychology of Sacred Spaces with Traumatic Pasts," based on his terrapsychological work with Indigenous tribes in a decimated South African forest.
- Unattended Trauma of the San Lorenzo River: A Terrapsychological Inquiry." This dissertation by M. Haber (2019) examined thematic correspondences between the troubled ecology of the river and the self-pollution of addicts living next to it.
- The edited volume *Terrapsychology: Further Inquiry into Self, Place, and Planet* (eds. Chalquist & Barnwell, 2023) follows up the earlier *Rebearths* by bringing forth new voices in terrapsychological thought and practice.
- This book will be translated into Mandarin and published in 2023 by China Press & Apparel in Beijing.

All told, terrapsychology has been used so far in at least forty academic studies, whether master's theses or dissertations. It has been taught to non-academic audiences in workshops, presentations, civic festivals, free public lectures, panels, and nature tours. Terrapsychology, then, is the field of imaginative studies, ideas, and practices for restorying and thereby reenchanting our place-oriented relations with the world, with each other, and with ourselves. Its practice arm is called Earthdreaming. Its research arm is TI.

Terrapsychology asks: What emerges when we listen, imagine, and feel into rich intersections of psyche, story, symbol, body, mood, and place? When we put the presence of *world* at the center of psychology?

Differences between TI, Jungian Psychology, and Ecopsychology

Although many fields and disciplines have informed the birth and evolution of terrapsychology, two particularly prominent ones are Jungian depth psychology and ecopsychology. Many who practice terrapsychology gratefully acknowledge this debt while continuing to be active in those fields as well. In my case, my doctoral work was in Jungian depth psychology, whose findings and practices I have taught and written about for more than twenty years, which is about as many as I have actively contributed to ecopsychology and ecotherapy.

As an offspring of these parents, terrapsychology has remained connected to them even while differentiating itself from them.

Jungian psychology focuses primarily on the individuation (becoming consciously whole) of individuals. It tends to see the operation of myths and archetypes as internal rather than outward as well. For most traditional Jungians, Earth and nature remain Great Mother symbols rather than active entities to be in conversation with. Even for James Hillman, the imaginal animal showing up in, say, a dream took precedence over the breathing animal, whose tending would amount to taking a symbol too literally. Additionally, Jungian psychology has remained true to its origins as a healing method, whereas terrapsychology is primarily exploratory. Overall, then, Jung's version of depth psychology privileges interiority, individuality, and explanations that stop at psychological archetypes, leaving much of the world beyond its focus. TI moves that focus outward while softening the implicit split between inner and outer, self and world.

As for ecopsychology, it focuses primarily on the health-giving aspects of the natural world versus the harmful effects of the built environment. At worst, this perpetuates a split between country and city, and nature and culture. Ecopsychology tends to examine place literally, as either beneficial or harmful, rather than probing the symbols and stories that link us to where we are. Very little in ecopsychology addresses animism, or, as discussed in terrapsychology, *interanimism*: how the presences outside us become aspects of our psychology. (When as a doctoral student, I first described my interest in the aliveness of place to an ecopsychologist, she could not understand why I studied not only in geology, ecology, flora, etc., but roads, houses, neighborhoods, and everyday objects as well. Do not all these live inside us too?)

Some ecopsychology practitioners have divided their efforts, or had them divided, into "first generation" (countercultural), "second generation" (ecotherapeutic healing), and "third generation" (social and environmental justice). All three are found in terrapsychological work, but without the categories because researchers and practitioners do what they feel called to do without any "generational" rivalries.

Additionally, ecopsychology offers no comprehensive research methodology. Some of its research is now quantitative, a paradigm that rests on the duality of human and nonhuman, self, and world. TI can provide ecopsychology with a suitable research approach.

All three fields remain vital and continue to play active parts in helping us understand how deeply we humans are embedded in the more-than-human world.

For Discussion:

1 In what ways does knowing the ancestry of a field enlarge one's view of it?
2 The Indigenous sense of place as animate vastly predates terrapsychology. Why is the field needed, then?
3 What fields, approaches, and paradigms inform how you relate to the natural world as well as to the built environment?

References

Ackroyd, P. (2009). *London: The biography*. New York, NY: Anchor.

Atwood, G., & Stolorow, R. (2014). *Structures of subjectivity: Explorations in psychoanalytic phenomenology and contextualism*. Abingdon and New York, NY: Routledge.

Basso, K. (1996). *Wisdom sits in places: Landscape and language among the western Apache*. Albuquerque, NM: University of New Mexico Press.

Bayley, S. (2004). From a narrative of some remarkable incidents, in the life of Solomon Bayley, formerly a slave. In M. Branchi (Ed.), *Reading the roots: American nature writing before Walden* (pp. 242–247). Athens, GA: The University of Georgia Press.

Berry, T. (2015). *The dream of the earth*. Berkeley, CA: Counterpoint.

Bortoft, H. (1996). *The wholeness of nature: Goethe's way toward a science of conscious participation in nature*. Hudson, NY: Lindisfarne Press.

Bullard, R. (Ed.) (2005). *The quest for environmental justice: Human rights and the politics of pollution*. Berkeley, CA: Counterpoint.

Butler, J. (2013). Name, place, and emotional space: Themed semantics in literary onomastic research (unpublished Ph.D. thesis). University of Glasgow, Glasgow.

Buzzell, L., & Chalquist, C. (Eds.) (2009). *Ecotherapy: Healing with nature in mind*. San Francisco, CA: Sierra Club Books.

Chalquist, C. (2003). In the shadow of cross and sword: Toward a psychoanalysis of place (unpublished dissertation). Pacifica Graduate Institute, Carpinteria, CA.

Chalquist, C. (2007a). Review of Howard Clinebell's *Ecotherapy: Healing ourselves, healing the Earth*. Santa Barbara Therapy News (CAMFT), September.

Chalquist, C. (2007b). *Terrapsychology: Reengaging the soul of place*. New Orleans, LA: Spring Journal Books.

Chalquist, C. (2009). *The tears of Llorona: A Californian odyssey of myth, place, and homecoming*. Walnut Creek, CA: World Soul Books.

Chalquist, C. (Ed.) (2010). *Rebearths: Conversations with a world ensouled*. Walnut Creek, CA: World Soul Books.

Chalquist, C. (2011). *Ventral depths: Alchemical themes and mythic motifs in the great central valley of California*. El Cerrito, CA: World Soul Books.

Chalquist, C. (2012a). *Edges, peaks, and vales: A mythocartography of California at the margins*. El Cerrito, CA: World Soul Books.

Chalquist, C. (2012b). Tracking the city's psyche: Terrapsychologizing in San Francisco. *Ecopsychology 4(3)*, 193–200.

Chalquist, C. (2013a). On ecological identity and terrapsychology. In M. Soltsys (Ed.), *Tangled roots: Dialogues exploring ecological justice, healing, and decolonization* (pp. 101–114). Guelph: Healing the Earth Press.

Chalquist, C. (2013b). *In the thick of things: Brief musings on living in an animate world*. El Cerrito, CA: World Soul Books.

Chalquist, C. (2014). Lorecasting the weather: Unhumanizing phenomenology for decoding the language of earth. In D. Vakoch & F. Castrillon (Eds.), *Ecopsychology, phenomenology, and the environment: The experience of nature* (pp. 251–260). New York, NY: Springer.

Chalquist, C. (2015). Integral education in light of earthrise. *Integral Review 11(1)*, 4–10.

Chalquist, C. (2018). *Myths among us: When timeless tales return to life*. Goleta, CA: World Soul Books.

Chalquist, C. (2019a). Can psychology heal itself? Terrapsych.com. Retrieved from www.terrapsych.com/index.php/Articles/can-psychology-heal-itself

Chalquist, C. (Ed.) (2019b). Earthspeak: Stories for a planet in transition. *Immanence Journal*, *3*(2).

Chalquist, C., & Barnwell, G. (Eds.) (2023). *Terrapsychology: Further inquiry into self, place, and planet*. London & New York, NY: Routledge.

Cheetham, T. (2004). *Green man, earth angel: The prophetic tradition and the battle for the soul of the world*. New York, NY: SUNY Press.

Clinebell, H. (1996). *Ecotherapy: Healing ourselves, healing the earth*. London and New York, NY: Routledge.

Coleridge, S. (1997). *The complete poems*. New York, NY: Penguin Classics.

Copway, G. (2004). From the life, history, and travels of Kah-ge-ga-gah-bowh, a young Indian chief of the Ojebwa nation. In M. Branchi (Ed.), *Reading the roots: American nature writing before Walden* (pp. 354–358). Athens, GA: University of Georgia Press.

Cunning, D. (2006) Cavendish on the intelligibility of the prospect of thinking matter. *History of Philosophy Quarterly* *23*(2): 117–136.

Davenport, K. (2010). *TerraPlaces: Powers of place initiative*. Retrieved from www.powersofplace.com.

Devall, B., & Sessions, G. (2001). *Deep ecology: Living as if nature mattered*. Layton, UT: Gibbs & Smith.

Du Bois, W. (2012). *The souls of black folk*. New York, NY: Signet Reprints.

Dudley, M. (1996). Traditional native Hawaiian environmental philosophy. In R. Gottlieb (Ed.), *This sacred earth: Religion, nature, environment*. London and New York, NY: Routledge.

Emerson, R. (2003). *Nature and selected essays*. New York, NY: Penguin Classics.

Filocamo, K. (2008). The alluring universe: Exploring an erotic relationship with the world (unpublished master's thesis). John F. Kennedy University, Pleasant Hill, CA.

Fisher, A. (2013). *Radical ecopsychology: Psychology in the service of life*. New York, NY: SUNY Press.

Freud, S. (1990). *The ego and the id*. New York, NY: W. W. Norton.

Gobaleza, S. (2016). Rocky mountains, Colorado trail (unpublished community fieldwork paper). Pacifica Graduate Institute, Carpinteria, CA.
Haber, M. (2019). Unattended trauma of the San Lorenzo River: A terrapsychological inquiry (unpublished dissertation). California Institute of Integral Studies, San Francisco, CA.
Hartmann, F. (2010). *Life and doctrines of Paracelsus*. Whitefish, MT: Kessinger Publishing.
Hillman, J. (1992). *Re-visioning psychology*. New York, NY: HarperPerennial.
Hippman, M. (2017). The psychology of salt (unpublished master's thesis). Environmental Humanities Program, University of Utah, Salt Lake City, Utah.
Humphrey, K. (2012). Anima loci, greening self: Reconnecting with place by meeting the mythic soul of Orange County (unpublished master's thesis). Pacifica Graduate Institute, Carpinteria, CA.
Johnson, R. (2001). *Elemental movement: A somatic approach to movement education*. Boca Raton, FL: BrownWalker Press.
Johnson, R. (2017). *Embodied social justice*. London and New York, NY: Routledge.
Jung, C., & Sabini, M. (Eds.) (2002). *The earth has a soul: C. G. Jung on nature, technology and modern life*. Berkeley, CA: North Atlantic Books.
Kohn, G. (2012). Hunukul: Archetypal reflections on the soul of place (unpublished dissertation). Pacifica Graduate Institute, Carpinteria, CA.
Lachmann, G. (2018). *Lost knowledge of the imagination*. Edinburgh: Floris Books.
Lahar, S. (1996). Ecofeminist philosophy and grassroots politics. In K. Warren (Ed.), *Ecological feminist philosophies* (pp. 1–18). Bloomington, IN: Indiana University Press.
Lakoff, G., & Johnson, M. (1999). *Philosophy in the flesh: The embodied mind and its challenge to Western thought*. New York, NY: Basic Books.
Leetch, A. (2017). Weaving meaning: Terrapsychological Inquiry and the historic industrial placefield of Lowell, Massachusetts (unpublished master's thesis). Prescott College, Prescott, AZ.
Macy, J., & Brown, M. (1998). *Coming back to life: Practices to reconnect our lives, our world*. Gabriola Island, BC: New Society Publishers.
McCrary, L. (2016). Deep genealogy [blog]. *Immanence: The Journal of Applied Myth, Story, and Folklore*. Retrieved from www.immanencejournal.com/deep-genealogy.
Metzner, R. (1999). *Green psychology: Transforming our relationship to the earth*. Rochester, VT: Park Street Press.
Miller, T. (2016). Applied ecobricolage: Mountain being(s)/mountain becoming(s) (unpublished dissertation). Prescott College, Prescott, AZ.
Mitchell, L. (2005). The eco-imaginal underpinnings of community identity in Harmony Grove Valley: Unbinding the ecological imagination (unpublished dissertation). Pacifica Graduate Institute, Carpinteria, CA.
Mitchell, L. (2014). Nomadic dimensions of education with the earth-in-mind. In D. Vakoch & F. Castrillon (Eds.), *Ecopsychology, phenomenology, and the environment: The experience of nature* (pp. 109–126). New York, NY: Springer.
Olivieri, C. (2015). Queer archetypal lifespan development theory and the "new" myth: Re-visioning the hero's journey through the practice of terrapsychological inquiry. *Journal of the International Association of Transdisciplinary Psychology*, *4*(1), 1–13.
Olivieri, C. (2017). Your church, my bar! A terrapsychological inquiry of the relationship between queerspace and queer spirituality in San Francisco,

California (unpublished dissertation). California Institute of Integral Studies, San Francisco, CA.

Parajuli, P. (2001). How can four trees make a jungle? In D. Rothenberg & M. Ulvaeus (Eds.), *The world and the wild: Expanding wilderness conservation beyond its American roots*. Tucson, AZ: University of Arizona Press.

Pauli, W. (1955). The influence of archetypal ideas on the scientific theories of Kepler. In C. G. Jung, W. Pauli, & P. Silz (Trans.), *The interpretation of nature and the psyche* (pp. 147–212). New York, NY: Random House.

Perluss, B. (2005). Desert dreaming: Tracking psyche through the landscape. *Psychological Perspectives*, *48*(2), 233–241.

Plato (2008). *Timaeus and critias*. Edited by T. Johansen. New York, NY: Penguin Classics.

Plumwood, V. (2002). *Environmental culture: The ecological crisis of reason*. London and New York, NY: Routledge.

Rankin, S. (2007). A terrapsychological study of the psyche of Petaluma as found in the stories of the land and as mirrored by my own psyche (unpublished master's thesis). Sonoma State University, Rohnert Park, CA.

Roszak, T., Gomes, M., & Kanner, A. (Eds.) (1995). *Ecopsychology: Restoring the earth, healing the mind*. San Francisco, CA: Sierra Club Books.

Ruffin, K. (2010). *Black on earth: African American ecoliterary traditions*. Athens, GA: University of Georgia Press.

Searles, H. (1960). *The non-human environment in normal development and in schizophrenia*. Madison, CT: International Universities Press.

Teilhard de Chardin, P. (1976). *The phenomenon of man*. New York, NY: Perennial.

Thoreau, H. (2012). *Walden and civil disobedience*. New York, NY: Signet.

Von Franz, M. (1997). *Alchemical active imagination*. Boston, MA: Shambhala.

Walker, A. (1989). *Living by the word: Selected writings, 1973–1987*. Orlando, FL: Mariner Books.

Wen, Xuan (2020). The yellow crane tower. Midterm paper at the California Institute of Integral Studies.

Wheelwright, J. (1988). *The ranch papers: A California memoir*. Culver City, CA: Lapis Press.

2

PHILOSOPHY OF THE METHODOLOGY

> To make full use of a research methodology, it helps to understand the basic premises by which it operates. These are included in its philosophy. Every field, and indeed every person, holds some philosophy; the question is not whether we have one, but how conscious of it we might be. Hence this chapter.

We start by considering terrapsychology's *ontology*: its assumptions about the nature of reality.

Ontological Premises

Denzin and Lincoln (2017) situate social science research in six major (and potentially overlapping) ontological paradigms:

1 Positivism

We met the negative or shadow form of positivism in the Introduction: the restriction of social/psychological inquiry to what can be studied with naturalistic methods such as measurement. Positivism at its strictest represents a paradigmatic counterreaction to centuries of speculative metaphysical thought, as though endless arguments about whether one, two, or three birds live in a nearby nest were answered with: Why don't we just look and find out?

Although the positivist paradigm no longer holds in microphysics, where the very act of observing changes what is seen, many social scientists seem unaware that this paradigm is antiquated. Its premises include:

DOI: 10.4324/9781003462965-3

- Materialist realism: there is only one objective reality, governed by discoverable laws.
- Science and experimentation offer the most effective ways to disclose this reality.
- Only what is tangible (e.g., already existing and available to the senses) shall be the proper study of science.

2 Postpositivism (Positivism Light)

Postpositivists concede that researcher values and background influence the research and that the goal of absolute knowledge of reality is not feasible given the limitations of human thought and perception. Even so, postpositivist research conforms to the methods of physical science.

3 Ontological realism

There is only one objective reality, governed by discoverable laws. Science backed by experimentation provides conjectures about this reality because we cannot rely on our senses to be truthful about it. Only what is tangible shall be the proper study of science.

4 Critical Theory (Includes Feminist, Race, and Class Theories)

Traditional theory tries to understand society. Critical theory seeks to change it, starting by questioning ideologies that support unequal power relations that create injustice. Its premises include:

- How we perceive reality depends on cultural, gender, social, and other lenses. It also depends on who has the power to conduct research and distribute it.
- Knowledge of reality is built through interactions between researchers and participants.
- This knowledge allows us to transform reality in the service of social justice.

5 Constructivism

Jean Piaget is often singled out as a theorist of the idea that although reality exists independently of us, we see it through the concepts we build. This, however, is an old thought – older even than the philosopher Kant – that undergoes rebirth time and again. Social constructivism focuses on how our sense of the world comes into being through our interactions with each other. Premises:

- We actively construct our realities through varying degrees of (un) consciousness.
- Science itself is a set of constructs for explaining what we perceive via the senses.
- Whatever "ultimate" reality is independent of us must be glimpsed through our constructs.

6 Participatory

Participatory research sprang forth from several influences, including Kurt Lewin, to emphasize the limitations of treating people (and animals) as objects and to invent possibilities for a more collaborative approach to research. Premises:

- Reality is co-created by human minds and the cosmos.
- We conduct practical research with people, in community, rather than on them.
- Research leads to action to transform the world in service to human flourishing.

Whereas quantitative research tends to favor positivism and postpositivism, most qualitative research falls under the critical theory, constructivism, or participatory paradigms. This does not mean that the researcher should stamp those paradigms onto the inquiry; rather, the topic drives the inquiry, which ends up falling within a particular paradigm.

Additionally, qualitative inquiry has moved over time from a structuralist to a poststructuralist emphasis and has been transformed by the voices of Indigenous researchers interested in story and experience.

Structuralism

This is the search for underlying structures in language as it shapes human relationships. Claude Lévi-Strauss is invoked for coining the term; before him, depth psychologists and, before them, the Romantics and members of various wisdom traditions stretching back through history attended to how concepts code experience. For this approach, knowledge depends on the structures of languages, signs, and symbols produced by cultural systems of signification (rituals etc.). Understanding these systems and codes helps the researcher understand the culture.

Poststructuralism

For this view, language is not a good description of reality, or of a people's world, which when decoded opens the doors to understanding. Rather, language refers mainly to itself, to its own signs and fictions. Here, nothing is determinate and everything is linguistically and philosophically created. (French poststructuralist writing is particularly and perhaps deliberately obscure in what it intends and does not intend to convey.)

What we think about reality depends heavily on our cultural and historical accounts of it. This is because discourses of public language create the subject, power, reality, truth, etc. A "text" (piece of writing, film, image, conversation, etc.) cannot be understood as containing a single meaning; instead, a multifaceted, multivocal approach best illuminates it.

Researcher and researched create multiple and changing meanings together, particularly if traditionally marginalized knowledges are involved.

Indigenous

No tribal group conducts research quite like any other. Nevertheless, common themes emerge when we hear what Indigenous researchers have to say about what they do and why:

- Inquiry need not to conform to Eurocentric standards, positivist ones in particular, about what constitutes valuable inquiry. That is for the researchers and their tribe to determine.
- Research is rooted primarily in relationships of various kinds, including long-term connections to the site of where it occurs.
- Indigenous researchers pay careful attention to tribal lore, including that held by traditional storytellers.
- Because so many Indigenous communities have been and continue to be subjected to the forces of colonization, by necessity much research focuses on possibilities for resistance and liberation.
- Knowledge is not just individual but belongs to the community and ultimately to the cosmos. Its uses and implications are decided by the communities involved in its production.

Where is terrapsychology in all this?

Terrapsychology and its research approach, Terrapsychological Inquiry (TI), are realist in their emphasis on a world beyond human projections, constructivist in tending the lenses through which we perceive the world, structuralist in emphasizing symbols and meanings, poststructuralist in taking multivocality and multiplicity of meanings into account, and participatory in exploring stories with multiple voices, including ecological ones. TI is also respectfully and nonappropriatively inspired by Indigenous research, and organic and interactive in assuming ongoing multidimensional participation between self and world.

This is what terrapsychological inquirers assume about the world we study and our place in it:

- Our terrain (locale, planet, cosmos) is verifiably and unmistakably real, not a veil of illusion or a purely human construct. It preceded us by billions of years, and our planet will orbit our sun long after we and our signifiers, discourses, and creeds are gone. We know reality best by participating in it as fully as possible, individually and collectively, recognizing our kinship with the other living beings who live here.
- The intimacy between self and world (the personal and the placed, thought and element, etc.) is an expression of the interdependency of all things. As a relic of empire, the atomistic view of nature opens unhealthy splits that prevent connection.
- When we think materialistically of the world as being "made up" of separate and independent entities, which are like building blocks, then we have got it backwards: the attempt to rationally reconstruct the world out of a collocation of "bits" contingently related to one another is as futile as the attempt to appreciate a symphony by sounding each note in isolation and then imagining a relation among them (Guigon, 1983, p. 100). Quantum physics has turned this conceptual corner by studying fields foundational, with subatomic particles constituting derivative field activities rather than coming first.
- Interiority (inwardness, subjectivity, an inner life) reaches wider and deeper than electrochemical activity in people's heads. It is more like a dimension or field of being, as Pythagoras, Thales, Ovid, Spinoza, Schopenhauer, Paracelsus, Goethe, Jung, Dewey, Teilhard de Chardin, William James, Bateson, Koestler, Whitehead, and a host of others have either hinted or said outright: a *matteriority* running all the way down, certainly to the molecular and bacteriological, and perhaps even into the subatomic (see section "Animism Reexamined").
- Like all other life on Earth, human beings are permanently, profoundly situated at every level of conscious and unconscious existence. Even in the midst of our most far-reaching speculations and dreams, even when our eyes and ears drift virtually around the planet, we are *here*. Dualisms that erect absolute walls between self and world, culture and nature, subject and object, spirit and matter, or us and them represent archaic splits valorized by the rise of monocrop agriculture, with its hardened distinctions of weed and crop, urban and rural, chieftain and peasant, army and civilian, reinforced ever after by institutionalized religion's disparagement of the tangible world and by the Industrial Revolution habit of treating nature and labor as commodities to be exploited.
- Manifestations of human psychic life, including patterns, images, symbols, and metaphors, link to correlates and correspondences in the natural

world across perpetually interactive fields and through complex systems. In other words, geological, geographical, ecological, meteorological, etc. forces are always psychological forces too.

- Jung, Corbin, Hillman, and others have posed the question of which archetypal-mythic position provides our lens: From which altar do we conduct our researches? That of Procrustes, as in positivism? That of archetypal Justice, as with critical theory? TI is terracentric, beginning with the root from which "gods" spring. That root finds itself situated in turn in *anima mundi*, the philosophic-mythic being of an animated cosmos. The core mythic figure is that of the continually speaking world soul.

Epistemological Observations

Terrapsychological action, whether carried out as research, prose, poetry, art, dance, wisdom practice, or some other way into the animate field, grounds itself in these observations about how we know the world:

- Research methodologies that assume up front, as positivism, postpositivism, and "realism" do, that human selves are separate from the world until proven otherwise remain saddled with an entrenched dualism that either nullifies their efforts or restricts them to relatively superficial findings (e.g., how temperature incrementally changes mood). Positivism reduces subject to object, postpositivism to conjecture, constructionism and poststructuralism to discourse. To understand the whole fish, we must abandon at least three habits of thought: the futile search for how its tail causes its head, that what we say about the fish constitutes it somehow, and the solipsistic conclusion that the fish is our own projection.
- Because we are always situated somewhere, we know whatever we know from right *here*. Knowledge transported around the world carries the flavor of its origins, places of interpretation, and transit points. We *begin* emplaced and connected – to nature, place, region, planet – and the quality of our knowing always reflects those connections, just as a branch implies the tree on which it grows.
- Environmental features translate into motifs operative within the human mind and body. From the perspective of unconscious psychic life, everything around us shimmers as potential symbol. Your home has a front door, and one fine day it flies open and cannot be shut. What in your life can't be kept outside any longer? What if we interpreted "outer" facts and events like images in our dreams? Metals would then be metalphors, landscapes inscapes, crowded parking lots holding up our drive, meandering tributaries tributarrying through our complex moods.
- Movements of mind and body echo movements of nature, surround, and place. Those moods and our dramas, symptoms, conflicts, and troubles

often, perhaps always, reflect those going on all around us: bulging waistlines and urban sprawl, spiritual epiphanies and sacred sites. Not only do we harbor within us the same earthly patterns that twist and curve around us, we act, feel, live, and die by them as well.

- Ignoring these connections between self and world pathologizes them and us. Although we now possess piles of research evidence for ecopsychology's contention that chronic disconnection from the natural world makes us physically, socially, and psychologically ill, we are only beginning to explore subtler disturbances resulting from what we ignore around us. Broken cities and barren rainforests wreak havoc in our psyches, diminishing us below and beyond the range of measurable illness as interiorized droughts and deserts encroach upon what remains of human sanity (Buzzell & Chalquist, 2008).
- We can include in our inquiries the facts, units, and quantities gathered by third-person or mixed-methods research by taking care to uncover their underlying forms, images, and reconnective motifs, highlighting the story in which the data are embedded. That a ranch in northern San Diego County was sold in the late 1800s to American settlers for $666.66 means little beyond the numbers until we know an important cultural and symbolic fact: that the ranch was named Rincon del Diablo.
- Working consciously with deep connections between self and world begins to heal the split driving environmental crisis and collective self-alienation and invites new delight in the complexity of our ties to nature, place, creatures, and things.

In brief, we know the world and its materials, storms, creatures, and sites by participating in it and with them in full, passionate, embodied ways. From the terrapsychological standpoint, knowledge arises from situated involvement with whatever fascinates us enough to study it. Tentative conclusions we draw about it operate like elements of fiction: plotlines, themes, and scenes carrying forward the story we walk into. No conclusion can be final because no story embedded in time and place is over for good.

Commitments of Terrapsychology

We do our work in the light of the following values and priorities, some of which will receive more emphasis than others in a given research project:

- Homecoming: the importance of longing for a felt sense of belonging consciously to place, planet, and cosmos. This includes welcoming home those voices, persons, impulses, beings, and even places repressed to the margins of culture and consciousness.
- Diversity: respect for and delight in variety at all levels, including those normally subdivided into "nature" and "culture."

- Agency: the right and privilege of forms and combinations of life, whether human or nonhuman, to flourish and direct themselves according to their own schemas of self-organization.
- Ecoliteracy: moving toward a basic awareness of ecology, nature, and environmental science.
- Sustainability: living as lightly as we can in the places we inhabit, and replenishing living systems or letting them replenish themselves.
- Ecojustice: using our work to highlight and give voice to those oppressed by industries and political systems that damage their environments.
- Appreciation: the aesthetic capacity for awe and love of what remains of Earth's natural integrity. We will not guard and cherish what we do not love and appreciate.
- Exploration: willingness to investigate the unknown even without a clear cause: the spontaneous and creative joy of finding out for its own sake.
- Collaboration: with all due respect to lone geniuses, recognition that our understanding of the world and our relations with it grows richer with every perspective added by researchers humbly committed to weaving a web of terrapsychological knowledge and practice.
- Responsibility: clarity about our obligations to do work that enhances the lives of our participants, their communities, the places we investigate, and the natural world itself. These obligations include alignment with Indigenous sovereignty.
- Integrality: the commitment to working as a whole researcher, conscious and unconscious, mental and physical, heartful and soulful.
- Terrania: a nickname or symbol for the just, sustainable, integral, and delightful world community of abundance, belonging, and truly international culture we will have to construct, network by local network and experiment by community experiment, if we expect to remain on this planet for longer than our extinct protohuman forebears.

These commitments reflect awareness of how the boundary we feel between our skin and the world remains a permeable one.

Sharing Flesh with the World

As a remedy for the now-customary philosophical habit of separative hyperindividualism, consider two alternative philosophies: one from a Vietnamese poet and Zen master, another from a French thinker and writer.

Thich Nhat Hanh coined the word "interbeing" to describe our deep interconnection with everything else. We cannot exist in isolation. Each of us represents part of a family lineage and a culmination of our ancestry. Our very bodies, themselves collections of cells, are filled with tiny organisms without which we could not move or live. "We inter-are with one another and with all life" (Nhat Hanh, 2017, p. 13). The entire planet is one vast, breathing cell.

In reflecting on the being of a single flower, we also see in it soil, rain, clouds, oceans, minerals, space, and time. Remove any of these "nonflower" elements and the flower ceases to be. This seems a simple philosophy of togetherness, but with it, Nhat Hanh has founded humanitarian relief projects, mindfulness ecovillages, monasteries for compassionate community, and engaged Buddhism for promoting social justice. For his efforts on behalf of nonviolence, Martin Luther King Jr. nominated him for a Nobel Peace Prize.

Maurice Merleau-Ponty, philosopher and anti-fascist war hero, drew on many sources, including Gestalt psychology, psychoanalysis, linguistics, anthropology, phenomenology, and the arts to present perception as primary and embodied rather than the unreliable faculty disparaged by Cartesian scientism. "The perceived world is the always presupposed foundation of all rationality, all value and all existence" (Merleau-Ponty, 1964, p. 13).

As the locus of perception, the body participates in the world's "flesh": not mere matter, analyzable and atomizable, but a field of relations between the sensing body and the things and beings it senses on every side. This field both underlies and activates sensor and sensed, self and things. Despite the turgidity of some of his writing, it seems to equate flesh with the world's animated ecology as perceived by a living body. As such, flesh precedes the split between subject and object, knower and known.

Flesh includes the world's elemental thickness, its perceptibility, its quality of incarnate being. Its relations differentiate, integrate, disintegrate, and reorganize with a flowing transience also observed by Thich Nhat Hanh. We learn the texture of this flow by receiving it with our senses. What makes the weight, the thickness, the flesh of each color, sound, and tactile texture, of the present, and of the world is how in sensing them we feel akin to them: the sensible returning to itself. When we witness this, language is no longer just personal or even human, but "the voice of no one, since it is the very voice of the things, the waves, and the forests" (Merleau-Ponty, 1968, p. 204).

This sense of kinship with the world unfolds through what Merleau-Ponty (1968) referred to as *chiasm*, a crossing back and forth between awareness of sensing things and awareness of being sensed. Touch your left hand with your right. Switch your awareness back and forth between your right hand as touching your left and your right hand as touched by it. This is an example of chiasm: the continuity and reversibility of subject and object, sensor and sensed. Notice that neither side of the chiasm is reducible to the other: not sensed to sensor (solipsism), nor sensor to sensed (materialism). Attempts at reduction end the conscious dimension of the dialog between them.

The chiasm of our embodied consciousness can, if properly sensitized, break through the split between mind and matter, body and Earth, self and locale, and culture and nature, and take its place as a member of the world's flesh. Merleau-Ponty (1968) had another word for this: *intercorporeity*. I see you seeing me; you see me seeing you. Instead of, "I think, therefore I am," it's, "We touch, therefore we are." Each thing stands forth in its differentiated particularity even as it remains related to other things.

Nhat Hanh and Merleau-Ponty came from two different cultures, and their philosophies reflect that. But the commonalities attest to their sharp sense of the world as a flowing place from whose activity we are never truly separate. We tend to view that world in terms of "finished" things separate from each other: a chair, a plant, and a mountain. They saw its continual becoming and concluded that relationality, not object or particle, is primordial. The world can indeed show up as object or particle, but its nature is continual, interdependent creativity.

Because the sense of the things around us as alive and conversing without words receives so much attention in terrapsychological work, we need a fresh view of animism.

Animism Reexamined

> Through this path of rediscovery, I found an undeniable call to action, to protect the place of my birth through custodial guardianship. I saw that the key concept that was missing from most efforts to restore or rejuvenate the San Lorenzo watershed area was a lack of understanding of the pathology of the river. This river was a living organism, shaped over time by natural events and by the hands of humans.
>
> *(Haber, 2019, p. 7)*

In 1871, E. B. Tylor published *Primitive Culture*. Influenced by Darwin and Comte, Tylor was on a self-appointed mission to destroy the superstitions of supposedly lower races and other pre-rational people. One of these superstitions was *animism*, the idea that aspects of nature can possess life and will (Tylor, 2016). Tylor had visited Mexico to improve his health in a climate warmer than that of London, but as an armchair anthropologist, he thought and read about "primitives" but never did any fieldwork beyond dressing as a ranchero to poke about among some Toltec ruins. Unaware that all cultures continually change and adapt, he tagged all forms of culture outside the European pretense of rationality with the label "early." To study how language originated, he visited the Berlin Deaf and Dumb Institute to look at inmates' gestures.

Anthropology has come a long way since Tylor, but his devaluation of animism as archaic and childish has embedded itself deeply in common notions about our relations with the natural world. Although he considered religion a precursor to scientific rationalism, he shared with scientism the denigration of matter and nature as passive and dumb. In this he aligned himself with Marin Mersenne and Pierre Gassendi, contemporaries of Descartes who sought in writing to refute the magical worldview of Renaissance Hermeticism (Bortoft, 2012). Alchemists like Robert Fludd, they accused, were not only ignorant of mathematics but also believed in a world soul and saw angels and demons everywhere (Yates, 1991). Their arguments of disenchantment laid the cornerstone for the ideological scientism to come. In the hands of Descartes, the world seemed to subside into passivity, a mere background to more important human affairs.

Of course, this has never stopped the background from intruding into the foreground. For example: "Inwardly, a molting dream monster named 'Babushka' chases a dreamer out of a building; outwardly, the polluted Russian River floods communities out of their homes and towns a month or so after the dream" (Chalquist, 2007, p. 23). Terrapsychological observation has found so many of these correspondences that the real question is not whether they occur but what they mean. At an unconscious level, animism seems to be a baseline psychology, a foundational template for how we encounter the world.

When TI first appeared as a research methodology, it distinguished between the *literalized animism* of explaining weather, fire, floods, or other natural events as caused by an arcane outer force like a spirit or demon and the *intersubjective animism* of experiencing such events inwardly as symbolically meaningful and full of significance (Chalquist, 2007).

Animism is often dismissed as a type of psychological projection, as if the world depended upon us for its aliveness rather than the other way around. David Abram critiques a common conclusion about how projection develops:

> The earliest experience of selfhood … co-arises with the earliest experience of otherness. So the clustered trees, the bricks in the floor, and the sunlight are not first encountered as inert or insentient presences into which, later, the child projects her own consciousness. Rather, the inwardly felt sentience of the child is a correlate of the outwardly felt wakefulness of the sky and the steadfast support of the ground, and the willfulness of the caressing wind; it is a concomitant of the animate surroundings.
>
> *(Abram, 2010, p. 38)*

Failing to understand the foundational depth of the self-other relation, we raise children to think of themselves as split off from a mute world. However, this cannot silence the world:

> *What the conscious mind is trained to see as nonliving places and things, the unconscious reacts to as animated presences and metaphors.* Borderlines and borderlands, sludgy bays and constricted moods, personal complexes and apartment complexes seem to resonate together as events in the world symbolize aspects of the human self and those aspects in turn point back to the features of the world that evolved our remarkable minds.
>
> *(Chalquist, 2007, p. 23)*

Intersubjective animism extends the psychoanalytic concept of the transferential field – the complex and mostly unconscious interplay of psychological dynamisms, postures, and behaviors in the therapy room – to include our relations with storms and streams, hillsides and valleys, streets and vehicles, and buildings and neighborhoods. Our sense of these things as responsive and ensouled arises in part as an emergent property of the psychological field between us and them, a property not reducible to simple causal relations (e.g., dim light causes low mood). This means we can interpret them, much as we interpret the symbols in our dreams.

That is one way to hold in mind the animate presences around/within us: psychologically. Another more radical and perhaps more ecological way aligns with panpsychism (everything has qualities of consciousness), panexperientialism (everything is capable of some level of experience), hylozoism (everything is alive), or Indigenous animistic worldviews. Subjectivity is then not a secretion of matter but the interiority of it: brain does not generate it, but brain and body complexify and differentiate it. That is why no science can pin down a thing that looks like subjectivity and show it to us under a microscope. All we can see from the outside are darting neurotransmitters and sparking neurons. Would it not make more sense to argue, then, that the more complex the form of matter, the richer the expression of its inner nature?

Versions of this argument reach back into prehistory, run through esoteric Buddhism, Shinto, Hinduism, and Judaism, acknowledge the vivid earthiness of the Yoruba orishas and recur in the folktales, fairytales, and myths of every land. Familiar names who have taken seriously this idea that everything experiences or lives include Aristotle, Ovid, Cicero, Seneca, Plotinus, and Plato, all of whom described Earth as ensouled; the long tradition of alchemy as a wisdom path in Egypt, the Middle East, and elsewhere; organizations and movements like the Neoplatonic Academy in Florence, *Naturphilosophie* in Germany, and Romanticism in Europe; and pagan, heathen, and goddess movements in many parts of the world. The United States has rich traditions of American Indian story and ritual praising the aliveness of land and place.

Among philosophers, Heraclitus, Pythagoras, Thales, Empedocles, Epicurus, Anaximander, Anaximenes, Leibniz, Spinoza, Goethe, Schopenhauer, Schelling, and many others took animism seriously. Pierre Teilhard de Chardin (1976, p. 53) considered subjectivity a "within of things" inherent in matter. Whitehead (1979) rejected the materialist fantasy of mind popping out of what is mindless, referring to it as the fallacy of simple location. Also on our list are Margaret Cavendish, William James, Charles Peirce, John Dewey, Paul Carus, Ernst Haeckel, John Muir, Aldo Leopold, Morton Prince, Owen Barfield, William Montague, and, more recently, Rupert Sheldrake, Charles Hartshorne, David Ray Griffin, Christian de Quincey, Freya Mathews, David Abram, Stephanie Lahar, Manuel de Landa, Val Plumwood, Stephanie Kaza, Jane Bennett, Karen Barad, and David Skrbina (2005).

Notable scientists include Johannes Kepler, Pierre-Louis Maupertuis, Sir Isaac Newton, Nicolas Copernicus, Vladimir Vernadsky, Joseph Priestley, William Herschel, Gustav Fechner, Ernst Mach, Emil du Bois-Reymond, Thomas Edison, Sir Arthur Eddington, Sir Julian Huxley, J. B. S. Haldane, Sir James Jeans, Sir Charles Scott Sherrington, W. E. Agar, C. H. Waddington, A. Cochran, Freeman Dyson, Gregory Bateson, Wolfgang Pauli, Sewall Wright, Bernhard Rensch, Stuart Hameroff, David Bohm, Stephan Harding, Derek McCormack, and Alan Latham.

We should bear in mind one psychological payoff in the culturally sanctioned rejection of animistic worldviews: a defense against punctured narcissism. Recognizing the world's needs and powers and intelligences relativizes our own. Having been removed from the center of God's universe, the solar system, and our own personalities, we stand now within the world of nature as one species among many. A unique one to be sure, but not its sole possessor of sentience. This is humbling. Why not deploy our human powers, then, to become more conscious of the animate presences conversing all around us?

For Discussion

1 What happens when we remain unconscious of the philosophy behind our researches?
2 Why is it important to understand and keep to our commitments while we explore?
3 Where do you stand on the question of animism?

References

Abram, D. (2010). *Becoming animal: An earthly cosmology*. New York, NY: Vintage.

Bortoft, H. (2012). *Taking appearance seriously: The dynamic way of seeing in Goethe and European thought*. Edinburgh: Floris Books.

Buzzell, L., & Chalquist, C. (Eds.) (2008). *Ecotherapy: Healing with nature in mind*. San Francisco, CA: Sierra Club Books.

Chalquist, C. (2007). *Terrapsychology: Reengaging the soul of place*. New Orleans, LA: Spring Journal Books.

Denzin, N., & Lincoln, Y. (Eds.) (2017). *The Sage handbook of qualitative research*. London, New Delhi and Thousand Oaks, CA: Sage.

Guigon, C. (1983). *Heidegger and the problem of knowledge*. Indianapolis, IN: Hackett.

Haber, M. (2019). Unattended trauma of the San Lorenzo River: A terrapsychological inquiry (unpublished dissertation). California Institute of Integral Studies, San Francisco, CA.

Merleau-Ponty, M. (1964). *The primacy of perception*. Evanston, IL: Northwestern University Press.

Merleau-Ponty, M. (1968). *The visible and the invisible*. Evanston, IL: Northwestern University Press.

Nhat Hahn, T. (2017). *The art of living: Peace and freedom in the here and now*. New York, NY: HarperOne.
Skrbina, D. (2005). *Panpsychism in the West*. Cambridge, MA: MIT Press.
Teilhard de Chardin, P. (1976). *The phenomenon of man*. New York, NY: Harper Torchbooks.
Tylor, E. (2016). *Primitive culture*, vol. I. New York, NY: Dover Publications.
Whitehead, A. (1979). *Process and reality*. New York, NY: The Free Press.
Yates, F. (1991). *Giordano Bruno and the hermetic tradition*. Chicago, IL: University of Chicago Press.

3

PREPARING FOR THE WORK

Whether academic or informal, research is systematic inquiry. *Deep research* moves below surfaces and mundane facts – below the simplistically linear and uniform, which complexity theory and current cosmological observations say are exceptions to reality's wiggliness – to tend the patterns and meanings that organize and live within and behind appearances. As Robert Romanyshyn (2007, p. 12) puts it, deep research is a "poetics of the soul" that attends "to the images in the ideas, the fantasies in the facts, the dreams in the reasons, the myths in the meanings, the archetypes in the arguments, and the complexes in the concepts."

As a deep research approach, Terrapsychological Inquiry (TI) explores the isles in the images, the fens in the fantasies, the dales in the dreams, the mountains in the myths, the archways in the archetypes, and the commutes in the complexes. We tend the metaphors, patterns, and symbols we share with our surroundings. TI provides tools, ideas, and examples for exploring how terrain, place, element, and natural process show up in human psychology, endeavor, and story, including myth and folklore. Understanding what we do and who we are requires understanding where we are, and when.

What emerges when we listen, imagine, and feel into rich intersections of psyche, story, symbol, body, mood, and place? How might we describe these emergences through research projects, storytelling, imagery, art, festival, ritual, and movement?

First, we need to know what sort of research TI can support.

What Kinds of Research Projects Are Suitable for TI?

Originally, research done with terrapsychology included

DOI: 10.4324/9781003462965-4

- Locianalysis: Studying a specific site for its ecological complexes or, as they were formerly called, placefield syndromes: wounds we symbolically share with a place, as when a mine dug there parallels a depression or litter a state of emotional confusion.
- Psychocartography: Charting myths and archetypes inhabiting particular places (e.g., Dionysus, genderqueer god of altered states, in San Francisco).
- Dialogical alchemy: Interaction with objects or natural elements as aspects of our own psychology – and ours of theirs.
- Archetypal geology: Matt Cochran's term (personal communication, April 2, 2014) for tracking the psychology of the underworld of buried geological rhythms (faulting, drifting, metamorphism).
- Lorecasting: Fanciful interpretation of natural events like epidemics, floods, and earthquakes as meaningful symbols (Chalquist, 2007).

Although the book *Terrapsychology* gave examples of animal behavior, weather, and even chunks of matter interpreted as metaphors like those which animate dreams, the primary three-phase methodology – preparation, assessment, and placehosting – focused mainly on specific geographic sites (Chalquist, 2007). So did subsequent research at first.

However, TI can study any deep connection with matter, nature, place, weather, animals (including interspecies communication), insects, plants, elements, or even earth or travels around the globe. It can be used as a formal research methodology, a framework for less methodical work, or even a genre or style of expression. (See the 2010 anthology *Rebearths: Conversations with a World Ensouled* for examples.) It can involve groups, entire communities, silenced voices, or solitary work.

Here are examples (not exhaustive) of topic areas in addition to the ones above and those found in this book:

- Emplaced folklore (including exploration of modern myths): Exploring how plots, images, or themes from myth, folktale, fairytale, or legend recur in particular places (Chalquist, 2018).
- Heartsteading (Appendix III): Building small communities around a compelling concern as a central focus or research question, then engaging in cycles of discussion, reflection, and next-step practices.
- Finding homeplaces or sanctuaries: How, where, when, and why certain kinds of people looking for belonging and homecoming congregate in specific places (Olivieri, 2017).
- Exploring the impact of ecological damage and healing on the psyches of people living near it (Haber, 2019).
- The lived relationship between unoccupied and occupied lands.
- Understanding how place or nature influence language.

- Storytelling, peacemaking, and childhood development.
- Sustainable food production (e.g., permaculture and agroforestry) as informed by the presence of the place where it occurs.
- Sea songs and myths as they enrich travel and oceanic exploration (Fay, 2018).
- Beauty as a means to appreciate, protect, and love nature.
- Making art with the natural world, or some aspect of it, as a full partner (Mitchell, 2005).
- Use of education, art, story, and nature practices for building ecoresilience in communities faced with climate change.
- Nature education for children using art, music, and gathering and telling local stories that include features of the ecosystem as characters.
- Appropriate and transformative uses of plant medicines, with the plants as emissaries of the intelligence of nature.
- Work with the presences found at sacred sites.
- Nature and healing (ecotherapy): Therapeutic and sensitizing practices that reconnect the psyche and body with the natural world (Buzzell & Chalquist, 2008).
- Ecological embodiment and embeddedness: Exploring the presence of nature, place, or the elements through how they talk to the body (Moynihan, 2018).
- How expatriates relate to place through story and community.
- Ecoliteracy education with an experiential or ecotherapy component.
- Community festival-organizing to celebrate or bring attention to neglected aspects of a local natural feature or locale.
- Studying parallels in declines and increases of human health with local ecological health.
- Planting and gardening that listen to the land and take the presence of place into account.
- Animal communication and community-building across species.
- Nature contact and presence as an emotional and communal resource for the displaced (G. Barnwell, personal communication, September 10, 2019).
- Place-based or nature-informed reconciliation among groups traditionally hostile to each other.
- Ecojustice: Focusing on the relationship between marginalized people and some aspect of nature or place (Olivieri, 2017).
- Terrestry: Working with recurrent metaphors and themes throughout one's ancestry, usually by tracing the earthly travels of those who have gone before.
- Eradigmatics: The study of how human history and life on earth shape themselves around vast controlling archetypes such as Mother Nature,

Heavenly City, Big Machine, and Earthrise (Chalquist, 2018) and express themselves in particular places.
- Ecospirituality ("tellusgnosis"): Developing reverent practices that appreciate the soulful or spiritual of aspects of the natural world (see Chapter 8).

This list of examples will expand as researchers feel called to investigate other aspects of how the things around us make their way into us, resulting in an emergent new story (or update on an old story) of how this transmutative interaction plays out and what it means to us.

Qualitative-research projects tend to emphasize either theory (hermeneutics), as when topics are put together to enrich one another, or knowledge gained from interviews and then subjected to thematic analysis (Chapter 5). TI can be used for either or both, as we will see in Chapter 4 when we go over how to proceed through a study.

Comparison with Other Methodologies

A *methodology* is an overall approach to exploring a topic of inquiry. The approach includes a plan for research, tools to use, a rationale for including them, goals of the inquiry, theoretical framework, and basic assumptions about the nature of inquiry (e.g., positivism, postpositivism, participation). A *method* is an inquiry activity like interviewing people and interpreting texts. Which methods you use depends on your methodology and inquiry topic.

Graduate students at the schools where I teach sometimes feel eager to make methodology smoothies, blending two, three, or more ingredients in the hope that this gives a more authoritative picture to their research. Students are also influenced by instructors who value bringing as many perspectives as possible into the study.

Unless done with care, however, mixing methodologies can water down the work, scatter one's energies, confuse the future reader, blur the research question that drives the inquiry, and force the researcher to explain the rationale for the combination and for how such different and often irreconcilable approaches must mesh. It involves extra work if done with any degree of rigor.

If you find yourself wanting to combine methodologies without a clear reason for doing so, your research question probably needs more refining. This is true whether you are working inside or outside academia. Also, in an academic study, just because your study has an experiential component does not make it either heuristic or phenomenological, both of which involve specific procedures to follow. All qualitative research brings in experiential material to some extent.

Additionally, avoid picking a methodology simply because it sounds like an approach you would enjoy working with. *Methodology should flow from the topic*, not the reverse. What you study dictates how you study it. You are pregnant with work that knows what it needs. Do not decide the baby will be an engineer or a psychologist before they even have a chance to emerge from the womb and start breathing.

To ease the novice researcher's anxious habit of mashing together methodologies without trying to integrate their differing values, worldviews, and basic assumptions, TI incorporates frequently used methods from a range of methodologies while holding its own foundational perspectives (Chapter 2). Components are built in from Heuristics, Phenomenology (including Interpretive and Existential), hermeneutic and theoretical approaches, Organic Inquiry, Grounded Theory, Critical Theory, Depth Inquiry, Collaborative Inquiry, Appreciative Inquiry, discourse and content analysis, Narrative Inquiry, Intuitive Inquiry, case study, action research, Mindful Inquiry, Alchemical Hermeneutics, Integral Inquiry, ethnography, autoethnography, arts-based research, Gaian methodologies, feminist research, Indigenous research, and other qualitative and theoretical methodologies.

Nevertheless, some research questions might require recourse to multiple methodologies. For example, if you wanted to conduct a TI that included all six Heuristic self-exploration steps as developed by Moustakas (1990), then combining methodologies would be appropriate so long as you explained why and how you did this. Studies involving Native researchers using Indigenous methodologies would be fruitful if following full tribal protocols and serving the communities of origin.

Below are some contrasts of TI with methodologies that otherwise fit well with it and to which it is indebted:

- Heuristics: Emphasizes self-exploration, whereas TI focuses on hearing the presence or "voice" of the world and its emplaced elements. Self-transformation occurs but is not the main focus. (Ancient alchemists were more interested in the aliveness of matter than in discovering themselves, a point some Jungians forget. Arguing that alchemists were unconscious of their projected strivings for wholeness is diagnosis from a distance.) Also, Heuristics tends not to emphasize systematic data analysis. (TI does not always either: see Chapter 5.)
- Organic Inquiry: Its philosophy conceptually splits the chthonic (earthly) from the numinous (spiritual) instead of holding them together. Also, it offers no substantive data analysis, and its reliance on in-depth interviewing is not always appropriate for TI.
- Transpersonal methodologies: Not developed primarily for ecological work, these exalt spiritual states that are normally secondary or ancillary to place-focused TI studies. Like heuristics, these methodologies also highlight individual transformation.

- Appreciative Inquiry: Does not explore or contain the shadow, darkness, or pathology of the topic.
- Phenomenology: Dwells entirely on individual human experience. Focuses more on obtaining the "essence" of an experience than on exploring underlying stories.
- Giorgi Phenomenology: Its emphasis on correct reduction to meaning units consumes time and energy that could be spent in dialog with the subject of research. Also, in a bow to Procrustes, it insists on sticking to fixed steps of analysis and replicability of results in order to appear scientific enough.
- Narrative Inquiry: Does not study the discourse of our relationships with the more-than-human world.
- Grounded Theory/Situational Analysis: Does not give importance to the ecological dimension, and when done properly takes years.
- Autoethnography: Focuses on oneself as a cultural entity, with place only a backdrop.
- Depth Inquiry: Not developed as an ecopsychological methodology, and needs other methodologies for data analysis.
- Alchemical Hermeneutics: Likewise; also, privileges the story of Orpheus as an archetypal mode of research but is silent about other archetypes that can inform inquiry. Unlike TI, it is not a stand-alone methodology.
- Indigenous methodology: Normally best done by Indigenous researchers or at the invitation of Indigenous communities; focuses from an insider perspective on local, tribal, and cultural concerns.
- Mixed methods: Although empirical/positivist research comes from a mechanistic worldview, its methods can be useful so long as we remember that they get only at the measurable, linear, etc., aspects of the study, aspects that are not deep truths but plot elements in the larger story as actually lived.

Although some topics demand more than one methodology, consider including whatever methods are needed in a TI study rather than dragging in entire methodologies and forcing them to adapt to one another on the spot despite their differences.

Formulating the Research Question

Before you devise a research or inquiry question, you will need to have found your research topic. Topics do not always show up where you expect them to. Or when. Sometimes a topic opens a path for a different topic beyond or behind it.

Topic hideouts stumbled upon by researchers being quietly or not so quietly pursued by a research idea awaiting exploration include: dreams, illnesses, psychological symptoms, past or present relationships, shifts in family situations, losses and endings, sudden beginnings, captivating new interests, nature encounters, weather fluctuations, surprising turns of events, unexpected news, "random" encounters, appliance or equipment misbehavior, mood shifts, workplace dynamics ... Anything changing unexpectedly can signal the entry of a topic.

Once you have the topic and it has you, the research question provides the primary focus, the pivot around which your entire study turns. Explorations in the field, literature review, interview questions, data analysis, detection and interpretation of key themes in what you collect, whether words, images, songs, movements, or texts: all derive from the key question that homes in on the topic that grabs you.

The question should testify to how the topic chooses you, not just you the topic. The question is your initial response to being singled out by the muted but persistent presence of what you wish to study and what wishes to study you.

To formulate your research question, begin by asking yourself what fascinates you, energizes you, and has an edge for you. Where is a gap in the fields you study? When you find yourself asking, "Why in the world hasn't anybody studied ... ?" then you may be watching a research question being born.

Write one page on where the energy is for you in your topic: what excites, what outrages, what brings up strong feelings, where the joy is, and what you wonder about. Once you have done that, reread what you wrote and asking yourself: "What questions must I ask about this topic? What must I know?" Write down your questions. Now, either pick the most urgent one or blend them into one question. That is your research question, for now. It will mutate.

Sometimes the question hides in exactly where the personal begins to shift into the more-than-me, as when the declining quality of air in Utah caught the attention of Maggie Hippman:

> There was a time – before we grew too high to stay whole – that to speak of air and atmosphere was to comment on the human soul and spirit. An individual could not have invoked one without implying the other ... If the air that sustains us is the keeper of awareness, and if the lungs are the organ of grief, then dirty air may be the physical manifestation of the grief that we repress. And if Utah does do one thing well, it is repression.
>
> *(Hippman, 2017, pp. 7–8)*

Another way to begin formulating the question is to ask someone receptive to listen while you talk about what moves you about the topic. Once you have finished, the listener should ask clarifying questions like: "What must you know about this topic? What unfinished story does the topic signify? What questions do you have about it? How do you want to see the story finished?"

Write down your questions and distill them into a single answerable question. Your question will evolve, especially when you and your dissertation chair, research adviser, or inquiry collaborators begin to unearth the unexamined assumptions buried in it.

Most research questions start out far too broadly stated. That is different from the question being open-ended, which is fine for explorations that require such an approach. Refine and concentrate your question until it can focus and empower your work. At each step of refinement, run the question by your dreams and by supportive people for comment. Be open to how the question might change as you proceed, remembering that the question is not only yours to labor over, but also, if you have listened carefully, what your research topic wants to ask about itself.

Levels and Degrees of Topic Involvement

How emotionally involved should you be with the inquiry? Below are some guides for gauging this. Terrapsychological research often brings up intense emotions, especially where ecological complexes (Chapter 4), climate-change fallout, or questions of social and environmental justice are concerned. Ideally, you want enough passion to carry through the inquiry but not so much that you drown in it. It's important to be honest with yourself about whatever wounds you bring into the study and about your capacity for managing them.

Be on the lookout also for the unexpected joys of the work. I have often heard reactions like, "Now I know where I am in the world." "So this is why X happened to me." "Even a building has a soul!" "The plants and animals are speaking to me, and I can actually hear them – they use gestures and symbols." "How intricately my story interweaves that of these cycles of nature."

Depth of Involvement

The depth of involvement has to do with where the promptings for research come from. For the most part, the depth has more to do with what the work itself wants than with the researcher's agenda for it, as everyone knows who has been possessed by a topic. The following levels overlap, and none is more or less valuable than the others.

Ego-consciousness Level

Inquiry performed at this level tends to be done to fulfill academic requirements or explore personal or professional interests. Subsets of this level include the *superego type* of project (picking a topic because you feel you "should" work on it), the *heroic/activist type* (the topic is done to create social change), the *wounded healer type* (done to tend or heal a wound in oneself), and the *career type* (taking on the topic in service to further a career), to name a few. Any desires for recognition should be noted.

Organismic Level

Work at this level meets needs for self-fulfillment or realization. The quality of involvement tends to include the somatic as well as the emotional and intellectual. The unconscious is a participant in the work as well, with its hints tended by watching dreams, fantasies, accidents, symptoms, and slips of the tongue. The researcher should ensure that the work, rather than oneself, remains the primary focus.

Relational Level

Relational-level work responds to the needs of others as though interlocked with one's own. There tends to be a community component also, implicit if not overt. Sometimes old family legacies (intergenerational wounds or themes) are addressed. A sense of mission beyond one's own fulfillment can characterize this level. One should watch for the triggering of a savior complex that could fuel emotional over-involvement.

Transpersonal Level

This work feels foundational and often includes mythological material, archetypal promptings, ecological concerns, or cosmological motifs. It is as though the work were initiated by something that transcends but involves the personal conscious and unconscious. The researcher does not select it so much as feel selected by it. This sort of work often acts as a barometer of the undercurrents of the time the researcher lives in. It will be important to remain grounded and not get lost emotionally or intellectually.

Degrees of Involvement

These refer to emotional intensity:

- **Minor**: Relatively undemanding emotionally, though sometimes intellectually and intuitively intricate.
- **Moderate**: Something is definitely cooking, and it fills the thoughts, senses, emotions, and imagination. The work has fire in it.
- **Consuming**: A sense of inescapability and profound commitment. Can become obsessional if not monitored consciously. Self-care and

time-management strategies are very important at this degree of involvement. Do not be isolated in the work.

Ranges of Involvement

- **Outside**: The research happens primarily outside the researcher. This range fits more traditionally scientific expectations of research.
- **Inside**: The research happens primarily inside the researcher. This fits more psychological approaches.
- **Intersubjective**: The research unfolds between the researcher, topic, and participants (including places, elements, plants, animals, objects, and buildings). This fits critical and participatory approaches.
- **Trans-subjective**: The research seems to happen everywhere you look: inside, outside, and between. This is the most frequent range for terrapsychological research.

Bear in mind that there is no optimal level or range. They depend on what the topic requires of you.

Understanding Symbol, Dream, Archetype, and Myth

Because the "psychology" part of terrapsychology includes insights from the depth traditions and the humanities, the researcher will need some adequacy in understanding aspects of human nature not studied by positivist mainstream psychology, with its emphasis on measurable behavior, cognitive schemata, sensory thresholds, and other surface aspects of consciousness. The deeper levels of psyche communicate themselves more clearly through symbol, dream, archetype, and myth.

Symbols

Emerging from many sources, the psyche's self-organizing and self-actualizing activity draws on the power of *symbolization*. From a psychodynamic standpoint, this means more than being able to communicate with numbers, letters, signs, and gestures. Beyond that, the psyche can invest objects, images, and events – in fact, just about anything – with psychological meaning. Through the magic medium of consciousness as it participates continually in what is outside itself, bridges become symbols of connection, chasms open deep places in the soul, peaks stand for heights of insight or mood, and rivers convey a symbolic motion of our journey through life, now calm, now meandering, rushing at times, and then flowing at last into the sea where all busy currents merge.

Even parts of the body can take on symbolic meaning:

- inexplicable hunger pangs in the gut announcing unsatisfied emotional longing;
- a backache testifying to a lack of emotional support;
- a medically healthy leg that won't bear weight making a statement about missing one's path in life;
- a headache forcing a transition from overthinking to sinking into feelings for a while.

Unlike a sign, an abstraction which stands for something definite (red light = stop; arrows in a triangle = recycle), a symbol, connected to the depths, always includes some mystery (Jung, 1976). How do we find out what a symbolic sensation, image, event, action, etc., can tell us?

In a class exercise in which I asked everyone to picture their dissertation topic and feel where it showed up in their body, one student said he felt as though someone were pushing down on his shoulders. When I asked him what popped into his mind as he felt that pressure, he replied that he felt blocked in his writing and overwhelmed by all the demands on him. As he spoke, I kept thinking of Atlas holding up the sky. When I shared this association with him, he felt a strong emotional resonance that included frustration and sadness at having to carry so much. I then asked him to name what was on his plate, and he said, "I'm an activist, and I feel worn out." He was also a full-time graduate student *and* had a family to look after. A lot indeed to rest on one man's tired shoulders. He liked my suggestion that the block was trying to protect him from even more pressure. The "someone" pushing down on his shoulders was, of course, himself. More specifically, what he expected of himself.

Notice what he and I did together to decode the symbol his body produced:

1 We felt our way into the possibility that a body event can hold symbolic message value: the unconscious speaking in the flesh.
2 We consulted our initial *free associations* (Freud, 2010) to that symbol.
3 We *amplified* the image (Jung, 1954) that came out of the association by discussing some of its details. (Further amplification would involve his learning more about the Atlas story and where it came from.)
4 We compared notes on all this on the assumption that psyche does not stay within you or me but lives between us too.
5 Then we asked what *purpose* the symptom (his writing block) served in his mental economy (Adler, 1964). These practices together allowed us to decipher the meaning or message in the symptom.

Notice too how this exercise demonstrates another power of the psyche: *identification*, in this case with a heroic mythological figure. We play roles all the time: lover, outcast, rescuer, mother, father, etc., but in identification we *become* the role with only a partial awareness, if that, of doing so. Probably all of us have heard ourselves say something in a familiar parental tone and thought, "That was my mother (father, grandparent, etc.) speaking." Identification.

This usually isn't a problem, but when the identification reenacts a wound and becomes rigid and unconscious, it can be. For example, what some call the inner critic can tear down self-esteem, amplify doubts, sabotage progress, and deepen depression. It then becomes necessary to identify the inner voice of the critic, step back from it, trace its origins (usually to an early authority figure who was harsh and demanding), and recognize it as one of many voices in the psyche no more important than any other. We can even negotiate with it and recruit it. This is the life-saving power of *disidentification*.

The roles we identify with aren't restricted to the purely human arena. As the example above demonstrates, we can fall as easily and unconsciously into the cultural fantasy of a mythological role. In fact, the society we live in prizes some of these roles over others. In the United States, men often find themselves pressed into folkloric roles like Hero, Warrior, and Savior. A dose of self-awareness can help prevent such role identification from degenerating into a lifelong psychological imprisonment. A knight who is only a knight and nothing else cannot raise his visor long enough to breathe properly. Nor is it easy to love with a heart trapped behind an unremovable breastplate.

When you think about it, the psyche's natural polycentricity and plurality resemble those of the natural world, which organizes itself effectively unless a single power tries to dominate it. Inside, that power can be the ego, the superego (Inner Critic), or some other role we identify with. Outside, in the world of nature, that dominating power is us, human beings, to the extent we remain ecologically blind. But we need not be. We can learn our place as responsible beings in the web of life.

Thus far we have considered several symbol-generating powers of the psyche, the fabulously intricate entity we live inside of, even when asleep. We are now in a position to consider another important power that can reveal our intimate bonds to the natural world: that of dreaming.

Dreams

Why do we dream? This remains puzzling when we ask the question purely from the outside, as though the brain were a machine generating nightly dramas. (Incidentally, this kind of externalization also interferes with our understanding of other species. Why do dolphins frolic? From an external perspective devoid of empathy, reasons include mating strategies, territorial definition, and skin care. But any poet or naturalist can tell you that dolphins frolic also because they enjoy it.)

For those of us who work a lot with dream content, the answer is fairly obvious: *Dreams bring back at night what we fail to integrate into our lives by day*. Even the neurological externals, the chemistry and circuitry, involved in dreaming serve this psychological purpose.

Consider that on a given night you pass through five stages of neurologically active consciousness:

1 alpha and theta frequency waves, also associated with relaxing meditative states;
2 sleep spindles;
3 slow-moving delta waves;
4 almost all delta; and
5 REM (rapid eye movement) sleep.

These stages move cyclically from one through five then start again with stage one. A complete sleep cycle takes an average of 90 to 110 minutes. From the busy pace of waking life, then, your brain slows and relaxes into the stately cycles of the natural world.

Dreams begin when the pons, an oval structure at the top of the brainstem, releases acetylcholine, a neurotransmitter acting in service to systemic self-modulation: in other words, realignment and rebalancing. As the generator of this chemical signal, the pons evolved 505 million years ago, which makes it older than the neocortex with which we think. "Pons," by the way, means "bridge": in this case, one spanning ancient mammalian past with active present, unconscious with conscious, sleep with waking, breathing in with breathing out, this part of the brain communicating with that, left ear coordinated with right, taste buds with each other, and movements on one side of the body balanced by those of its other side. The pons, then, is not only a literal organ but also a highly symbolic one.

Other parts of the brain involved with dreaming include the deep gray matter above the eyes (depth of tissue and of consciousness), the prefrontal cortex, which in dreaming slows down ego-involved activity and suspends touch with the hippocampus (memory), and the parieto-temporal-occipito (PTO) junction of gray matter in the back (depth again) of the brain. The PTO sits where the temporal and parietal lobes meet: time and the senses joined by streams of impulses from motor, perceptual, and emotional activities, all mingling in moral decision-making and in sensing the minds of other beings. Damage to these lobes impairs empathy, physical balance, time sense, and many other operations involved with self-regulation; diminished REM sleep shrinks our understanding of complex emotions. (We also dream during non-REM sleep, but the dreams tend to be less colorful.)

Dreaming, then, is when the brain sets the will aside to drop us into a slow, deep, reintegrative flow of image, emotion, and memory transfigured. When we wake, serotonin – involved in the rational construction of experience – floods the brain, often carrying our recollections of dreams away on the neurochemical tide. "Serotonin" comes from "serum," which in turn derives from the image of a flowing river.

Psychologically, too, dreaming rebalances the psyche by returning to daytime consciousness what we fail to integrate into it by day – *but in symbolic form*, as when we dream of driving a powerful new car just before deciding to take firmer control of our direction in life. The dream is a precise image and, in this case, hints about the actual psychological state of affairs. Dreams can be difficult to understand in part because they show us what we fail to see and in part because they speak in symbols rather than reasoned arguments. Reductive explanations of dreams as somatic trivia or "anxiety dreams" hide their import. Once we decipher them, we receive invaluable guidance from sources of organismic wholeness deeper than conscious reasoning.

When psychotherapists and analysts work with dreams, they pay especially close attention to initial dreams because they often signal the course of the work. This is also important when beginning a TI. The state and direction of the inquiry may appear in symbolic form.

As will be evident in the following chapter, dreams can offer guidance throughout the inquiry. The San Diego dream mentioned in Chapter 1 is an example of how places personify as dream figures to be conversed with even after the dream ends. Other aspects of the work personify as well: animals, insects, storms, and floods – just about any aspect of the natural or built environment can reappear as a dream character. Free associating to and amplifying it will indicate whether a particular dream symbol represents such a personification or is more an aspect of ourselves.

The inquiry itself can personify, as when a doctoral student starting their work on how plant medicines act as emissaries of the natural world dreamed of a baby boy who could already speak. He was highly vocal. By day she was filled with ideas to jot down.

Archetype

Birth. Life. Death. Heroine or Hero. God. Rebirth. Initiation. Return. Child. Crone. Trickster. Matter. Spirit. Love. Take one of the big truths of our existence, give it capital letters, think of it as a theme both external and internal, and you have probably named an archetype. In all our minds lives Wholeness, Seeking, Conjunction (Sacred Marriage), and other primal patterns that organize human experience while linking it to the greater-than-human world.

Archetypal images appear in dreams and fantasies; works of art and literature; gods and religious rituals; the villains, heroes, spirits, monsters, and helpers inhabiting folklore; stock characters in plays, festivals, and films; the sacred stories we think of as myths ... and, of course, the natural world, unless we prefer to assume our minds did not evolve from it.

First point of potential confusion about archetypes: thinking of them only as nouns, as things. Peel back a skull and find archetypes? No. Did you ever take a literature class and hear about analyzing a story's themes? *The Odyssey*, for example, unfolds the theme of a grand journey homeward – what mythologist Joseph Campbell (2008) would identify as an archetypal Hero's Journey. A Hero's Journey isn't something you can measure, pin down in a word count, or otherwise handle. It's a thematic pattern holding a story, or a life, together.

Because archetypes are thematic patterns or motifs rather than things, we don't so much perceive them directly as perceive events *through* archetypes. They work like psychological templates that structure perception and imagination. Let us say your approach to a problem is to confront it, fix it, forcibly if necessary, and in that way become a champion over it. Well, that's what a Heroine or Hero does; that's heroic psychology at work. Say instead you wish to find the enchanting word or idea or ritual that dissolves the problem. That's a Magician approach. Or perhaps you must give up something important, even your style of life, to bring the problem into a new state of reconciliation. There we have the archetypal theme of Sacrifice.

Useful, then, to know which archetype we look or listen through in particular situations. This knowledge gives us a wider view not only of the situation but also of *how we perceive it*. How others perceive it, too. Hero, Warrior, Lover, Trickster, Queer, Peacemaker, or Artist will tend to see different sides of things, pointing to a need to combine viewpoints for a fuller picture.

Archetypes have a long intellectual history across cultures. *Arche* refers to origins, and *-type* to "strike" and also to "impression" or "model." They have been called Platonic, elementary, or primordial ideals or Forms. Jung studied Gnosticism, an arcane tradition in which celestial powers pattern mundane reality and its inhabitants by projecting copies of themselves. Gnostic tales are one source of the idea that we each have a higher or angelic self.

Second point of potential confusion: being thematic, archetypes are not directly visible. They are akin to the natural laws that order the physical universe: invisible, but discernible by their effects. You cannot see the Second Law of Thermodynamics, but you can see someone's neglected kitchen getting messier over time (the archetype of Chaos). The same applies to the archetypal presences that haunt our collective psychology: ineffable as such, but, like literary themes, discernible through their actions upon what we can perceive.

How do we know when they operate? Jung, from "The Psychology of the Child Archetype":

> An archetypal content expresses itself, first and foremost, in metaphors. If such a content should speak of the sun and identify with it the lion, the king, the hoard of gold guarded by the dragon, or the power that makes for the life and health of man, it is neither the one thing nor the other, but the unknown third thing that finds more or less adequate expression in all these similes, yet – to the perpetual vexation of the intellect – remains unknown and not to be fitted into a formula.
>
> *(Jung, 1981, p. 155)*

In other words, if we label the archetype expressing itself above Daytime (or Ego) Consciousness, that tells us a little, but, ultimately, what the sun, the lion, and the other images express is finally beyond our definitions, which are at best working fictions to get at a truth. The same with the archetype of the Unconscious: moon, fish, queen, dragon, etc., only bring us so far when we try to pin them down intellectually. What matters is to receive their influences. And, by the way, all these symbols are *archetypal images*, not the archetype itself. Third point of potential confusion: mistaking the symbol, which is personally and culturally conditioned, with the archetype, which is ubiquitous.

Particular archetypes emerge and cast their spell – in other words, *constellate* – in specific response to fluctuations in psychological circumstances, whether personal or collective. During important rituals like graduation or marriage, for example, we often feel as though we step into a place where many have gone before. It's more than just knowing that a lot of people graduate or marry: a sense of weight, even awe, descends upon us to the degree the event holds importance for us. Beginnings and endings, births and deaths, usher in a similar weight and awe. Pageantry recognizes this. So does ritual.

For an activated archetype strikes and seizes us. Cosmic dream imagery, *numinous* (fearfully charged and awe-producing) spiritual conversions, great works of art and dance, falling in love, adrenalized dashes into danger to save a life, heart-stopping visions, the upending of a lifetime's values, the sudden abandonment of our customary style of living for another, and untried style: these are just a few examples of what can erupt in states of archetypal possession. The more one-sidedly we occupy a fixed psychological position – cynical disbelief, pie-in-the-sky idealism, routinized office or factory work, religious zealotry, and prudish abstinence – the more energy our lack of balance feeds the counter-position in the unconscious. When the pressure building in the depths reaches a certain point, the appropriate archetype emerges, and, almost overnight, it seems, we are ready for a position opposite to the one previously held: open-eyed wonder, grounded sensibility, creative unemployment, radical free-thinking, spiritual conversion, or hedonistic adventure, as the case may be. (It seems to be a rule of the psyche that *One-sidedness always feeds its waiting opposite.*)

When such an inner breakout happens, it's important to try to find out which archetype has seized us. As mentioned above, amplification helps here. As we work with the archetype and its surrounding images, they lose their compulsivity and suggest new ways to feel, think, and imagine. When death carried off my father, an event heralded by an underworld goddess visiting my dreams the week before, I faced it not just as an event, but as an image expressing itself in many ways. Holding it like this opened a door in me to the presence of other endings, and to what they brought: feelings to sort, decisions to make about what to keep and discard, adjustments in self-definition, gifts of learning. I mulled other deaths: deaths of some career goals, of relationships, of that which no longer suited me. From these losses came new beginnings. This is how to proceed with an archetype unfolding in the inquiry topic as well.

However, be aware that the literal, fixed mind tries to freeze the archetype into a stereotype. Supposed archetypes like "the Masculine" (described as active, bright, yang) and "the Feminine" (passive, dark, yin) are especially problematic. Claiming to be universal and trans-cultural, these stereotypes foreclose experience instead of enriching it. It's as though Procrustes the mythic innkeeper had snuck in long enough to impose his inelastic categories. Sometimes he is accompanied by Nihansan, the Arapaho Trickster who thought he saw red plums in a river, dove in after them, and was swept downstream – in this case in the rush of enthusiasm for inventing archetypes with no basis in tradition, lore, or myth.

A related error is identifying sex or gender with a given set of supposed archetypes: King, Warrior, Magician, Lover for men, for instance. Why can't those work for women too? What about trans people? What about the male-identified friend of mine who protested, "What, we only get four?" Misidentification also occurs, as when Jung takes obvious Magician figures for archetypal Wise Old Men.

How then do we tell when an actual archetype is at work on us or in the work itself? Here are some archetype detection criteria for guidance:

- We become possessed, especially emotionally, as noted above.
- The archetype strikes during or just before a key life transition.
- It brings sweeping existential motifs along with it.
- It brings numinous imagery to fascinate our attention.
- It invites a radical change of supposedly fixed viewpoints and values.
- It can be identified in a variety of mythologies.
- Indigenous lore describes it.
- World events resonate with its themes.
- You can identify versions of it in the natural world.

That last criterion sets terrapsychology apart from the traditional Jungian position for which archetypes remain an exclusively psychological possession. Archetypes are to be found outside us as well as within, as Jung began to recognize late in his career.

In his book *The Archetypal Cosmos*, Keiron Le Grice (2011), who views the cosmos as archetypally structured and refers to archetypes as the basic powers of nature as they are perceived through the psyche, writes of archetypal images that they:

1 are not invented;
2 appear in consciousness spontaneously and complete;
3 are autonomous, not subject to human will;
4 are purposive, subjects in their own right;
5 possess mana (a felt charge) or numinosum;
6 point to an unknowable transcendental background.

As organizing principles within/behind all we perceive, archetypes are where inner and outer, personal and collective, meet. To identify them, we must think associationally, symbolically, animistically, concretely, and in embodied modes of sensory and emotional awareness. Archetypal patterns evade Procrustes, but they appear to imagination and emotion, and art and dream. Their motifs connect us to what we study, forcibly, breaking down any artificial wall we erect between self and world and culture and nature.

If Jung's comment that there are as many archetypes as typical situations risks plunging you into despair over the lack of a definitive list of archetypes, do not worry. Archetypes are drawn naturally into the kinds of stories we can get to know. Especially myths.

Myth

We can't escape it. Archetypes gain specificity through their embedment in mythic tales. When Earth appears as Ala, Ana, Anahid, Anu, Anu, Asase Yaa, Atargatis, Atlantentli, Changing or Turquoise Woman, Cybele, Danu, Dennitsa, Don, Eanan, Fjorgyn, Folde, Gaia, Haniyama-hime, Hutuch, Hvov, Jord, Kishar, Kunapipi, Mati Syra Zemlja, Muziem-mumi, Nehalennia, Nerthus, Nzambi, Papa, Papatuanuku, Po, Rhea, Semele, Tellus, Terra, Thyone, Zemyna, or Zlotababa, each appearance or telling reveals another side of her beyond the label "earth goddess." The advice to show cleverness in the face of adversity takes on more meaning when we see it demonstrated by Manawydan, Oonagh, Metis, Merlin, Morgan, and Scheherazade, each magical in a different fashion.

Mythic images encircle us: a giant Apple logo with a bite out of it, zombie apocalypse, online avatars, UFOs, New Age, and esoteric schools of witchcraft and wizardry. In finance, we encounter angel investors, witching hour, Invisible Hand, Alpha stock, Omega leveraging, and Black Friday. Spacecraft names like Orion and Hutu. Medical logos that contain the double-serpent caduceus symbol of Hermes, who guides souls to the afterlife. Days of the week, months of the year, names of planets, and signs of the zodiac: all from myth.

Less conspicuous myths and mythic imagery await within the symbolism of everyday things: smartphones as today's magic wands; the return of the Golem in artificial intelligence; Gaia and Artemis in environmental activism; Demeter promoting agroecology; fossil fuels that bring the Underworld to the upper world with fire and death; the elevation of celebrities to a godhood even they come to believe in. The Fountain of Youth hides behind the cosmetic surgeon's scalpel. The priest's robe is now a lab coat.

Mythic themes and motifs, images and dramas recur again and again, endlessly. An education in mythology can highlight where they come from, what they seem to want of us, how they react to current events, what they say about our lives, and perhaps how to embrace a more fluid and Earth-honoring style of life reenchanted by tending the stories appearing on every side.

When asked to define a myth, the more rationalistic among us would give one of two answers: that a myth is a lie (e.g., "the myth of the liberal media"), or that a myth is an archaic explanation for some natural event like lightning that science can now explain. If we are religious, we might define our beliefs as The Truth and other beliefs as myths. For atheists, all religions are myths but, again, one's own standpoint is the true one.

Myth has been studied for centuries by scholars and philosophers. Many seek to render myth down, defining it by its simplest elements: language structures, social rules, superstitions, allegories, historical events, binary codes, and simple motifs. This is somewhat like "explaining" Shakespeare's plays as products of Elizabethan power politics, Will's early toilet training, Sir Francis Bacon in uncharacteristic anonymity, or ink scrawls on parchment. The meaning, the relevance, the deep wisdom, and the self-renewing aliveness of myth are then lost.

Myth has fared better among theorists and tale-tellers who work with it psychologically, but that approach brings limitations as well. The symbol might receive more attention than the story, for example, especially from those hunting for archetypes. Also, to psychologize the grand motifs and powerful images of myth shrinks the animated profusion dancing ever across the wide world of culture into a confining interior space between the ears. Nor will we get far by making of myth a return to a glorified past, although such has proved useful for dictators manipulating reactionaries.

What such maneuvers show us, be they reductive or glorifying, is that myth has become a stranger to us. That is why we think of it in such dismissive terms. The dream suffers a similar mistreatment. Something was "only a dream," we are assured, or "only a myth." (Even the imagination, a foundational power, is belittled: "only a fantasy.") Myth seems problematic mainly in societies that have lost the knack of mythologizing, of polishing old tales until they glow with entertaining images and handy truths. For storytelling societies still awake to their living traditions, collective stories are relevant, traditional lore matters, and tellings connect their hearers to nature and cosmos and each other. The quality of our consciousness, personal and collective, is only as clear as our tale-telling is rich, diverse, and abundant.

Let us consider a working definition of myth. By "working definition" I really mean description because myth resists being pinned down. *A myth is a collective, entertaining, and imaginative sacred tale of the existential conflicts and relations between grand, more-than-human marvels or mysteries and human beings, and as such is a sacred story believed in by most hearers but held as instructive or metaphoric by wisdom teachers.*

We could add that the tales occur in a timeless present, the marvels and mysteries are often personified and named (unlike in folktales and fairytales, where the entities are usually stock characters), various realms of being are described, spiritual entities are present, the myths tend to collect in groupings we call mythologies (again, unlike folktales, which often fly solo), and these mythologies often, but not always, accompany religious rituals.

A shorter description: *Myths are fanciful collective sacred tales about interactions with and among mysterious beings, forces, or dimensions of existence.*

If myth, as basic a production of the cultural psyche as dream is of the individual one, returns continually to life within and outside us, how is it possible to "lose" myth and live in a supposedly mythless age?

We lose myth by failing to acknowledge it as an active force in our lives. But myth does not lose us. The notions of a culture as post-mythical or of myth as "primitive," for example, push reemerging mythic motifs and images into the unconscious, where they fester like symptoms. The mythic-spiritual urge to transcend one's limitations then degenerates into making machines to do our thinking and, some day, feeling (which we already refer to as "processing"). Possessed by the archetype of the ebullient soaring Divine Child of fairy tales and myths, self-improvement gurus preach the gospel of unlimited freedom and success – and then create workshops on getting back up after the inevitable fall from illusory grace: perhaps we should call this "disaster spiritualism," with a nod to Naomi Klein (2008). The desire to make magic descends to paying too much for smart gadgetry. Stories once open to multiple interpretations harden into dangerously exclusive ideologies: the Golden Age of the American 1920s, for example – for White people.

The result of repressing myth out of consciousness – if not out of the resulting anxieties, depressions, phobias, nightmares, wars, market crashes, self-division, self-sabotage, or fights between angry people – is what Rollo

May (1991) describes as "loss of myth": loss of unifying social narratives and ideals and visions; loss of tools for interpreting our time while keeping our souls alive; loss of inspiring models for noble poise and ethical action; loss of lenses for seeing through divisive binaries of sex and gender; loss of meaning in an increasingly bewildering world; and loss of psychological protection from mass ideologies that sweep millions overnight into international aggression and domestic terrorism.

"Without myth," May writes, "we are like a race of brain-injured people unable to go beyond the word and hear the person speaking" (1991, p. 23). We might add: unable to hear Earth speaking too. Without meaningful tales featuring animals and insects, and rivers and landscapes as characters worthy of love and respect, we are deprived of inspiration to care for what remains.

Because myths encompass so much experience and reach into more-than-human dimensions, knowing something about them is useful in studying themes or patterns that link inner and outer. The Golden Gate Bridge, for example, is a notorious jumper magnet, a site of hundreds of suicides. As it was being built, some of the construction workers fell off, were caught in the safety netting, and afterward formed a Halfway to Hell Club. The bridge was left flame orange, the color of its primer coat. Strollers out along its length often drop coins in the center in unconscious tribute to Charon, who collected them to ferry souls to the Underworld. A wind-catching railing put up in 2020 makes the bridge sound like it is screaming. These few of many examples of Underworld motifs that gather around the bridge offer a mythic frame for understanding its presence or "soul" as a gateway of mortal transition. Facts alone could not get us there.

What confronts us in myth, as in fantasy, folktale, and dream, is apt to be strange at first. A hill-sized giant with a club. A woman with hissing snakes for hair. A gigantic tree being nibbled on by a dragon. A blue boy with four arms and piercing eyes. A wolf who takes a bite out of the sun. In folklore and myth, blessings result when the stranger is greeted with respect. Receive whatever appears, no matter how odd or disturbing, with gracious open-mindedness, and it is likely to bestow gifts of rare insight.

To be receptive, we must move beyond literalistic interpretations of mythic entities and forces and listen into them as symbols: images and themes that represent something beyond themselves. Represent, not stand for, because the meanings are not fixed, as they are in mere allegories. Apollo, for example, chasing Daphne, who fled from him: What could this mean, symbolically? To one reader or hearer of the tale, it might bring to mind male privilege and the rapist behavior it enables. That is legitimate. To another, it might also reflect the act of fleeing from what Apollo represents, be it healing, order, or the power to foresee. To run from Apollo can mean evading one's intuitive gifts, abandoning reason, rejecting healing, or being allergic to one's own light. True symbols do not have fixed meanings, for they are not rational explanations. Their potential for illuminating the mysteries of consciousness they refract cannot be confined to a particular perspective.

To unpack what a mythic symbol means to you, try the following:

- Describe a symbol (event, character, setting, action, and theme: virtually every element of a myth can serve as a symbol) to someone else as though they had never come across it before. What insights arise while hearing yourself speak and answer questions?
- Dwell on details. Ponder the symbol long enough to start knowing it, turning it as you would turn a jewel recently given to you. Listen to it. Talk to it. Describe it vividly in writing. Linger with it instead of rushing to interpret.
- Find out what the stories mean to the people who grew up hearing, watching, telling, reading, and performing them.
- Bring up free associations to unpack what the symbols might mean to you. In a tale you come across a magic mirror. What does this stir in your memory and imagination? A mirror you gazed into in childhood? "Mirror, mirror, on the wall"? A crystal ball? Your tablet or laptop? Do this kind of associating to the symbols that call to you, then retell the story through the associations you've gathered. Has your grasp of the symbols' relevance deepened?
- As you consider a symbol that stands out, what feelings emerge? Sit with them for a time. Record them if need be.
- Check your body to see which parts respond to the symbol as you hold it in imagination. What additional symbolism do these responses offer? Do suddenly heavy legs indicate a difficult way forward? Does a tingling between the legs suggest generative energies at play?
- Give form to the symbol: paint it, collage it, collect graphics of it, dance it, build an altar for it, and create a ritual for it. Do this with the story too, or with any part or aspect of it that speaks to you.
- Check around for how the symbols are used in other stories and in other mythologies. Where do they show up in literature? In history? Art? Film? Elsewhere? What symbols mean in a variety of settings can shed light on what they indicate in the story you're reading or listening to.
- Slip into a state of reverie then summon forth the symbol and allow it to express itself on the stage of your imagination however it wants. Does the symbol have something to say? To give you? Can you step into the scene with it and move the story forward? Do other objects or characters want to be a part of the action?

As for myths that appear during a TI:

- How is the topic mythic? Where does it feel fabled, epic, or folkloric?
- What seems to be the primary myth of the place where you conduct the study?
- What mythic role or situation do you occupy as a researcher?
- Ask yourself: Through which mythic stance do I view this myth? Do I harbor a Saturnian desire to structure or restructure it? Nail it down like Procrustes? Hammer with it like Thor? Mother it like Demeter? Battle it like Shango? Flirt with it like Oshun?
- Engage in imaginal conversations with the mythic aspects of the topic and see how they respond. What do they have to say for themselves? How do they feel about how the tale frames them? How you do? What would they like to say to each other? To you?
- Explore within yourself your reactions to other people's interpretations, especially when you find them strange or jarring. Something inside requests your attention.
- Do homework or self-analysis on whatever resonates in the story, fires you, stirs enthusiasm, bothers you, makes you curious, or has an edge for you. Find ways to learn from this fire or this edge.
- Watch for the appearance of mythic figures and situations in your dreams and in unexpected happenings around you. Myths do not stay in books or films.
- Look for thematic parallels between a resonant myth and your life, past or present. How are you living inside the tale? Where do you want to go with it? Where does it want to go? What is the next phase of your journey?

Not all terrapsychological inquiries focus on myth, but those which do add a layer of enriched meaning, as we will see in Chapter 4. We now turn to method.

For Discussion

1 What topic of inquiry is up for you at this time? What must you know?
2 Try turning your topic into a theme. Does the theme feel archetypal, like a basic quality of existence?
3 What emerges if you turn the topic into a mythic character, call it up in imagination, and have a conversation about what it wants from you?

References

Adler, A. (1964). *The individual psychology of Alfred Adler: A systematic presentation in selections from his writings*. Edited by H. Ansbacher & R. Ansbacher. New York, NY: HarperPerennial.

Buzzell, L., & Chalquist, C. (Eds.) (2008). *Ecotherapy: Healing with nature in mind*. San Francisco, CA: Sierra Club Books.

Campbell, J. (2008). *The hero with a thousand faces*. Novato, CA: New World Library.
Chalquist, C. (2007). *Terrapsychology: Reengaging the soul of place*. New Orleans, LA: Spring Journal Books.
Chalquist, C. (Ed.) (2010). *Rebearths: Conversations with a world ensouled*. Walnut Creek, CA: World Soul Books.
Chalquist, C. (2018). *Myths among us: When timeless tales return to life*. Goleta, CA: World Soul Books.
Fay, L. (2018). Human connection with the ocean represented in African and Japanese oral narratives: Ecopsychological perspectives (unpublished dissertation). California Institute of Integral Studies, San Francisco, CA.
Freud, S. (2010). *The interpretation of dreams*. New York, NY: Basic Books.
Haber, M. (2019). Unattended trauma of the San Lorenzo River: A terrapsychological inquiry (unpublished dissertation). California Institute of Integral Studies, San Francisco, CA.
Hippman, M. (2017). The psychology of salt (unpublished master's thesis). Environmental Humanities Program, University of Utah, Salt Lake City, Utah.
Jung, C. (1954). *On the nature of the psyche*. Edited by R. Hull. London: Routledge & Kegan Paul.
Jung, C. (1976). *Psychological types*. Edited by R. Hull. Princeton, NJ: Princeton University Press.
Jung, C. (1981). *Archetypes of the collective unconscious*. Edited by R. Hull. Princeton, NJ: Princeton University Press.
Klein, N. (2008). *The shock doctrine: The rise of disaster capitalism*. New York, NY: Picador.
Le Grice, K. (2011). *The archetypal cosmos: Rediscovering the gods in myth, science, and astrology*. Edinburgh: Floris Books.
May, R. (1991). *The cry for myth*. New York, NY: W. W. Norton.
Mitchell, L. (2005). The eco-imaginal underpinnings of community identity in Harmony Grove Valley: Unbinding the ecological imagination (unpublished dissertation). Pacifica Graduate Institute, Carpinteria, CA.
Moustakas, C. (1990). *Heuristic research: Design, methodology, and applications*. London, New Delhi and Thousand Oaks, CA: Sage.
Moynihan, T. (2018). The phenomenology of ecological embeddedness (unpublished dissertation). California Institute of Integral Studies, San Francisco, CA.
Olivieri, C. (2017). Your church, my bar! A terrapsychological inquiry of the relationship between queerspace and queer spirituality in San Francisco, California (unpublished dissertation). California Institute of Integral Studies, San Francisco, CA.
Romanyshyn, R. (2007). *The wounded researcher: Research with soul in mind*. New Orleans, LA: Spring Journal Books.

4

TERRAPSYCHOLOGICAL INQUIRY IN PRACTICE

At its best, methodology organizes and deepens how we study a research topic. It suits the topic rather than the reverse. It suggests a choice of methods.

As previously discussed, the mechanistic paradigm of unreflective scientific ideology, namely *scientism*, has used methodology to dominate and control the work while deadening emotional responses to it. In Terrapsychological Inquiry (TI), by contrast, we are guided by the topic as well as enlivened and transmuted by it. We provide a structure, a scaffolding that holds the topic while assuring it creative space for growth by its own emergent paths.

Because deep research is a kind of alchemy, the following three phases, each with seven steps, unfold like alchemical operations. At times the researcher takes the lead; at other times the content of our study becomes the process by which we study it and the work directs itself, a philosopher's stone telling the adept how to bring it into being. Always, even while adapting, we seek to maintain a practice of disciplined inquiry while retaining an optimal psychological posture, neither emotionally distant nor chaotically possessed.

The framework for achieving this is: (1) prepare, (2) investigate, and (3) coagulate.

Phase 1: Prepare for the Work

(1) Engage with and be Engaged by the Topic

What has seized you? Only by allowing the topic to take hold of you can the work shift your involvement from mere ego to deep soul (Romanyshyn, 2007, p. 6). Katherine Humphrey's exploration of the soul of paved-over,

DOI: 10.4324/9781003462965-5

master-planned, big-boxed Orange County, where she had grown up, opened with a painful wondering:

> Finally, upon my last return, deep in grief and preparing to embark on the course of study that has culminated in this thesis, I began to ask new questions. Questions like: What is it about Orange County that draws me back, and why does it hurt so much to call it home? How has this place shaped me, and what part of me truly belongs here?
>
> *(Humphrey, 2012, p. 1)*

Michael Haber sought a close connection early on with the San Lorenzo River, whose ecological troubles he believed paralleled those of the down-and-outs of Santa Cruz:

> Since I am asking the San Lorenzo River area to tell me its story of trauma, I need to connect with that terrain on a personal level. I plan to walk the banks of the San Lorenzo daily for a period of no less than 120 days for at least one hour and take in any ideas that come into my mind, while inviting the river to display things like symbolic references, examples of pain that I can understand as a human inhabitant in this region, and other encounters that may or may not relate to my research.
>
> *(Haber, 2019, p. 43)*

He writes of this as engaging the river as an active partner, participant, and ally in the research.

Kevin Filocamo's call to work with the erotic presence of nature and matter arrived with a visceral sense of being physically and emotionally penetrated by Hell's Peak in California. After practicing holistic sexuality techniques at Wellspring Renewal Center, he walked silently near a river and felt it and the soil calling out to him:

> This is what I sensed in those moments: a palpable sense of the intrinsic aliveness of the land that seemed in some way to be reaching out to me, touching me, and allowing me to touch him/her/it. As I write this, I recognize the similarity between this encounter and the experience of engagement initiated by Hell's Peak: in both, the land reached out and made contact with me in energetic ways felt deeply in my own body.
>
> *(Filocamo, 2008, p. 17)*

His inquiry stemmed in part from a desire to understand such intimate encounters between him and these natural features.

> I cannot explain what caused the experiences of energetic interconnection and interpenetration with the land and river at Wellspring, nor with Hell's Peak at Saratoga Springs. But these experiences have led me to believe that there is indeed an erotic nature to matter – a living energy that can and perhaps wants to connect and commingle with human energies – and I believe that we humans can and must find ways to connect with this erotic potential in the matter (body) that forms our own beings as well as that of all beings in the universe.
>
> *(Filocamo, 2008, p. 17)*

For this step in the inquiry, call in the subject of research as to an autonomous entity, living and breathing in its own right, while rendering yourself transparent to what it asks of you. Look for its signature in synchronicity, fantasy, and unexpected encounter. Listen carefully to help it take on shape and coherence. Think of it as a partner to be in dialog with throughout the entire project. We invite in the soul of the work and wait for how it wants to show up: in the body, in our dreams, from our past, in the field, etc.

(2) Research the Topic

Do your homework on the topic, including its history, cultural background, ecology, geography (where relevant), previous studies, documentation, interview material, and whatever helps you triangulate on it through multiple sources of knowledge. Collect books, articles, and online resources. Talk to experts and elders. Much of this can go into your literature review, if you required to write one: a series of nods to the ancestors in the fields you engage (see Chapter 7). Research can serve as ritual, as Filocamo shows in his preparations to begin by sitting with and listening carefully to a particular tree in San Francisco:

> I conducted library and internet searches to find scientific and historical information on Monterey Cypress trees and the part these trees have played in the creation of Golden Gate Park in San Francisco, California. I also attempted to find out information about the particular Monterey Cypress tree I engaged during the research, and the land from which the Monterey Cypress grew.
>
> *(Filocamo, 2008, p. 60)*

For her master's project on the presence and imagery of Petaluma, CA, Sarah Rankin visited sources suggested by her research interest:

> I used the local museum archives, State Historical Society collections, and informal interviews with older Petaluman natives to research the scientific

> and geographic presences of the lands in Sonoma County. When possible, I used the help of different wildlife groups affiliated with the schools in which I teach.
>
> *(Rankin, 2007, p. 32)*

Michael Haber kept his research objectives in mind while collecting knowledge:

> The personal accounts, historical surveys, and in-depth examinations into the past at the local library and in county historical records will serve as background information and evidence of historical or ancestral decay or trauma. Geological surveys and reports will amplify this evidence and serve as validity checks.
>
> *(2019, pp. 44–45)*

(3) Gather the Resources You Will Need

Collect whatever you will need for your work. Some of this might be equipment: cameras, recorders, maps and guides, art supplies, writing pads, computers, an artist's sketchbook, etc. Some of the tools will be internal or attitudinal. Example: Cultivating a *sensitized innocence* that moves back and forth between what you know of the topic and a freshness of mind and body able to receive whatever plays across your senses, moods, thoughts, associations, and dreams. Consider setting up an intention-strengthening opening ritual to call in the topic and whatever helpful influences surround it.

Another tool you will need is a research journal for jotting down what you do and your rationale for it, reflections on the work as it unfolds, fresh ideas to pursue, inner conflicts that arise, how you deal with them, dreams along the way, changes you make as new findings arise, what you are reading, holes in the literature, how your codes and themes relate to each other (if you use coding: see Chapter 5), conversations with your research associates, reactions to interviews, and the overall path of the study, including the later data analysis and whatever surprises and novelties emerge. The journal tells the study's creation story, keeps the history, provides an audit trail, and warms you up to write. Feel free to be creative with it.

For the first phase of her inquiry, Amanda Leetch regarded her place of study as a mentor for how to study it, and with which tools:

> During that phase, place was teaching me how it can best be known through the many layers of my perceptual being during our initial encounters and engagements. It was teaching me how better to ask the questions, what tools to use and how to use them. Material tools included notebooks and pens, markers, chalk, artifacts from the field like bobbins and patent

> medicine bottles, maps and historic archives, cellphone and tablet, and the terrain weaving supplies.
>
> *(Leetch, 2017, p. 114)*

In earlier versions of TI, this step mentioned "engaging the transmarginal": consciously making use of whole-person resources like dream, fantasy, ritual, meditation, and other kinds of guides (Chalquist, 2010) as mentioned above. Michael Haber, who has Lumbee and Choctaw ancestry, compares this practice to spirit-walking in the Native American traditions.

(4) Select the Place for Your Work

In Indigenous methodologies, *where* we work is nearly as important as what we work on and how we work on it. As philosopher Ed Casey points out, a place is not just an empty or filled space: it is "the immediate environment of my lived body – an arena of action that is at once physical and historical, social and cultural" (2001, p. 683). Its presence is felt in the thickness of the conversation between us and what and who is there.

Decide where to reflect, study, and write. Explore the history, geology, and presence of the place. Imagine it as a person or being and ask it for dreams in response to your interest in being there. Then select where your desk and study space should be and whether to honor the work by adorning your work space with images, reminders, or altar objects. To establish good study boundaries, let people know that you cannot be disturbed at certain times.

For her thesis "Weaving Meaning," Amanda Leetch selected, and was selected by, a place whose history informed the process by which she studied it:

> Lowell ... was a textile mill city at the heart of the American industrial revolution. Everything that transpired there, everything that it is still unfolding, is deeply tied to tapestry weaving. Weaving is one of my methods for the arts-based educational research component, and the weaving metaphor is appropriate for trying to repair the snagged and distorted narrative fabric of historic material unfolding.
>
> *(Leetch, 2017, p. xv)*

In locianalysis (the type of TI that focuses on specific places), it is important to identify the central, most prominent geological feature of the site because the primary symbols of the place emanate from it, and whatever mythologies are abroad in the area gather around it:

> Everything starts with the river ... The force of the falls is the beating of the heart of the city, rooted in this thrumming deep time rhythm; lub dub

> the flow is churned, aerated and accelerated. This does something to the ecosystem; it agitates it. Awakens it. Catalyzes it. Lowell is a site of rapid complexification related to that agitation.
>
> *(Leetch, 2017, p. xxxvi)*

A locianalytic study includes four domains to explore: location, infrastructure, community, and genius loci. The first three domains fill in a *place history*: a case history of place. The fourth draws on the place history for sifting out recurrent themes or images that delineate the felt presence or soul of the place: the "placefield."

Of particular interest are the *placefield motifs*, the recurring themes shared by people and places alike. Think of them as outlining the place's character structure:

> When people inhabit a particular place, its features inhabit their psychological field, in effect becoming extended facets of their selfhood. The more they repress this local, multifaceted sense of environmental presence, the likelier its features will reappear unconsciously as symbolic, animated forces seething from within and from without.
>
> *(Chalquist, 2007, p. 7)*

When the motifs signal pathology of place and people dwelling there, most often evident in a decline of health in both, we see placefield syndromes called *ecological complexes*. We tend these ("placehosting") by shaping a response to them: a series of ceremonies, a master's thesis or dissertation, a book or article, local activism, a festival in appreciation of the genius loci, sharing findings with the local community, launching an enchantivist project: some kind of empathic ethical giving back to the place from which we learned so much (Chalquist, 2007).

C. K. Olivieri studied San Francisco with her own internal stresses in mind:

> In metaphoric alignment with San Francisco's flag symbolism, I too needed a rebirth. Like San Francisco of 1906, I needed my own personal phoenix rising. Like her motto, I too sought to be gold in peace, iron in war. If she could rebuild six times following fires and twice after earthquakes, I could too.
>
> *(Olivieri, 2017, p. 56)*

(5) Refine the Research Question

This is the question that will guide your entire inquiry (see Chapter 3). What fascinates you? Where is a gap in the fields you study? Most initial research questions are too broad. Concentrate yours until it can focus and encompass your work. At each step of refinement, run the question by your dreams and by supportive people for comment. Be open to how the question might change as you proceed.

> The primary question that I addressed in this research is, "How might humans relate erotically with the world?"
>
> *(Filocamo, 2008, p. 17)*

> What is the "felt experience" of engaging in a relationship with the "soul" of Queerspaces in the Castro and Mission districts of San Francisco when Terrapsychological Inquiry (TI) functions as a spiritual practice?
>
> *(Olivieri, 2017, p. 30)*

> How can the exploration of archetypal symbols and patterns of a place and the amplification or deepening of these symbols allow for the recognition of, and identification of, particular predominant themes?
>
> *(Rankin, 2007, p. 7)*

For one study, this served as an initial working formulation: "The central question of my research seeks to understand if it is possible to reframe the placefield encounter for guests to experience it as more holding" (Leetch, 2017, p. 5). The question evolved:

> This research explores how the connection to place, specifically the industrial place of historic Lowell Massachusetts, is carried in the regional psyche, reproduced through place encounters, and iterated through the self and as culture across scales. It wonders specifically about the ways place narratives are being reproduced in the regional psyche through a process of normalized historic retraumatization.
>
> *(Leetch, 2017, p. 6)*

At this point, the researcher tried on a tentative supposition to follow up:

> It is my position that this retraumatization is avoidable through ethically enacted field-embedded awareness that trouble persistent narratives and teach more expansive and receptive interpretation and responses to the field's varied symbolic communication. This research goes on to propose the role educators can play in disrupting retraumatization by honing and deepening our own place-based relationships, as an ethical embedment, and incorporating that wisdom into our praxis.
>
> *(Leetch, 2017, pp. 6–7)*

You might wish to add a summary of what your study intends. Saran Rankin wrote this about her overall objective:

> My thesis project is a rethinking of place, not just as the backdrop for our lives, but as the keeper of our natural selves, the holder of our personal and collective stories, the place of our birth and subsequent rebirth, and a sacred entity in its own right. Without this awareness and intrinsic knowing that the Earth is a complex and powerful entity which is conscious and evolving, we become deaf to its voice, its healing potential, and its destructive capabilities. We lose the wild animal in us, the wild animal that knows how to read the land for tracks, knows when a storm is coming, and knows how to listen to the songs of the wind.
>
> *(Rankin, 2007, p. 6)*

(6) Design the Study

Research projects that are primarily theoretical/hermeneutic (in simpler language, interpretive) will benefit from an outline of which directions to pursue and which sources to consult. This outline can evolve into a table of contents or literature review for the final product. It can be helpful to briefly summarize your research plan. Leetch's began with a situational context:

> From May 8 to September 3, 2016 I designed and implemented youth programing in conjunction with the Interpretive Rangers of Lowell National and Historical Park. I observed and implemented typical programming designed by the institution. I ran programs, lead tours, and hosted projects with hundreds of park visitors over the course of the summer. I worked with visitors of all ages, but with a specific focus on visitors under the age of 11.
>
> *(Leetch, 2017, p. 88)*

She then described some key activities of the inquiry at Lowell:

> I designed a drop-in curriculum with the placefield that suited the developmental needs of mixed-age groups while inviting a creative, openhearted and sensory engagement with the placefield, which was attended weekly by a small core of local children. Weekly sessions worked with children to attune their perceptions … We did activities ranging from weaving to water Ph. testing, chalk earth and body mapping … and started each session with a brief somatic grounding activity that focused on the breath …

> Over the summer the participants built a museum within the museum to showcase their art and experiences.
>
> *(Leetch, 2017, p. 88)*

Filocamo summarized his initial research goals and participant involvement:

> Using written accounts of my own experiences interacting with a particular entity of nature (a tree in San Francisco's Panhandle) as the primary data, I explored whether or not I could experience relating with non human entities in the world erotically, how I might prepare myself to interact with this entity erotically, what forms this erotic interaction might take, and what I could learn about myself and the world through such experiences. I also facilitated a brief experiment with four volunteers using similar techniques that I used during my own exploration, and asked them to write about their experiences, which I analyzed using hermeneutic methodologies.
>
> *(Filocamo, 2008, p. 18)*

Olivieri described her approach to asking queer-identified participants about feeling safety and belonging in certain San Francisco neighborhoods:

> The placehosting phase contains within its parameters the one-hour terrapsychological experiential activity in the co-researchers' queerspace of choice within the Castro or Mission districts and the subsequent one-hour semi-structured heuristic interview regarding the nature of the felt experience of the activity. The opportunity for a 30-minute verification interview via phone, email or Skype was also provided and incorporated in the placehosting in order to give the co-researchers an opportunity to expand or clarify their initial statements. The data from the activity was generated in the forms of journal entries, poems, images, symbols, stories, and other creative media.
>
> *(Olivieri, 2017, p. 29)*

She also laid out the course of the inquiry in steps:

> Ceremonial opening of the assessment: asking permission and guidance;
> Textual assessment: the four domains;
> Heuristic interviews;
> TI experiential activity/placehosting;
> Additional triangulation/supporting documentation;
> Personal/research journals;
> Generation of findings/explication;
> Creative synthesis;

Terrapsychological data analysis;
Summations and conclusions;
Ceremonial closing.

(Olivieri, 2017, p. 30)

(7) Inventory Yourself

Take careful note of both the pre-understandings (initial ideas and opinions about the area of inquiry) and potential blind spots you bring to the topic. Include consciously selected delimitations: deliberate boundaries setting out and limiting the scope and method of your explorations. Delimiting is vital to stay focused and to keep the study from ballooning into a giant project impossible to finish. A concentrated research question will help do that as well.

Discuss this self-inquiry with research partners and mentors inside and outside the field of your work. Expect to uncover more biases and blind spots as the work proceeds. In fact, be troubled if none appear.

Make use of culture-of-origin resources. "I am deeply connected to the understanding of an Indigenous mindset. It is a part of my heritage and I have connections to that heritage in my local community" (Haber, 2019, p. 44).

Self-preparation includes immersion in sensitized innocence, the openness that willingly suspends ingrained attitudes and past learnings long enough for the individual or team of researchers to open sufficient psychological space for whatever the place, element, event, etc., under study might reveal. As awareness moves back and forth between outer and inner, associations to what one senses spring forth in the activated imagination, presuppositions are challenged or destroyed, impressions arise and are stored as one moves through the terrain nonpossessively, questions become more important than answers, and conclusions give way to fresh perceptions and wandering wonderings.

Olivieri noted the following as part of surfacing her biases:

Initial Assumptions

1 I believe that the discipline of Terrapsychology and methodology of TI is a real and valid way to approach the "psychoanalysis of place."
2 I believe that TI is a spiritual practice, as well as an academic discipline and qualitative research methodology.
3 I have a "lived" experience of interacting with San Francisco terrapsychologically. Specifically, I have a personal ongoing dialogue with both queerspace and queer communities of San Francisco that I would personally define as psychospiritually transformative.
4 I have a desire to see the queer community experience social justice. I am mindful that I must acknowledge this.

5 I have a bias against organized religion in that queer populations have been discriminated against consistently by dogma and doctrines. I am mindful of this and of my innate assumption that spirituality is differentiated from any one organized religion

(Olivieri, 2017, pp. 119–121)

Phase 2: Investigate the Topic

(1) Explore the Terrain

Initiate an opening ritual if appropriate and begin. Your topic can home in on various kinds of terrain: a site, an object, weather, the Earth, animal, plant, or insect behavior, myths in certain locations, yourself in relation to nature, a particular place, its ecology or geology, a cross-place investigation, the elements, natural ingredients or substances, environmental wounding, relationships between people or cultures and locales, travels or pilgrimages, visits to sacred sites, urban spaces … the range of possibilities is limitless. Be wholly focused on the terrain of the study before you embark.

For hermeneutic studies, the “terrain” will include texts. Pay attention to where you read them, take copious notes, write down your thoughts and reactions in your research journal, and converse with people who are experts on the texts you have selected.

In the end, of course, there is no substitute for being in the field:

> I walked along the river and across bridges on both sides, snuck through back alleyways along the sections of the Concord river … around and under the bridge by the homeless encampment tucked by the highway. I walked till I knew the churches and the neighborhoods they served, part of the history of the immigrant sections of Lowell. I explored University of Massachusetts, Lowell’s campus and the whole length of the canal walk, down to the Mills artist studio and along the Northern Canal. I roved whenever I was able, and chose places to sit, connect, be still, to indulge the depth of my senses, to look, listen and feel.
>
> *(Leetch, 2017, p. 115)*

Sometimes exploring the terrain of the study reveals the need to develop new capabilities:

> In order to experience the erotic nature in the world or in matter (matter being in this case the actual *substance* or material of all that exists), I needed to learn to relate to the world in a very different way, with a different, more embodied, more receptive sensitivity. A large part of this

> thesis involved an exploration of this "new way" of being and relating with the world.
>
> *(Filocamo, 2008, p. 8)*

Be alert for symbolism in the locale:

> Look at a satellite image of the Great Salt Lake. It is a rather oddly shaped blob, with a slightly pink north arm, and a southern portion that is blue. The color variation is due to a transportation route that bisects the lake which ... causes the northern portion to become saltier and welcoming to bacteria called halophiles (literally: salt-loving) which turn the water pink. Now look at a diagram of the human heart. The top left portion of the heart is the half that is fully oxygenated (and therefore red), while the lower right half is deoxygenated and blue. The lake is our functioning heart.
>
> *(Hippman, 2017, p. 8)*

Why is this significant? Perhaps because of the question it raises: What does it mean that people living nearby almost completely ignore the very heart of the ecosystem they occupy, there in the chest cavity of the Great Basin? "It is more than a pool of elements in various proportions, just as the heart is more than a mass of cells and tissue" (Hippman, 2017, p. 8).

Be sure to ask for dreams and other promptings from the psychic depths to guide you along your way. In TI, the unconscious is a project partner. Call in whatever powers can help you do the work, making research a sacred endeavor.

Doctoral student Michael Haber reported the following dream at the start of his locianalytical study of the San Lorenzo River, whose flow carves indentations into round rocks caught in the sandstone wall:

> I was swimming in the river. The river's current was carrying me. I was on a journey ... In my dream I can see the carved deep indentation bowls in the walls of the river ravine and the rounded rock. They are both larger than I have ever seen in real life. The rocks are carved by rolling around in the beautiful bowls. And then I saw a large rock in one of the bowls that had been carved into the shape of a rounded heart ... To me, the rock shaped like a heart was a metaphor of being shaped by the river. It caused me to think about I have been shaped by the river as a part of participation in this project.
>
> *(Haber, 2019, pp. 1–2)*

His dissertation work became a bowl or container for the flow of what he learned in his deep exploration of the river and its thematic psychological influence on the people living near it. He also dreamed of an amphitheater being built on a triangle of land near the river: "I feel like the building of theater space was about how we as a community are building our relationship with the river" (Haber, 2019, p. 4). A river restoration celebration whose planning he had not heard about took place there several months after the dream.

Beyond faculty advisers or a dissertation committee, guides can be imaginal figures who appear in dreams or outer helpers who appear spontaneously – as they so often do, as every inquirer can attest – during terrain exploration. Keep an eye out for them.

(2) Collect Data through Multiple Modes of Perception

Do this through all your senses, including somatic responses, moods and emotions, dreams on site or after, intuitions, ordinary and nonordinary states of consciousness, on-site conversations, and analytic and nonlinear ways of working with data. Note existential motifs by attending lived space, body, time, births, deaths, rebirths, and relationships. Concentrate on recurring symbols, images, themes, stories (legends, fairytales, and emplaced or free-floating myths), or ecological complexes: thematic knots or junctures where human and ecological wounding combine (Chalquist, 2010).

Some researchers will want to make use of interviewing to collect data. For those studies, a semi-structured format with questions decided in advance will be suitable so long as the interviewer puts forth spontaneous clarifying questions ("How did you feel about that?" "What do you mean by…?") that follow the natural conversational pattern. Highly structured inquiries are seldom if ever used because they turn participants into passive respondents who must stick to what matters to the researcher's theory.

In TI, respect and empathy, not cold clinical distance, spreads out an interactive field in which fresh insights emerge about the storied complexity of participants' full experience. Unlike a questionnaire collecting hundreds of potentially shallow answers, a live researcher can engage the interviewee's interest while reflecting back what was said and modifying the questions. However, do not rule out surveys to gather preliminary data or to follow up after interviewing.

> Before they participated in the two-day process, I asked them to complete a brief questionnaire (Appendix Two) in which I asked about any previous experiences they may have had communing with nature, any current spiritual practices with which they are working, and which offered them a chance to relate any expectations they may have for the weekend or how they thought their relationship with me might affect their experience.
>
> *(Filocamo, 2008, p. 55)*

Alternatives to one-on-one interviewing could include Nominal Group Technique (group brainstorming) and sharing individually written stories with a group of interviewees who then create a collective story, art project, or text (see Chapter 7).

If you are new to interviewing, consult an interviewing expert and consider asking someone to watch you practice interviewing to advise you on tone, body language, etc. Piloting interviews are another option.

To select interviewees, consider theoretical sampling (picking people who meet certain criteria). Also available are site sampling (whomever is at hand), opportunity/convenience sampling (whomever you can get who might be suitable), and snowball sampling (asking study participants to invite others). Researchers who include a quantitative component to the study should also consider systematic sampling (every tenth, eighth, etc., of a population) and stratified sampling (making sure certain groups are represented). In general, though, it is better to use fewer interviewees and go deeper with each than the reverse.

If you interview, try informal personal or group conversations, attending to discourse, nonverbals, and metaphoric patterns, followed by a creative activity. In community settings, determine beforehand how your research can benefit the people you talk to and strengthen your relationships with them. Consider using co-researchers as full partners as well as heartsteading circles (see Appendix III) to pool knowledge and create a group project supportive of or inspired by the topic under study.

For hermeneutic studies, find concrete examples of what you're engaging with, no matter how theoretical, and interact. For example, if you compared nature spirit practices, you might try them and track the results, involving as many of your senses as possible. If you studied the symbolism of subtle interactions between horses and humans, consider being around horses in various settings and collecting your own impressions.

(3) Let the Phenomena Speak

Treat what you study as having a psychical presence, or a soul. What is it saying? Where does its "speech" show up in your life, perhaps in unexpected ways? How does it speak in your dreams, moods, body states, relationships? This applies to texts and bodies of thought as well as to soils, clouds, animals, everyday objects, and geographical sites.

During her research on the presence or "soul" of Petaluma, California, a place where she found many images of the phoenix motif, Sarah Rankin discovered the two wings of the fabulous bird reappearing in how she wrote about them:

> Petaluma is indeed split in half, in the physical world, by Highway 101. In the psychic world, I found myself, about halfway into the study, unable

> to integrate an exploration of the two separate spheres of Petaluma: the places where people live and the places where they don't ... There is the older, historic downtown to the west and the newer, modern subdivisions to the east. There are the older residents who want Petaluma to be the sleepy town it once was and there are the newer ones who want more development, more progress.
>
> *(Rankin, 2007, p. 131)*

Go back and forth between tending the motions around you and watching for motions within, taking up the topic and relinquishing it, taking it up and relinquishing it, nonpossessively.

A theory you engage is also a living being. Ask it into your imagination and converse with it regularly. The same with a model or set of practices you are developing. Let them have their say as you go, allowing the conversation to deepen and grow richer.

> Lowell showed me how to get underneath what is being communicated by the repetition and reproduction of these skewed patterns. To interpret how the pattern is brought out of balance by the way it is enacted, and to listen to what it is telling you it needs by the way it expresses itself. This is how we catalyze a regenerative and ethical form of liberation, by interpreting and addressing the field emanations as emergent outcomes of localized actions.
>
> *(Leetch, 2017, pp. xx–xxi)*

During his meetings with the entity he called Tree in the San Francisco Panhandle, Kevin Filocamo received distinct impressions of being reached out to by his research partner. As his research journal records,

> At some point I felt a deeper connection to the tree. The connection came after my attention and intention began moving more deeply into my body ... I felt the contact of my body to the tree, with its relative softness in relation to the relative hardness of the tree ... And what was amazing about this experience was that I felt that the tree had somehow reached out its sense of hardness – had in some way "bumped" me to get my attention.
>
> *(Filocamo, 2008, p. 70)*

On other occasions, he felt "held" by Tree as he leaned into it. Instead of analyzing this perception at the time, he allowed it to play out fully.

Naturally, the question eventually surfaced about whether his perceptions of Tree's part in the conversation – including a sense of warming energy and a holding presence – came down to human projection. Admitting he could not answer this question scientifically, he wrote:

> My intuition tells me that "no," my body was responding to something that has life. More: that this "some thing" – this tree – was not only alive but was in some way responding to the contact in its own way. Could it be that we were "waking each other up" to each other's existence through this contact?
>
> *(Filocamo, 2008, p. 89)*

Sometimes the "speech" of what and where you study includes recurring motifs from folklore, myth in particular.

> In exploring myth I first turned to the stories of the people native to this land ... This is based on my underlying conviction that once a mythic story is enacted on a land it gains strength and potency and if not consciously recognized and reconciled, repeats itself. Because of the repetitions that make the story noticeable, a person may begin to identify with it. An examination of repetition refers to the ways in which stories repeat themselves, in different forms, in the recorded history.
>
> *(Rankin, 2007, p. 34)*

Noting that the city sign of Irvine depicts a face separated from a tree by a wall, a motif that recurs throughout the history and development of Orange County, Katherine Humphrey (2012) spotted a new billboard depicting Jesus standing next to Poseidon, a prominent figure in the myth of King Erisychthon and his daughter Mestra, whom he sold into slavery. Elements of this myth recurred on site as well, with local construction of malls and other large structures recalling the king's manic and greedy building program. (While studying Orange County on my own, I had come across similar motifs of giantism and overdevelopment; see Chalquist, 2009.) Mestra seems the redemptive aspect of the myth, an aspect older than the county's colonization by Americans and, before them, Spaniard settlers, soldiers, and missionaries. Although the king's insatiable hunger, inflicted on him by Nemesis when he cut down a sacred grove, made him eat everything in sight, Mestra used her shape-shifting ability to free herself from captivity. Her figure, co-collaged by the researcher, seems to echo in local Indigenous lore as the shapeshifting being who, seeing death on every side, reentered the land:

> If the story of Erysichthon and Mestra is a story about passage from colonizing to relational ego, it would not be the first time that, in the mythology of this very place, the all-consuming hunger of a father yields a

metamorphic flight resulting in peoples' re-emplacement in the more-than-human community and in a newly ordered world.

(Humphrey, 2012, p. 86)

(4) Record and Document

Methods for recording data include documenting direct participation and observation, journaling and thick description, video, art (personal or group or performative), disciplined reminiscence, empathic identification, noting ecotransference (see below), photographing public art, signage, memorials, and infrastructure, and collecting prior documentation (milestone official papers, letters, essays, programs, news articles, photographs, ecological studies, etc.).

Screen data you collect through your research question: keep what's relevant and look for gaps. Attend Jung's four functions of consciousness – feeling, intuition, sensation, and thinking – and, knowing which you favor, bring in the others. Questionnaires and surveys can be useful if you bear their limitations in mind: response rates tend to be low; you cannot alter the questions; and those who choose to respond might be atypical.

> I cultivated and attended to impressions and inferences, patterns and perceptions, dreams, fractals, stories, and interpretations that were present and communicating in the field ... I roved the paths of the park taking in the sights and sounds, exploring well-trafficked areas and seeking out hidden nooks. I recorded these encounters and experiences through reflective journaling, art, poetry, diagram, research memos, videos, and photographs.
>
> *(Leetch, 2017, pp. 104–105)*

Recording also helps later with checking the validity and sourcing of one's perceptions. On March 6, 2008, Filocamo approached his research partner Tree "with concerns about work and income." Although he did not want Tree to mirror his own concerns, during one visit Tree's twisting branches seemed somewhat sinister. On March 28, however, when the researcher felt more taken care of and emotionally stable, he also felt more connected to Tree during their contact (Filocamo, 2008, p. 68). Going back over dates also helped him identify times when, and why, he felt he was "objectifying" Tree instead of staying in conversation (Filocamo, 2008, p. 70). (The sense of another being's aliveness tends not to arise through projection, which instead sets up a deadening objectification that splits perception.)

For studies that involve creating a practice or model of some kind, write down some case examples of how you apply it and what results occur, including surprises leading to innovations or modifications.

(5) Receive Feedback

Check in regularly with a panel of thoughtful listeners (a formal or informal research committee) outside the interactive field. These should be people who know and support you and can provide critical honest appraisals of what you bring to the study as it unfolds.

> I received feedback from the thesis committee through the process, feedback from participants, from the participatory presence of place, and from self-awareness and self-perception across scales ... This sort of self-awareness has been actively cultivated through my counselor training, and I was prepared to process ecotransference through the data gathering process as research memo, digital media and art. I was wary that wounds I thought healed might be encountered from newly awakened understanding, and this proved to be an invaluable tool in my study.
>
> *(Leetch, 2017, pp. 118–119)*

> It is necessary for me to hold an awareness of the complexes that I have a tendency to exhibit. I know that I can very easily fall into the role of the victim. So it is necessary to hold this awareness and move through it when it surfaces as a possible diagnosis for a theme I discover within the land. Also, sharing my feelings with the members of my committee at different stages of the exploration will be a valuable method for identifying possible personal projections.
>
> *(Rankin, 2007, p. 39)*

Ask for dreams throughout, and keep track of moods and free associations to aspects of what you explore. Go over interview material (if any) with participants to check their version of what they gave you.

> I began keeping record of my dreams, intuitions, and ideas as they were revealed to me. I started to feel as though I was following a cosmic trail of breadcrumbs. As I began picking up the small and strategically placed symbolic clues, my relationship with place deepened. I later came to understand that I was listening to the "soulscape" (Chalquist, 2010, p. 2).
>
> *(Olivieri, 2017, p. 6)*

(6) Maintain Self-Care

In TI, ecological countertransference – ecotransference – arises from deepening involvement with the topic. We can detect ecotransference when the style or discourse our work begins to move as the content we examine becomes the process by which we examine it. It lands in us as the sum and weight of unintegrated emotional responses to the characteristics of what is under investigation (Chalquist, 2007, p. 59).

> My attendant realizations and reactions required me to back off of this project for several months to tend to my personal material before I could reapproach *anima loci* [soul of place] and the myth and be able to work with them on more-than-personal levels.
>
> *(Humphrey, 2012, p. 88)*

> There are things in my mind, in my memory that can no longer be ignored. My stomach convulses, my back stiffens, I begin to sweat as I hold onto the things that need to be set free. My body fights its own experiences and my heart is kept prisoner. I know I can, I know I will set free the woman within me. She will take flight, but she needs my help. Dropping down (Personal Journal, September 8, 2006).
>
> *(Rankin, 2007, p. 99)*

> I thought about the river, feeling restrained by its cement barricades, and I wanted to tear them down with my bare hands.
>
> *(Haber, 2019, p. 59)*

On the one hand, step away from the research as needed, especially if the intensity begins to interfere with your life. On the other hand, if some part of the work loses energy, focus on what where your interest still is while tracking any dead zones (e.g., ecological damage, injustice/oppression) in what you are studying. When possible, work with other TI researchers in a group, even if each member is exploring a different topic.

> I experienced ecotransference in the area of self-care because of my own personal history of internalized industrial norms (which is introduced with the researcher, and presented as part of my findings) … By paying close attention to the way the *genius loci* manifests in my own reactive ecotransference, I was better able to map an understanding of the way the place-field pushed me and disrupted the stability of my personal field, pressuring me to accommodate its processes and tendencies.
>
> *(Leetch, 2017, p. 95)*

She also engaged in self-care when needed, especially when the "standardizing, industrial, consumerist" aspects of the place were influential enough to interfere with the research:

> Practices like eating clean, ethical food, staying well hydrated, making art, meditating, spending time in nature, and having warm social interactions

> with human and more than human beings are all ways of nourishing the self to support the likelihood of generating states of flow, inviting and cultivating e/mergence with the placefield ... These methods made me better able to create adequate holding for the emergent complexities I was hosting, transmuting, and helping to express.
>
> *(Leetch, 2017, p. 95)*

Ultimately, self-care opened up the research directly:

> Tracking this proved a useful measure for when I was being over-influenced by the intensity of the field, and when I might not be able to connect to the depth necessary to produce research findings. It ended up birthing an entire suite of ecotransference findings.
>
> *(Leetch, 2017, p. 96)*

(7) Withdraw with Thanks

Some researchers give gratitude and thanks to whatever places, elements, lifeforms, informants, interviewees if any, and imaginal beings were involved in your inquiry. Promise to share the results (see Chapter 7), and be open to how you can return the favor in the future. For primarily scholarly research, thank the experts consulted. Initiate a closing ritual to bring your psyche back into itself.

Sarah Rankin went outdoors to a site she felt close to, faced each of the four traditional directions, and lit a small fire to honor the phoenix motif that echoed throughout her work in Petaluma. She then poured water on the ashes.

> What is left for me to do? What else does the place need from me? ... With my eyes closed, after sitting on the bench in meditation, I was met with: silence, reverence, providing tools ... I am a member of STRAW, Students and Teachers for Restoring a Watershed. Through this curriculum and thematic instruction that integrates scientific exploration with core subjects, I am providing a forum for young people to engage.
>
> *(Rankin, 2007, p. 136)*

Filocamo expressed gratitude for what he had learned with a May Day ritual:

> On May 1, 2008, I carried a small green silk bag filled with ten dollars in loose quarters to Tree. Placing the bag in a hole in Tree's trunk that opened into the ground, I prayed that this offering would cause no harm to Tree or to any being that might live in that space. I later wrote, "May this ritual, this gift, bring blessings to Tree and to any being that happens upon it" ... I imagined somebody, someday, discovering this bag of coins

and wondering at this unexpected gift, perhaps wondering too what kind of being Tree might be to inspire such a blessing being left with her.

(Filocamo, 2008, p. 96)

Phase 3: Coagulate the Results

(1) Begin the Harvest

With some of your awareness on your inner responses, immerse yourself in what you found. Go through it, sampling impressions. Clear inward space for heuristic "indwelling" (Moustakas, 1990, p. 23), incubating new learnings while elaborating the research question and allowing core themes and images to emerge from the data. Tend intuitive breakthroughs as patterns in the material reveal themselves, but for this step impose no particular structure. Fool around with what you collected. Play attention.

After selecting some of your findings – stories, key images, dreams, textual analyses, interpretations, recordings, and interview transcripts – and staying with them in reflection to let them awaken and work on your psyche, consider them from different angles through different sensory modalities and psychic functions (thinking, feeling, etc.), imagining which aspects of them seem essential to their being or essence and which seem incidental. Allow the primary themes, symbols, patterns, ideas, images, etc. to arise gradually from the materials you've collected. Allow them to connect with each other. These motifs or images are not objects or generalizations but knots in the weave of the interactive field between you and your terrain of investigation: as Van Manen (2018, p. 90) puts it, "Themes are the stars that make up the universes of meaning we live through. By the light of these themes we can navigate and explore such universes."

Kevin Filocamo read his journal notes several times before attempting any thematic analysis (see Chapter 5). He also reread the accounts and surveys conveyed by his research participants, allowing his intuitive awareness to flow through the gathered material without trying as yet to pin anything down. Consciousness of the themes arising in the research came later.

(2) Modify Initial Lenses

Return to the pre-understandings you collected during the preparation phase and round out the hermeneutic circle, the iteration of your inquiry from segments to gatherings and back again, by modifying what you thought you knew with what you have learned. Build in new understandings and, if needed, return to the field for fresh data. *Horizontalize* your perceptions by temporarily dropping the focus on what has been figural and prominent throughout the research and tending instead to what rises from the background. Fit what emerges into your growing picture of your topic.

Add tools as needed. In working with place, Amanda Leetch realized fairly early on that her inquiry needed the lenses of feminist materialism, Barad's (2007) agential realism, and arts-based research methods. The work also required that she add other perspectives along the way.

Filocamo's initial idea was to spend time with a series of trees to gauge his erotic and emotional reactions to this form of nature activity:

> I didn't decide to work with *one particular tree* until the November 28, 2007 visit. Before that date, I chose different trees to spend time with during each visit. And even though, on this date, I began to refer to the Monterey Cypress tree that I consistently worked with as Tree, this did not become consistent until the beginning of the new year. Therefore, there may be times when I refer to Tree as "the tree," but these are not mistakes. These are accurate recordings from my journal reflecting earlier stages of the process.
>
> *(Filocamo, 2008, p. 65)*

(3) Analyze the Data

The delicate task in analyzing data is to preserve the butterfly of living results without recourse to the killing jar (Coppin & Nelson, 2017, p. 266). In TI, the primary goal of analysis is to distill the data into a story that reveals the character and depth of what was studied. In most cases of finding things out, the story is what we are after anyway, not dry collections of facts or explanations. We want to know not just what, but *why*: the underlying meanings.

First, we reread the research question and swim for a while in the data collected. Then we take the data apart, and, after our analysis, resynthesize it, following a formula from medieval alchemy: *Solve et coagula* (dissolve and coagulate). Chapter 5 covers how to do this.

> I analyzed the written accounts of their [i.e. participants'] experience with the land using a similar methodology that I had used to examine my own journal entries: by immersing myself in their writings and identifying labels, categories, and themes with which to discuss their experiences. This process began as I concluded analysis of my own journal entries.
>
> *(Filocamo, 2008, p. 57)*

A *theme* is a motif, image, or other prominent pattern that emerges from the data. *Codes* are abstract labels ("launching," "eruption," "resurrection," and "motherhood") that help us pick out the themes. We search for recurring images, statements, metaphors, events, actions, transitions, absences, and similarities/differences: signs of what has been silenced and seeks to return to personal and cultural awareness.

Working with themes can provide richer pictures than content analyses that do not distinguish between implicit and explicit themes or that concentrate on certain words while missing their synonyms. The happily fulfilled might never use the word "joy," for example, and places and elements exhibit recurring movements and cycles without ever speaking a word.

Not all studies will need coding or thematic analysis. For those that do, the oversight panel of colleagues and supporters needs access to whatever analyses are applied so it can examine how the researcher thematizes and stories the findings. Participants can be asked to pick out as key phrases from summaries of their stories or their own written accounts.

This thematic data can be further analyzed narratively (as dramatic plot structures), heuristically, intuitively, or even quantitatively while running it through different states of consciousness. We will consider data analysis in detail in Chapter 5.

(4) Reflect on What Changed

Reflect on yourself and your work. How you are different because of it? How has your relationship to your topic changed, and how have you been changed by it? What does your committee or group of colleagues say about these deep transmutations? At which points did the study investigate you?

"There are things I know now which were not possible for me to comprehend at the beginning of my research. Understandings had to be matured in the field to become meaningful" (Leetch, 2017, p. xvii).

> Learning to partner with place and to cultivate an open-hearted receptivity toward place communication has helped me to mature my consciousness into a more expansive, alive, interconnected, reciprocal sensory frame, evolving how I define and experience selfhood ... I feel it in my body, connect to it emotionally and somatically, register the patterns intuitively and cognitively, and express it creatively.
>
> *(Leetch, 2017, p. xx)*

One shift of awareness had to do with listening not only to nonhuman nature but to the built environment too:

> I did not learn to hear the earth from the birds up on the Mogollon rim ... I learned to hear her in the bricked in and boarded up back alleys of America's original urban laboratory. In the shaking rhythm of a vintage

> weave room, and the rush of the falls as it blends with the rush of the highway into one voice in concert; the same road that was once one of the first automotive racetracks.
>
> *(Leetch, 2017, p. 208)*

> I've had some injury to my thigh, and now there's a circular part of me – the wound, or where the wound was – made of earth, fertile earth with a fuzz of green, I am active toward it, and it is active, greening and prone to lose a few crumbs of earth as I/we move to examine it.
>
> *(Humphrey, 2012, p. 96)*

What surprised you? If nothing did, you might have missed something important. Finding no surprises raises the issue of whether the inquiry was conducted such that it merely confirmed what you already thought about the topic. If so, then the inquiry should change direction, deepening into an exploration of the defensive measures served by the project and their possible relation to any themes arising from the topic.

While going through his research journals and comparing them to the data, Filocamo noticed a discrepancy between the lack of emotional content in his "Emotions" theme and how often emotions came up in his journal entries (2008, p. 83). This prompted him to reevaluate some of the data and revise the story of the project.

(5) Create the Report

Assembling all materials, begin writing up the final description- and theme-rich *transmutative exposition* (see Chapter 6) on your topic, including the meanings that emerged, their relations with each other, any important cultural, spiritual, autoethnographic, ecological, or psychological implications, and how they deepened your understanding of the topic. Be sure to situate yourself culturally: e.g., ethnicity, socioeconomic status, sex, and gender; "middle-class white woman in America" (Rankin, 2007, p. 38).

When writing a thesis or dissertation, consider organizing it thus:

- Include whatever is relevant from the preparation phase in the "Delimitations" and "Methods and Procedures" sections.
- Outline what you did in Phase 2 for the "Methods and Procedures."
- Describe the actual work done in those steps in "Results and Findings," with the final transmutative exposition – the story of the inquiry – appearing in the "Discussion" section.

- In the "Conclusions," offer implementable suggestions for benefitting the terrain and your co-participants. Consider offering photography, video, art, drama, or other media, online or otherwise, alongside the final report.

> I will be leveraging art, diagram, video, photography, sound, poetry, and prose as appropriate to draw the reader into a multi-layered experience of meaning making, with the explicit intent to connect with the reader across multiple learning styles, types of knowing, and avenue of entry into this work.
>
> *(Leetch, 2017, p. 7)*

In the deepest inquiries, the presences tended stay with the researcher throughout the write-up or final project:

> Even as I write this I am allowing the place patterns, themes and motifs to guide how I weave this report. The lessons of the project are distilled and communicated as a placehosting artifact: the finished thesis. The thesis will serve as a gift created through collaboration with the *genius loci*, meant to honor the process and teach its lessons, feeding back into the deeper resonance of the field-effects of Lowell.
>
> *(Leetch, 2017, p. 124)*

(6) Share the Findings with Co-researchers

> Verification interviews were conducted once the original interview data had been transcribed and a depiction compiled. The information was be sent via email to the co-researchers for review. The verification interviews themselves were conducted via email, phone and Skype ... Co-researchers could add or clarify anything depicted in the original material, as well share any new insights or feelings since the time of interview.
>
> *(Olivieri, 2017, p. 39)*

Include this as part of a post-interview debriefing. What do the participants make of what you (and your committee/colleagues) found? What are points of agreement and of disagreement? How did the work change them? Have you been careful to honor their stories and, where necessary, protect their identities? How have they benefitted from the study? All this too is data. It also opposes the objectivist oppression of making oneself the expert, from the outside, on others' experience.

Leetch (2017) included photography and videography as an appendix to her thesis. She also asked people overseeing the inquiry to participate:

> I invited members of the resonance panel to create their own circular terrain weaving in as a means of processing their personal connection to and experience of the placefield. I conducted a basic demographic survey and video recorded the activity and discussion. I collected artist statements and weavings. After the thesis presentation, I will solicit the park to host a temporary exhibit of researcher and participant terrain weavings, to complete the circle of placehosting and to empower place to voice itself.
>
> *(Leetch, 2017, p. 118)*

She also included educators and others from the site of the research:

> I led the participants through a guided mindfulness activity, connecting them to the deep time thrumming of Lowell, through the lenses of shared experience. I introduced them to the concept of the placefield and invited them to use my stash of yarn to weave the connection they felt to place in the moment as we discussed the sum of my findings. In addition to the weavings, each member of my resonance panel produced an artist's statement and answered a small demographic survey. All survey questions asked for self-identified categories, rather than applying restrictive labeling.
>
> *(Leetch, 2017, p. 170)*

(7) Present and Host

The ways to present your results are endless: webinars, slideshows, videos, workshops, art projects, speeches, group presentations, movement activities, guided meditations, dramatic performances, poetry readings, study circles, heartsteads (see Appendix III), articles, books, ceremonies … Bear in mind a point made by information theory: all things being equal, sounds and pictures convey more information content than words alone. For combined impact, mix the media and draw on many voices in order to converse with your audience instead of just reporting. Tell the story of the inquiry. Use excerpts of interviews (if any) so the participants' voices will be heard. Include your contact information to continue the discussion.

> The process of placehosting requires that a gift from the process be returned to the community. This thesis, the associated presentation, and the art installation are the last in a series of gifts to Lowell based on the outcomes of my work. If I have attended to the needs of place, staying with what it needs from me instead of what I needed from it, this hosting

> is an act of ethical participation in catalyzing a transformative approach to meaning making, cultural reproduction, and (ultimately) consciousness.
> *(Leetch, 2007, pp. 185–186)*

These last activities of the inquiry can bring forth a community-based creative endeavor:

> As part of developmentally appropriate placehosting, students and rangers crafted a museum within a museum that showcased the art, technology and design innovations of our young participants. Building week to week, we enshrined collaged rivers and bean plants, circular weavings and water wheels, recycled "planned" cities, clay pots, water sample surveys, photographs of body mapping, and our future casting art project (which layered tracing paper over vintage photography and invited the participant to draw what they wished the future would be like over the old photograph) ... This iterative style of reciprocal making turns human participants and place into mutual co-creators.
> *(Leetch, 2017, p. 89)*

As you present your work, explore what ongoing obligations you feel toward the subject of your study and those who participated in it.

Managing Ecological Complexes

These wounds, knots, or points at issue we share with what we study make the inquiry real, emotional, and embodied. A hillside beaten into a golf course seems like someone else's business until we feel the flattening impact inwardly or recognize it in our relationships.

Ecological complexes show up as ecological countertransference:

> Ecotransference is the sum of unintegrated emotional reactions to the characteristics of the place under investigations. These reactions always carry an unconscious component normally tied to woundings in the investigator ... The presence of an unconscious identification with a place or some aspect of it distinguishes ecotransference from empathy. Empathy with a troubled place can hurt, but ecotransference hooks the empathizer by the unconscious.
> *(Chalquist, 2010, p. 59)*

During his research, Haber's theater dream warned him of a delay in finishing the inquiry:

> I then met some of the people from the city who were working on the project and I said, "Oh when is this going to be complete? When can we

> use this wonderful space by the river? It is going to be so perfect, it is so beautiful." And they said, "We are still working on it. We don't know when it is going to be done"
>
> *(Haber, 2019, p. 3)*

He also dreamed of a powerful snake he could not let go of. Such a snake was known to the Uypi tribe who lived near the river (2019, p. 4). The snake recalled the shape of the river (p. 6).

Leetch described tending ecotransference as maintaining a "diffuse permeability," achieving a depth of inquiry requiring a degree of bravery and vulnerability:

> A useful metaphor might be that, for the purpose of this study, I made myself into a windsock for the conditions and emanations of place; when the winds blow that way, I shift with them so I can observe and study the change of how my co-constructed self-field is constituted through the exchange.
>
> *(Leetch, 2017, pp. xix–xx)*

Leetch imagined the ecotransferential field as a person:

> The field I partnered with to complete this research is an active, vocal, and significant one. Her stories are woven through and tightly around the multiplex ecological and sociological issues that proliferate under late-stage capitalism. This was a heavy presence to host, and there have been points of resistance, instances of reactivity, and moments of personal difficulty all along the way, testing my capacity to tend the obligations of place and complete this research.
>
> *(Leetch, 2017, p. 92)*

Ecotransference works its way into how we conduct the study. Inquirers often get lost in familiar settings, for example, only to discover aspects of a place they never suspected. Or unforeseen obstacles arise:

> My sensitivity notwithstanding, Lowell also resisted me for a long time. "The entry into the space confounds me. 'The park is the city' yet the place encounter starts on strangely ill-defined terms" (Research memo, 5/30). My attempts at altar making failed over and over again as the points in the field that felt like thresholds and the way into the park from the parking lot were incongruent ... After trying to leave gifts, I choose another symbolic language to communicate with, and this time I picked sound. The field was much more receptive to my singing bowl meditations, responding with both cacophony and quietude.
>
> *(Leetch, 2017, p. 158)*

While on a pilgrimage on the Colorado Trail in the Rocky Mountains to feel in the flesh how the abused land feels, Sherry Gobaleza grew bloated and nauseous. The idea of purging came to her. As she realized that her sickness expressed that of the environmentally stricken place where she walked, a stranger who took a wrong turn showed up and helped her get to a hospital. Doctors told her that her mineral levels had been depleted: exactly what mining had done to the land (Gobaleza, 2016).

In ecotransference, *ecoreactivity* refers to the force with which what we study induces in us, emotionally and somatically, its current state of being (Chalquist, 2007, p. 59). Some examples involving place:

> Lowell was not just an industrial city. She was on the forefront of violent settler expansion, a thriving indigenous fishing community, a glacier shelf that retreated to change the course of an entire river. She has been a hub for immigrants and refugees, and the transmutational alchemy of immigrants on cities and cities on immigrants is part of this spiral patterning as well. Lowell embodies a drawing, sucking, swirling spiral, drawing in energies to its center, and through this motion shaping and transmuting everything that comes in contact with its historic narratives, shaping an entire community, an entire nation, the entire planet, all by way of a swirl through the stories of the river city.
>
> *(Leetch, 2017, pp. xv–xvi)*

The persistent swirling, spiraling motif embedded in the land resurfaced in the actions of colonizing inhabitants:

> Settler women, disconnected from their homeland and, ultimately, terrorized away from building sisterhood, were enticed to the city to join the productive work in the cotton mills. Here, a lost sisterhood was fomented among the spindles. Leaders of rebellion, voices of resistance, young women who resisted to create more humane labor conditions for the workers who made the industry possible: women and children.
>
> *(Leetch, 2017, p. lxi)*

How reflectively the researcher manages ecoreactivity is often central to conducting deep terrapsychological work:

> When I moved back to Orange County for the last time, I often dreamed of flooding: tidal waves and swollen rivers ... I first made the connection last winter between the physical floodplain of Orange County, the maldevelopment represented by its dammed river and flood-prone, overbuilt housing, the feeling of dissociation conjured by the endless walls of the local a(n)

> esthetic, and the psychic flooding that occurs as fallout from dissociation as a response to trauma. The very same night, while I sat on my grandmother's couch pondering these connections, she turned on the television to the nightly news report of the worst flash-flooding in decades of Orange County history.
>
> *(Humphrey, 2012, p. 89)*

> Lowell's hydrophilic symphony entangled itself with this researcher's experience of ecotransference and ecoreactivity … as due dates for my thesis artifact were met with flooded basements and overflowing sinks, the floodplain of the river coming to dominate my own psychological infrastructure as aspects of uncertainty, unable to be contained despite the engineered intentions of human systems.
>
> *(Leetch, 2017, p. 141)*

> Once I relaxed into my emotional body, new textures began to emerge in the physical landscape. In tending to my inner world the outer began to reveal itself. That sensitivity cultivated to hear myself was intercepting messages from the world beyond my skin. As I've found myself working with my own limitations I find correlates in my environment.
>
> *(Hippman, 2017, p. 3)*

While investigating and listening in on various locales throughout California, I was often accosted by locals who turned out to be perfect guides for showing me the underside of wherever I was at the moment, whether or not I felt ready. This happens to all of us and is an expression of ecoreactivity, as though the place "wants" us to know it better.

> A few months later [after the flood dream], in a Starbucks parking lot, a very old and very drunk Irishman with a Mexican name and accent approached me and, for no apparent reason, began quizzing me on Fountain Valley history. He was impressed that I knew its previous names (Talbert, Gospel Swamp). As a reward for this knowledge, he began to regale me with stories of his boyhood during the great floods of the 1930s and 40s – how he and his gang used to punt around on rafts atop the sudden, transient lakes stretching as far inland as Bolsa.
>
> *(Humphrey, 2012, p. 89)*

Places also show us, through dreams, art, and by other means, their true nature prior to any injury. On the morning of meeting the Irishman, Humphrey had the following dream:

> James Hillman left a piece of writing, just a small sentence in a book that gives directions to an underground diner, a place we never knew existed, and we're excited to go and find it. There seems to be nothing here but blank OC and then as we descend into it, it opens up into a big, lively, open-air diner space – wonderful! Delicious food served on colorful, very big plates. This is a place I've always wanted to exist! And as we take it in, the field deepens and it's as if a whole vista is suddenly revealed, a depth of field, the wide sublime springtime canyon hills and sky, hills going on and on, the real OC land here; my heart leaps with the sight of it.
>
> *(Author's personal journal, March 13, 2011, p. 89)*
>
> At this point, roughly halfway through my exploration of Orange County history and halfway through my master's studies, and at a major personal turning point, Orange County seemed to be showing me another face. It was as if I suddenly had depth perspective, the field of my life opening up as in the dream. Perhaps the most striking feature of the dream is its shifting of the Erysichthon motif of clear-cutting the sacred land to turn it into a personal banquet hall. Here, instead, is an image of a secret diner integrated perfectly into the sacred hills themselves, a delicious communal experience of possibility.
>
> *(Humphrey, 2012, pp. 89–90)*

This is also an example of how the placefield, though traumatized, begins to heal as we work with it. (Numerous examples appear throughout my *Animate California Trilogy*.) The changes delineate a road map of our path through the work, with dreams as markers along the way.

> Dream:
>
> I planted and tended a garden in the backyard that was once a safe house for my childhood grief. As I did so, I slowly began to be drawn back into research beyond the personal. And so the Orange County of my dreams began to appear again, and to change. The appearance of the color orange in dreams came to represent commentary on the progress of my research. I dreamed of shape-shifting into Huell Howser, dressed in orange, on the hunt for California's gold; of cradling an infant swaddled in orange who spoke to me the words "I am."
>
> *(Humphrey, 2012, pp. 92–93)*

Eventually she dreams of a healthy, shape-shifting bear holding forth the possibility of restoring local relationships with a place that once hosted the largest subspecies of American grizzly on record:

> She showed us the permeable edge of the fence where home and wilderness can be neighbors, where human and nature can have their respective

> homes, their respective boundaries, and yet can play and learn together as cubs: all overseen by a fierce local feminine, an empowered, embodied, ensouled, and emplaced *anima mundi*.
>
> (*Humphrey, 2012, pp. 94–95*)

Finishing the Practice Phase

When this phase ends, the terrapsychological inquirer enters a transitional space that requires its own observances before plunging into working with the data (themes, stories, images, etc.).

Even with compelling academic or professional deadlines at hand, it serves the work well to take at least a little time and embrace the shift of psychologies (and archetypal stances) from investigator to interpreter. (Think of Odysseus in the underworld: upon encountering the ghosts and hearing their sad tales, he shifts from Hero to Storyteller. In Korean folklore, Princess Bari changes from woman of the woods to initiated healer.) Even with a few last leads to run down, it's important to feel and embody the change of roles as the next phase approaches.

Your mind might be filled with all the things you think you should have done, what could have gone better, what you missed, and mistakes you think you made. There are no perfect inquiries.

Pause. Breathe. Time out.

In the phase just ending, you were like the alchemist preparing the laboratory, the altar, and the fire, which you gradually turned up as your energy increased. Now comes the *separatio* of analysis, including decisions about what belongs and what does not; the *circulatio* of going over and over the material; the *vera imaginatio* ("true imagination") of listening to the themes emerging from it; and the *coagulatio* of watching the pieces find their places in the picture of what it all means. This is also a good time to watch for dreams that might bear on the work of interpretation and meaning-finding.

For Discussion

1. In thinking over the unresolved issues you might bring to the study, how would you predict they would be triggered? How would you manage them?
2. At the end of the study, your dreams should shift. How might you expect them to?
3. What are your lasting obligations, if any, toward the places involved in your inquiry? For example, an ecologically damaged locale won't magically repair itself. What steps might you recommend based on what you learned?

References

Barad, K. (2007). *Meeting the universe halfway: Quantum physics and the entanglement of matter and meaning*. Durham, NC: Duke University Press.

Casey, E. (2001). What does it mean to be in the place world? *Annals of the Association of American Geographers 91*(4), 683–693.

Chalquist, C. (2007). *Terrapsychology: Reengaging the soul of place*. New Orleans, LA: Spring Journal Books.

Chalquist, C. (2009). *The tears of Llorona: A Californian odyssey of place, myth, and homecoming*. El Cerrito, CA: World Soul Books.

Chalquist, C. (Ed.) (2010). *Rebearths: Conversations with a world ensouled*. Walnut Creek, CA: World Soul Books.

Coppin, J., & Nelson, E. (2017). *The art of inquiry: A depth-psychological perspective*. Thompson, CN: Spring Publications.

Filocamo, K. (2008). The alluring universe: Exploring an erotic relationship with the world (unpublished master's thesis). John F. Kennedy University, Pleasant Hill, CA.

Gobaleza, S. (2016). Rocky mountains, Colorado trail (unpublished community fieldwork paper). Pacifica Graduate Institute, Carpinteria, CA.

Haber, M. (2019). Unattended trauma of the San Lorenzo River: A terrapsychological inquiry (unpublished dissertation). California Institute of Integral Studies, San Francisco, CA.

Hippman, M. (2017). The psychology of salt (unpublished master's thesis). Environmental Humanities Program, University of Utah, Salt Lake City, UT.

Humphrey, K. (2012). Anima loci, greening self: Reconnecting with place by meeting the mythic soul of Orange County (unpublished master's thesis). Pacifica Graduate Institute, Carpinteria, CA.

Leetch, A. (2017). Weaving meaning: Terrapsychological Inquiry and the historic industrial placefield of Lowell, Massachusetts (unpublished master's thesis). Prescott College, Prescott, AZ.

Moustakas, C. (1990). *Heuristic research: Design, methodology, and applications*. London and Thousand Oaks, CA: Sage.

Olivieri, C. (2017). Your church, my bar! A terrapsychological inquiry of the relationship between Queerspace and queer spirituality in San Francisco, California (unpublished dissertation). California Institute of Integral Studies, San Francisco, CA.

Rankin, S. (2007). A terrapsychological study of the psyche of Petaluma as found in the stories of the land and as mirrored by my own psyche (unpublished master's thesis). Sonoma State University, Rohnert Park, CA.

Romanyshyn, R. (2007). *The wounded researcher: Research with soul in mind*. New Orleans, LA: Spring Journal Books.

Van Manen, M. (2018). *Researching lived experience: Human science for an action sensitive pedagogy*. London and New York, NY: Routledge.

5

ANALYZING THE DATA

Data Analysis as Ritual

The purpose of data analysis is to examine the data you collected systematically, with help from a plan, model, or schema that reveals what you seek even if the data contradict what you expected. The analysis is an act of refinement that moves your work toward the presentation of its results. Hence, this chapter is written for use in research requiring systematic work with the findings. If you are not conducting formal academic research, you may skip this chapter, although it may contain some ideas about assessing information during whatever project you have conducted or are planning to. Even an informal inquiry should tend whatever themes emerged.

The common notion of data is that it means numbers. It can, but it needn't. ("Data" became associated with numerical facts only in 1897; the word goes back to *datum*, the "thing given.") For purposes of terrapsychological research, data is results in the raw. It can include narrative accounts, transcripts of interviews, photographs, field observations, articles and papers, news accounts, documented emotional and somatic responses, primary and secondary literature, dreams ...

Before you plunge into the harvest you brought back from your explorations, plan a routine for working with this material. What hours of the day or week will you set aside for the analysis? Where will you do it? How might you turn your desk or computer into an altar for honoring the research? What objects and images will witness your efforts? What steps will your routine include? How will you open and close each session? What methods will you use to get back on track during periods of apathy? Will you require any artistic materials or media? What presences (if any) will you call in for

DOI: 10.4324/9781003462965-6

assistance? (My laptop has a sticker of a face peering from under the keyboard to remind me that the machine too is a presence.) Whom among your research allies will you enlist for assistance? Will you play nature sounds or music? Burn incense? Meditate to ground yourself? To whom will you turn when you feel overwhelmed? (Picture mythic Psyche aided in her chores by helpful ants and eagles.) These and other questions can help you create the ritual by which you begin to sort the lentils from the chickpeas.

The ritual includes deciding on the type of data analysis your research project needs, if any. Terrapsychological Inquiry (TI) presently uses these methods, which can be carried out in this order or used separately:

1 Sorting
2 Coding
3 Thematic analysis
4 Creating a transmutative exposition (see Chapter 6).

Sorting

A mass of disorganized findings will not help you paint your picture. Sorting begins to bring order to your data before you write it up and present it. All data collected should be filtered through your research question to separate what is relevant from what is not. As Deah Curry and Steven Wells (2013) observe in their *Organic Inquiry* primer, the researcher must distinguish between what is related (which is pretty much everything) and which relations are actually relevant to the study. "Terrapsychological Inquiry requires an expansive approach to data collection and interpretation, and my inquiry has produced a mountain of data that needed to be transcribed, sorted, coded, second-string coded, and analyzed" (Leetch, 2017, p. 127).

Start by doing breathing, movement, or other exercises to get your mind back into your body and bring your senses and feelings to full wakefulness. A ritual can help. Call in whichever unconscious presences or archetypes you believe can serve as guides to help you sort the data.

Once you are centered and ready to tend the work, go over what you collected, refamiliarizing yourself with the total picture. Make brief notes on whatever images, themes, or other patterns stand out as your attention continues to rove over the material.

> The goal of working with the data was to distill the content of the journal entries into themes that could be used to describe the contents of that data, as well as provide a foundation from which to draw some conclusions about what insights this data offered in relation to the research question. I started working with the data … by simply reading through the journal. I

> read through the journal three times over a two-week period without doing anything with the material. In a sense, I wanted to prepare my mind for the deeper work that I was about to embark upon with this data.
>
> *(Filocamo, 2008, pp. 50–51)*

Now, carefully reread the research question that guided all your collecting. As you sit with the question, imagine it as a filter or net holding on to what is relevant to it and letting the rest pass through. Ultimately, you store all the documentation, but what passes through the filter will not appear in your final summary of the findings.

Let this delimiting alchemical image of net or filter guide your analysis and prevent you from hoarding data. Discarding some is a necessary act of ferocity. *Keeping in what should be left outside the circle of the research focus distracts attention from what matters most about the study.* The alchemists' colorful term *terra damnata* refers to ingredients left in the mix too long. Out they must go.

A caution, however. As you decide, item by item, what to keep and what to let pass through the filter, ask yourself always: "Do I want to discard this because it's irrelevant, or because it makes me uncomfortable or contradicts my expectations?" Not only keep the latter but also give it special analytical attention and mention it in your findings. Discovering disconfirming evidence creates opportunities for deep learning. When in doubt about what to discard, run it by your committee or other research allies and get their opinion. (You will want them to know what you got rid of anyway.)

If you are rereading an interview transcript, cross out what neither literally nor metaphorically bears on your question. For example, say you are interested in what kinds of nature encounters help people feel kinship with Earth. You begin the interview by asking, "Can you give me an example of a time when you were outdoors and something deeply moving happened?" The participant begins with:

> Sure, but I'm a little nervous. I hope I don't babble too much. I tend to go on and on in interview situations. I think it's because when I was little, my noisy family made it hard to get anyone's attention. As a result, I sometimes run off at the mouth for a while ... Your question is so interesting. I never thought about that before. Outdoors, and something transformative happened. Hmmm, let me see. Oh yes, just the other day I came across a poppy blooming where I had never watered. It was a lovely orange, and it got me thinking, What makes *me* bloom?

As you read this excerpt, ask yourself: Is anything about nervousness, noisy family, getting attention, running off, and so on symbolically or literally reflective of either the research question or the setting in which the interview takes place – for instance, near a babbling brook? If the answer is "no," then:

> ~~Sure, but I'm a little nervous. I hope I don't babble too much. I tend to go on and on in interview situations. I think it's because when I was little, my noisy family made it hard to get anyone's attention. As a result, I sometimes run off at the mouth for a while… Your question is so interesting. I never thought about that before. Outdoors, and something transformative happened. Hmmm, let me see.~~ Oh yes, just the other day I came across a poppy blooming where I had never watered. It was a lovely orange, and it got me thinking, What makes *me* bloom?

At this point your inner critic voice might stir and ask: *What if you chop something that belongs?* Well, that's what keeping all the documentation is for. You can always revisit, and you should at least once before the final exposition. Also, important symbols and themes recur. You may miss them in one place, but they will pop up again elsewhere. The far more common error is not getting rid of enough.

The alchemical *separatio* you perform on the data will continue, eventually expanding to include unnecessary sources in the literature review, irrelevant observations cut from the final texts, paragraphs that do not truly belong, and other bits of *terra damnata* in need of dumping and, possibly, eventual recycling for a later project. Reassuring yourself that the data will be reborn somewhere else helps quell *separatio* anxiety even if the somewhere else never materializes.

Coding

> I logged more than 500 memos over the research period. I collected research memos, process memos, and field observations. I first transcribed, sorted and coded my observations and reflections using qualitative coding software. After determining themes, I created a shorthand for significant memos and wrote them on sticky notes which were sorted into folders several different ways, first looking at themes, then connections, continuing to distill the ideas into smaller and smaller units.
>
> *(Leetch, 2017, p. 128)*

Are you scared yet? Actually, not every inquiry will require coding the data.

Coding refers to tagging your data with category labels aligned with your research question. We code data to see how the meanings we mark in the data illuminate what we want to know. Coding can help with identification of themes (recurring symbols, images, and motifs) in the material we have collected (see "Thematic Analysis" below). It's a bit like the reminders some of us scrawl into the margins of paper books. A used book I read contained the scrawl "peasant ecology" near a section on how dwellers, not agri-giants, look after their land. An uplifting if less pertinent scrawl from another reader exclaimed, "Doug is a good man." Well then.

Codes answer such questions as, "What is going on here?" "What is this an example of?" "What actions are being performed here?" "What assumptions are implied?" "What is surprising?" and "How would I categorize this interaction, statement, or event?"

For example, in a study about styles of education, the interviewee statement, "I found his active style of engagement very helpful for bringing me out of myself in class" might be coded, "Encouraged student participation." In the interview example above, a code might look like this: "Oh yes, just the other day I came across a poppy blooming where I had never watered. It was a lovely orange, and it got me thinking, What makes *me* bloom?" Code: "Surprising blossoming."

Where do the codes come from? Usually, the researcher invents them and provides a rationale for their use. Codes emerge from the imaginal space between your data content and your research question, with one eye on each. To code is already to begin to interpret. As coding expert Johnny Saldaña explains,

> A code in qualitative inquiry is most often a word or short phrase that symbolically assigns a summative, salient, essence-capturing, and/or evocative attribute for a portion of language-based or visual data ... Just as a title represents and captures a book or film or poem's primary content and essence, so does a code represent and capture a datum's primary content and essence.
>
> *(Saldaña, 2015, p. 3)*

According to Boyatzis (2018), a good code comes with

1 a label.
2 a definition of its characteristics.
3 a description of how to know when the theme occurs; how to flag it.
4 a description of qualifications or exclusions.
5 positive and negative examples to help with detecting something codable.

Many researchers create a "start list" of possible codes and subcodes for use with the material (Miles, Huberman, & Saldaña, 2019). These contain labels or categories for grouping the findings. One possibility is to create codes collaboratively: researcher, allies/committee members, and participants working together. Some codes will emerge from pondering the data, finding what Coffey and Atkinson (1996) describe as a codable moment.

Whether to code or not, and to what extent of formality and detail, depends on your research question, the results you wish to obtain, the level of rigor you prefer or are required to uphold, and your own facility with coding. Questions to ask before deciding include:

- Do the data in this study lend themselves to coding? (Try it out.)
- Do the codes thoroughly address various aspects of the research question? (Try them on.)
- Do the proposed coding schema and categories fit the study? (Try it out.)
- Does coding any of the material lead to fresh insights? (Try it out.)

Some researchers feel concerned that coding can deprive the research material of its living presence. "For example, in working with dream images," Coppin and Nelson (2017, p. 266) caution, "rather than simply naming the image, or worse, assigning it a reductive analytical interpretation, you would try to represent the image more in the context of the dream and allow it to continue moving"; they call this "keeping the data alive." Few things kill living experience more quickly than categorizing it before it has drawn a long breath.

However, if we have taken time to honor the experience and allow it to come to voice, we might then use coding as a kind of tag of convenience without taking the labels too seriously, like titling a new digital folder "vacation photos." "A code can sometimes summarize or condense data, not simply reduce it" (Saldaña, 2015, p. 4). The normal procedure is for a first cycle of coding the data, then refining the codes, then a second cycle.

Qualitative researchers like Saldaña (2015) have identified types of codes commonly used for the first cycle of coding. These include:

- Open coding: seeing what codes spontaneously emerge from the data you review.
- Process coding: capturing an action with an "-ing" word, as was done above ("surprising blossoming").
- Descriptive coding: a one-word tag for tracking what's going on ("wonder").
- In-vivo coding: using a word or short phrase from the actual text or transcript (works well with interviews).
- Emotion coding: codes with an emotion word or short phrase.
- Magnitude coding: using a word or number to describe frequency or intensity.
- Values coding: notes beliefs, attitudes, and values.
- Versus coding: tags conflicts or polarized attitudes (this vs. that).
- Dramaturgical coding: coding with terms from theater; e.g., identifying the actor, plot elements, main conflict.

- Motif coding: noting recurring symbolic roles, archetypes, or themes (hero, victim, and threshold crossing).
- Narrative coding: tagging by type of narrative structure, such as genre, setting, plot, characterization, and point of view.
- Verbal exchange coding: classifying types of conversation along these dimensions: (1) Phatic Communion or Ritual Interaction; (2) Ordinary Conversation; (3) Skilled Conversation; (4) Personal Narratives; (5) Dialog (Goodall, 2000, p. 121).
- Simultaneous coding: applying more than one code to a datum.

All of these can be used for terrapsychological data analysis. Because of TI's focus on story, the narrative-dramatic types of first-cycle codes can be particularly useful. Also, consider these adaptations and additions:

- Ecotransference magnitude coding, e.g., for an intense bout, "high" as opposed to "medium" or "low."
- Placefield motif coding to tag patterns in people as well as in places they inhabit (e.g., a dream of contamination echoes a recent oil spill).
- Indigeneity coding to register data that reflect the beliefs, stories, or practices of a place's original inhabitants.
- Terrestry pattern coding to mark themes or dynamics running through family lines.
- Ecorole coding to indicate roles showing up in how participants relate to nature, place, or whatever is being studied: Rescuer, Warrior, Martyr, Guru, Lover, Channel, Champion, Trickster, Artist, Scientist, etc.

Methods used for the second cycle of coding concentrate, refine, and synthesize data coded in the first cycle. For example,

- Pattern coding identifies emerging patterns or themes in large portions of data.
- Focused coding singles out the most useful and relevant first-cycle codes.
- Axial coding amalgamates and codes relationships between first-cycle codes.
- Theoretical coding puts all the codes together into a central category that summarizes what all the data are about or point to.
- Elaborative coding takes the theoretical constructs from previous work and further develops or modifies the theory.
- Longitudinal coding for long-term studies marks changes in participants across time in terms of insights, emergences, decreases, turning points, and other kinds of transformation.

As you go, write out rules for inclusion for each category of codes you decide to deploy. Also, make notes in your research journal about the process of coding, noting resistances, emergences, insights, conflicts, unanswered questions, problematic codes, etc. Mark material you are not sure how to code on the first pass with "unsure" and come back to it later. Using computer-assisted qualitative data analysis software – known by the spiny acronym CAQDAS – is also an option.

For still more thoroughness, try asking research allies who haven't used the codes to code some of the research material (text, images, etc.). The resulting overlap of results between coders is known as "intercoder agreement." Above 85 percent agreement is considered reliable; 70 percent is average. The usual formula is: reliability = number of agreements / total number of agreements and disagreements. (Coders who like to find broad, inclusive categories have been nicknamed "lumpers," whereas coders who create tight, separate categories are known as "splitters." *Coagulatio* and *separatio* fans.)

When coding with others, establish expectations and levels of magnification so they know how widely or narrowly to focus.

And so, to code or not to code the data or findings of your TI? I have often been struck by how many of the qualitative studies I read presented conclusions that were obvious well before the data-analysis phase. Sometimes this was because the writer's knowledge of the analysis results showed up early in the write-up. But not always.

Some years ago, having taught qualitative research and supervised many dissertations, I came across a sample text in a book on the methodology of Grounded Theory. A sample text reprinted in the book had been subjected to careful coding and thematic analysis. This prompted me to try a little experiment. Reading the text carefully before looking ahead to the coding or analysis, I wrote down what seemed to me the clearest themes running through it in light of the research question. I then checked the results of the elaborate GT analysis carried out on the sample. It was nearly identical to what I had come up with in a few minutes of examination.

After that I stopped using coding in my own terrapsychological work. But thorough analysis aids some researchers, looks scientific, impresses funders, and speaks to the need for rigor in research.

Codeweaving

The data analysis continues from data to codes to combining the codes into larger and larger categories. This is *codeweaving*: forming more abstract and general codes from the codes already at hand.

Codeweaving involves merging like categories of codes. The example above included the process code "surprising blossoming." Perhaps another code elsewhere marked examples in the data of "sudden awe." Depending on the research question, these codes might be woven into the code "unexpected awe." Instead of two codes, we now have one. Multiplying this synthesis reduces the number of initial codes and grows the list of themes that will inform the transmutative summary of the research findings.

Some might protest here that moving from living specifics like landscapes, elements, conversations, gestures, and even texts into abstractions is too heady. We forget that even the body categorizes. If someone blows a sharp breath into one of your eyes, a mere gestural hint of a repeated exhalation is enough to cause a blink: the body has already classified such as unpleasant or dangerous. The problem isn't categorizing. The problem is forgetting that categories are working abstractions.

In addition to merging codes, codeweaving involves writing a statement of how the codes relate to each other interactionally, thematically, causally, emotionally, or in some other way. Try writing several versions of these statements, attending to which are supported by the data and which might be challenged or disconfirmed by it. (That is another advantage of coding: putting similar data together can make it easier to identify contrary examples.)

If what you are writing follows organically from data to codes to codeweavings, you should be left with several statements that indicate basic themes that hold together and make sense of the mass of material you collected. Finding such underlying patterns helps interpret terrapsychological material because the world approaches us on bridges of symbol, image, and movement, coded or not.

Thematic Analysis

> As the primary researcher, my role has been to chronicle my own process of conducting this inquiry, to bracket my assumptions throughout the duration, and to utilize this information to triangulate the co-researchers' data. Throughout the course of this study, themes have emerged and cross-referenced my own experience. The additional data provide a place from which to generate further questions.
>
> *(Olivieri, 2017, p. 115)*

Themes are recurrent patterns of experience that link inner and outer, psychological and ecological, literal and symbolic, and manifest and latent. Very often, one aspect of the theme is tangible (seeds opening after a fire) and the other intangible (rebirth). A symbol is an image that holds these aspects together: for example, a cross symbol as both visible crossroads and the idea of convergence. (See Chapter 3 for more about symbols.)

Themes matter greatly in terrapsychological exploration because they join and organize so many aspects of human and nonhuman existence. It's amazing after feeling like one is going in circles to step outside and see whirlpools forming in a stream, one after another. The stream encircles the region, which sits upon vast funnels of granite formed long ago. We always find ourselves within the thematics of places and things, cycles, and elements. TI studies those thematics to bring them into consciousness. They are what the data is about, what it means, and their implicit unifying structure.

> When the first levee was built in 1958, the path of the [San Lorenzo] river was straightened, as a deeper canal was formed … This area has since been developed with light industrial buildings, small car dealerships, some second-rate hotels, and this mental health facility. Working in this facility, I always thought it was strange that this historic place of turmoil, destruction, and divided river became the future home for people suffering from what R. D. Laing referred to as a divided self.
>
> *(Haber, 2019, p. 13)*

Note how this kind of theme, a placefield motif, reaches across locale, land, time, and even psyche, involving people and places alike. In Santa Cruz, a site of splitting and interrupted flows, dams and bulkheads built to hold back water, the repeating ecopsychological trauma shows up early on as a result of colonization:

> Had the *padres* heeded the warning of the Indians at the mission, they may have been able to avoid this disaster by seeking a better location on higher ground. This first site for the mission is also the current location of a corridor between the downtown business district and the Homeless Services Center. This area has been a major thoroughfare for drug addicts and criminals seeking support services, drugs, or victims.
>
> *(Haber, 2019, p. 13)*

A problem with guessing at themes intuitively while poring over research data is that to the nonintuitively inclined, the conclusions look flimsy and arbitrary. Another problem is that intuition can be wrong, although it nearly always feels right. You simply *know* that man is a stranger in town … except he isn't.

A thematic analysis allows us to be explicit about how we detect and organize themes that arise in the work. Boyatzis (2018) compares it to tracking: once an expert points out the pattern clearly, others can see it too.

> Central to the Castro district is Market Street, the "obtuse angle no traffic plan will ever solve." Market Street was designed to integrate the competing northern and southern grid system of the 1800's. Measuring 412 feet by 475, Market Street was, and is, literally off kilter, that is, *not straight*.

> This single angular street has literally been the walkable path to queer enterprise and financial success. The revolutionary explosion of queer-owned and -operated businesses began an era of political capital based on disposable income. Eccentric and enduring, this "hills-be-damned geometry" forever shaped the experience of queer San Francisco.
>
> *(Olivieri, 2017, pp. 93–94)*

Seeing discarded needles that bore unwitting testimony to larger threats to the flow of the San Lorenzo River, Haber noted the intuition but proceeded systematically:

> I plan to do this [thematic analysis] by tracing underlying and prevalent themes, ideas, and psychosomatic reactions or responses from my reflections, grouping similar ideas into categories and then analyzing the recurrence of unifying or symbolic motifs. These motifs will help illustrate and illuminate the San Lorenzo River and its story of neglect, abuse, and trauma.
>
> *(Haber, 2019, p. 47)*

Sometimes it's easy to see a theme because its pattern recurs regularly and forcibly. Fire and renewal, for example, repeat over and over throughout the history of Harbin Hot Springs in California; the place has burned down over and over, and the fiery recurrence shows up in other ways as well. At other times, themes are more difficult to detect. Try taking each code and adding "is a symbol of" and see if that reveals a theme. Look for anything that recurs, including absences. A generative theme does not so much explain as draw together large portions of data.

> I reviewed the categories and scanned the labels that each category included until I began to identify commonalities between categories that suggested a broader perspective that encompassed the categories. These became the themes under which I organized the contents of the journal entries for analysis and discussion. The themes that I identified were titled *Experiences/Relationship with Tree and Environment; Named Experiences during Visit; Presence and Awareness; Techniques or Methods of Engagement; Somatic Experiences; Emotions; Expressions of Erotic Connection; Thoughts and Questions; Relationship to Self and Process; Post-Visit Effects; Communicating Experiences*; and *Benediction*.
>
> *(Filocamo, 2008, p. 52)*
>
> Soon, I started to see a connection between the mental state of these lost souls and the degradation of the San Lorenzo; both had been left behind, forgotten, denigrated, left without purpose or intention. Healing could begin by telling

> the stories, of the river and of the people. As much as the river needed the help of the people, the people may have needed the help of the river more.
>
> *(Haber, 2019, p. 54)*

As in literature, art, dream, and life itself, themes place foundations beneath the stories behind the events we wish to understand. Whether or not we code to trace themes, we should be clear about how we detected them, what significance they have for the study, and how their implicit meaning becomes explicit for us and our research participants.

Because they are foundational and gather in so much experience, we should avoid simplistic labels for themes and try not to impose them from the start (Braun & Clarke, 2006). At the same time, "Descriptive or interpretive methodologies do not preclude scoring or scaling of themes and then using this numeric representation to check the consistency of judgments" (Boyatzis, 2018, p. 129).

How many themes should researchers deal with? It depends on the study, what's being studied, and the time available. Braun and Clarke (2006) suggest a maximum of three for a paper. A place tends to have one primary theme (the placefield motif symbolizing the central geological feature: a ravine, a river, and a hill of skyscrapers) and other subsidiary themes that spin off from it. These we might want to cluster to show how themes relate to one another (Boyatzis, 2018). An easy way to map this is to write down the central themes, write the subthemes below them, and draw lines to show meaningful connections. Themes running all over the place can indicate either a lack of focus or specificity of the research question or the same issue with how the central themes are identified and described. Try refining them.

Once you have a theme map or its equivalent, write a summary of the relationships, with the central themes as key characters in the story and their actions as plot developments. Fill out the characters and trace the subthemes (minor characters whose interactions constitute subplots). Be sure to check in with your body, your dreams, and your research allies as you do this.

Go back to your data, recheck your codes (if any), then compare them with what you have written. Is anything significant missing? Do the themes align with the data?

If your research study involved participants, you have some creative options if you wish to involve them in the thematic analysis. These include:

- asking them to search for themes emerging from their own experience of the study;
- meeting with them as a group to discover themes in the data together;
- running what you have summarized by the participants, then documenting their feedback;
- making a creative project together to highlight the emerging themes (see Chapter 6).

During her research, C. K. Olivieri taught her participants basic locianalysis and asked them to write descriptions of what they discovered. She then melded the descriptions and extracted the themes, beginning first with context:

Composite Depiction

> This depiction is a composite of the four co-researchers' experience of conducting a terrapsychological activity in their locale of choice. This composite seeks to describe felt experiences of the terrapsychological relationship to queerspace. These qualities, consistent with TI methodology, display themes that are "arrestingly consistent, symbolically rich and thematically meaningful" (Chalquist, 2007, p. 49). The composite depiction was generated and compiled throughout a four-month time frame. A return to immersion and incubation was conducted after the initial interviews. Subsequently, immersion and incubation were revisited during the month-long gap between the compilation of the individual depictions and the initial workings of the composite.
>
> Then the themes:
>
> Thematic Qualities of Felt Experience
>
> Safe Space
>
> Physical, emotional and spiritual safety, both the need for and creation of, dominated every aspect of the co-researchers' felt experience. In effect, the definition of queerspace itself holds the prerequisite of being a safe space.
>
> Holding the Tension of Opposites
>
> All locales in this study contain interactions and descriptions of juxtaposition of opposites through both manmade and natural phenomenon. This tension of the opposites creates a "seeing through," an experience of inner and outer reality as one. Terrapsychological Inquiry presupposes a concept of interiority (inwardness, subjectivity, and inner life) which participates in a place as a functional terrapsychological interactions.
>
> *(Olivieri, 2017, pp. 109–110)*

> Unconventional Conventions
>
> Terrapsychologically, each chosen locale commonly reflects a disregard for conventional mores. All geographic and psychic spaces contain a system of rules and boundaries that are queer-specific, rooted in the dissent from heteronormative heterosexual culture … These behaviors include social structuring, the definition and meaning of success, and sexual norms.
>
> *(Olivieri, 2017, p. 111)*

> Church-likeness
>
> One of the most consistent qualities of queerspace has been the felt experience of spiritual space or church-like capacity. Queerspaces are utilized in both joy and sorrow, providing a container for counsel that is ripe with symbolism, ritual and community:

> I mean, it makes me really happy and joyous to just see people breaking out into song and people breaking out into their little jam sessions downstairs, even if they are ridiculous sometimes. it just feels like there is a really overwhelming sense of...just happiness and comfort and like, there's a lot of love there...I can go there anytime and in whatever mood I'm in, I can go there and find something that's going to work for me and that's been the case the entire time I've been going there.
>
> *(Olivieri, 2017, p. 112)*

> The Future of Queerspace
>
> A theme woven throughout the heuristic interviews was the presence of an optimistic future for queerspaces and their role in the lives of queer-identified individuals as well as their function within the larger collective consciousness.
>
> *(Olivieri, 2017, p. 114)*

A final pass through the hands of allies or committee members and incorporation of their feedback into the final summary or *transmutative exposition* (Chapter 7) of what was studied completes the thematic analysis. Now it's time to look more carefully at what the findings mean.

For Discussion

1 In what situations and arenas might data analysis be useful?
2 What themes can you detect running through your topic of interest and how you arrived at it?
3 Why is it important to enlist participants in analyzing the data or findings of the study?

References

Boyatzis, R. (2018). *Transforming qualitative information: Thematic analysis and code development*. London, New Delhi, and Thousand Oaks, CA: Sage.

Braun, V., & Clarke, V. (2006). Using thematic analysis in psychology. *Qualitative Research in Psychology* 3(2), 77–101.

Chalquist, C. (2007). *Terrapsychology: Reengaging the soul of place*. New Orleans, LA: Spring Journal Books.

Coffey, A., & Atkinson, P. (1996). *Making sense of qualitative data: Complementary research strategies*. London, New Delhi, and Thousand Oaks, CA: Sage.

Coppin, J., & Nelson, E. (2017). *The art of inquiry: A depth-psychological perspective*. Thompson, CN: Spring Publications.

Curry, D., & Wells, S. (2013). *An organic inquiry primer for the novice researcher*. Kirkland, WA: Infinity Publishing.

Filocamo, K. (2008). The alluring universe: Exploring an erotic relationship with the world (unpublished master's thesis). John F. Kennedy University, Pleasant Hill, CA.

Goodall, H. (2000). *Writing the new ethnography*. Oxford: AltaMira Press.

Haber, M. (2019). Unattended trauma of the San Lorenzo River: A terrapsychological inquiry (unpublished dissertation). California Institute of Integral Studies, San Francisco, CA.

Leetch, A. (2017). Weaving meaning: Terrapsychological Inquiry and the historic industrial placefield of Lowell, Massachusetts (unpublished master's thesis). Prescott College, Prescott, AZ.

Miles, M., Huberman, A., & Saldaña, J. (2019). *Qualitative data analysis: A methods sourcebook*. London, New Delhi, and Thousand Oaks, CA: Sage.

Olivieri, C. (2017). Your church, my bar! A terrapsychological inquiry of the relationship between Queerspace and queer spirituality in San Francisco, California (unpublished dissertation). California Institute of Integral Studies, San Francisco, CA.

Saldaña, J. (2015). *The coding manual for qualitative researchers*. London, New Delhi, and Thousand Oaks, CA: Sage.

6

WHAT THE FINDINGS MEAN

"Findings" is an apt word. Terrapsychological Inquiry (TI) seeks to lend voice to that which has been ignored or silenced in how we relate to the world and how it relates to us. The work is a project of recovery in the spirit of the alchemical *opus*, the great work of sustained labor and love that led in the operation of *coagulatio*, the bringing together of what was previously mixed up or sundered.

The primary step forward in this part of the research journey is taking up the findings gathered up – for a formal academic study, from the thematic analysis (Chapter 5) – and understanding them before crafting a comprehensive story about what they mean (Chapter 7). Because the story's the thing; even in experimental studies, what we look for is not so much the data, facts, or proof as a deep understanding of how what interests us came to be (beyond quanta or chemicals), where it originated (beyond oversimplified isolated causes), and where it is going (beyond statistical probabilities). In other words, we want the tale behind the detail.

Making Sense of What Was Found

Researchers often gain a new level of understanding of findings by putting them in some kind of presentational order. This is especially so when the sheer amount of data, information, or experience collected exceeds early expectations (as it often does in TI work). Leetch supplemented her text with diagrams like Figure 6.1:

> The magnitude of terrapsychological data gathered during the process is beyond the scope of a master's thesis. Instead, what I have done is identify

DOI: 10.4324/9781003462965-7

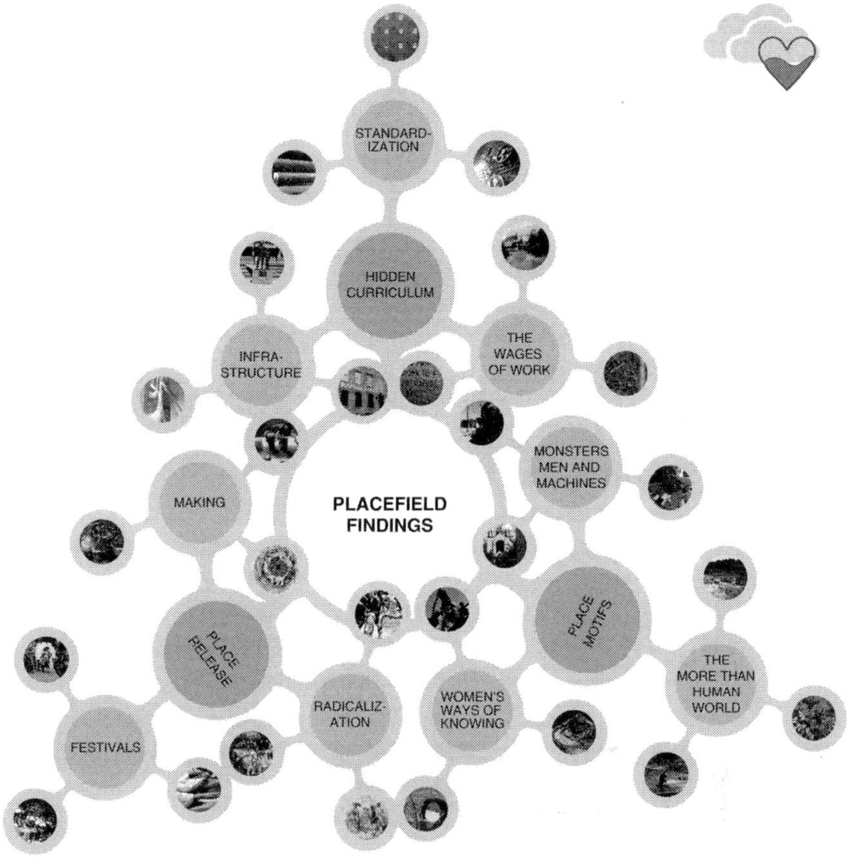

FIGURE 6.1 Finding molecule 1: Placefield findings.

Source: Amanda Leetch (2017).

> three larger headings that contain my findings, and selected findings within each of these subject areas to focus on in this findings chapter. Each finding section opens with a molecule diagram to illustrate the findings that will be covered in that section.
>
> *(Leetch, 2017, p. 133)*

Findings 1 (a), 1 (b), and 1 (c) represent central theme categories (place intensification, place motifs, and hidden curriculum) from the presence of the place (Lowell) being researched. The letters (i), (ii), and (iii) indicate subthemes (Leetch, 2017, p. 136). The diagram indicates the interrelationships. Even without delving deeply into the diagram, we can get a sense of how detailed the findings were.

When I first studied San Diego, I began with the land. San Diego is a seaside port and city riven by canyons. Sharp edges – splits, borders, and crossroads – recur continually in San Diego, beginning with the geography. Its original name was Miguel, the sword-wielding angel. It may have been named after the swords (*diegos*) carried by the sailors of Captain Vizcaino, one of whose ships was named *San Diego*. This edgy recurrence signals a central placefield theme under which various subthemes fall like plotlines in an unfolding story. In other words, we cannot understand San Diego deeply, as a complex entity, without understanding its multidimensional edges and splits.

A question to ask about any theme or subtheme is: *Why does it matter?* In this case, because we can now look for splitting in other aspects of San Diegan life. The International Border expresses it. The shape of the Bay – a near-vertical split between Coronado and the city – seems to be another, one that happens to run along a major earthquake fault. Unconscious identification with the features of the largely ignored landscape – ignored because not thought of as anything more than lifeless bulk – results in acting them out, whether personally or collectively, like "smart" fences built over fault lines in Jerusalem, like revolutions in river-spoked Moscow, like rises and falls of fortune in once-hilly Manhattan.

Aside from place, dynamics in ancestry show up in personally felt conflicts, as when a student of mine seized by the desire to drop out of school discovered in her family history a pattern of women dropping educational opportunities when right on the verge of completing studies. (Learning about this persuaded her to stay on course and graduate.) In terms of objects, we buy cars we think express something about who we are, but which of their mechanical qualities do we unknowingly take on after long use? How might our bodies reflect our homes, or the neighborhoods we occupy? What might the emotional overheating (internal combustion) of entire nations tell us about climate change?

In Figure 6.1, Finding 1 (b) included three important subthemes:

> The genius loci communicates symbolically through place motifs that are clearly recognizable patterns and emanations. In the Lowell placefield these communications manifest to this researcher from three categories: women's ways of knowing, the more than human world, and monsters and machines.
>
> *(Leetch, 2017, p. 137)*

Leetch unfolds the first theme:

> Lowell deeply underscores the ecofeminist relationship between women's bodies and the living earth. The factory conditions which made many women sick with tuberculosis also poisoned the river; the women were

> the symptom-bearers for the land, and the symptoms a catalyst for resistance. Lowell's revolutionary feminist labor history echoes into the park's priorities as strong women are placed in prominent positions and enact feminist leadership, liberation pedagogy models, and ethics of care and reproductive value.
>
> *(Leetch, 2017, p. 138)*

She then mentions a link to another significant theme:

> Finding 1a, *making*, is resonant with women's ways of knowing as fiber arts have long been the essence of what is traditionally considered *women's work*. My data terrains are a reclaiming of weaving from the mechanized and industrial world, and a cultivation of expressive and intuitive methods of meaning making. The place intensification process of making was particularly well articulated by one of the resonance panel weaver's artist statement.
>
> *(Leetch, 2017, p. 138)*

As for some consequences of the findings:

> In the most radical and open interpretation of the phrase, attending to place is attending to self, and place care and place partnership are radical acts of self-love. These findings trouble established Western notions of what selfhood is and how one should approach it. Cultivating sensitized innocence and partnering with the placefield is a profound and transformative experience, one with outcomes which cannot be fully understood from the state of consciousness that has theorized but not experienced this type of placefield connection.
>
> *(Leetch, 2017, pp. 163–164)*

Even though these kinds of findings – including findings not specifically about place – are deeply meaningful and connective, how do they relate to customary research standards of generalizability, reliability, and validity? Standards upheld in physical science?

Validity, Reliability, Generalizability

Our biases inevitably filter how we perceive. Science seeks to limit the error factor.

However, the positivist model of verifiability makes at least five problematic assumptions:

1 that the world is made up of discrete things;
2 that self and world are separate until joined;

3 that the complexity of reality can be fathomed by isolating simple chains of cause and effect;
4 that inner knowings are accurate only when compared with some fixed outer reality;
5 that subjectivity is a contaminant.

These are the standards of efficiently operating factory machinery, not of mature inquiry able to deal with mess, uniqueness, or ambiguity. This mess is anxiously defended against by an overemphasis on rigor.

> Terrapsychological Inquiry asks its readers to step outside of normal Western and Eastern thought patterns and epistemologies and embrace a more indigenous or ancient mindset, one of careful observation, in a world where all living things are interdependent, with nature as a central unifying body, as teacher and spiritual guide. To frame this way of thinking in terms of standard quantitative or even qualitative research methodology denies the importance of developing a reciprocal relationship with our natural environment.
>
> *(Haber, 2019, p. 39)*

TI starts with the inner integrity of the researcher. More than two centuries of psychotherapy have taught us that systemic biases often herald unconscious factors that lose their potency when brought to light. Also, as Carl Rogers (1995, p. 22) noted, a researcher drawing on the entirety of one's "organismic wisdom," unconscious as well as conscious, through sustained reflection strengthened by feedback from other people, is less likely to be ruled by unseen distortions of perception.

In social science of the kind still anchored to natural science standards of rigor, *validity* refers to whether research really measures what it claims to measure. *Reliability* means whether the results are predictable and stable enough to repeat. *Generalizability* has to do with whether the findings apply to people or situations outside the study. Qualitative research has modified these three standards to be friendlier to human experience, but they remain problematic, especially for TI, as ideals of accuracy.

Validity

To begin with validity, the truly objective kind is impossible anywhere, but in a Euclidean world of objects, we remain detached from and view only from outside. Relationships, meanings, and minds cannot be measured the way the length and width of a computer screen can be calculated. Because of interanimism, TI would have to ask how the flatness of the screen recurred symbolically in the very act of measurement.

Is validity a useless criterion, then, in terrapsychological research? No. Even for work outside the academy or the laboratory, it makes sense to look into whether what we think we study is really there. TI leans on Denzin and Lincoln's (2017) redefinition of validity as trustworthiness of research design and practice: the more careful, transparent, systematic, collaborative, self-consistent, and self-reflexive the study, the greater its validity. Note that this standard is more rigorous than is usually applied to natural science research, where the researcher's inner life is usually ignored because held as separate from the study. In actuality, bias comes not from too much subjectivity but from too little. Ambition, aggression, uncritical conformity to authority, projection, privilege, splitting, repression, fear of being defunded, greed, hierarchy, and other forms of unconsciousness remain in shadow – which is why "objective" science has provided poison gas, mass surveillance, pharmaceutical monopolies, and nuclear bombs, and why fully a third of scientific papers are highly inaccurate or even fraudulent.

Rosemary Anderson's "Intuitive Inquiry" relies on *resonance validity* and *efficacy validity*. The first has to do with the quality of emotional resonance within the participant. "Research can function more like poetry in its capacity for the immediate apprehension and recognition of an experience spoken by another and yet (surprisingly and refreshingly, perhaps) true for oneself, as well" (Anderson & Braud, 2011, p. 36). Resonance should occur across multiple domains of experience, including the intuitive, the emotional, the aesthetic, and the somatic. Resonance validity also includes a "resonance panel" of peers or experts who track the research; in graduate programs, this is usually the master's project or dissertation committee. The second standard, efficacy validity, depends on the extent to which the research fosters inspiration, delight, insights, and creative leaps.

Liberation psychology, for which research is critical participatory action, includes contextual validity, the fruitfulness of how the research effort and questions are framed and the relevancy of data collection to those involved in the research; interpretive validity, which increases as people come together from various social locations and levels to discuss possible meanings of dominant social narratives and to consider alternative interpretations; and catalytic validity, whether the research leads to creative, liberatory transformation in the individuals who participate and in the world at large (Watkins & Shulman, 2010).

TI accepts these types of validity and adds six more:

1 Ecotransference *resonance*, the deeply felt and even dreamed discovery of consciously or unconsciously enacting themes resonating in the place, object, plant, soil, building, animal, etc., under study, as when a dream figure in Orange County criticized me for omitting an important local motif from my initial explorations there.

2 Endurance *validity*, which is how consistently themes identified as expressions of an ecological complex continue to resonate and develop during and after the study.
3 *Transmutation validity*, the deepening of the relationship between researcher and researched.
4 *Community response validity*, which is how consistently people who live at the research site resonate with or recognize the findings.
5 *Ecological validity*, the extent to which findings make sense in their natural settings instead of being confined to the artificiality of a laboratory (Ciceral, 1982).
6 *Sustenance validity*, the degree to which the study contributes to the aliveness, sustainability, and ecological integrity of the research site. In addition to acquiring knowledge, research should open a conversation with the place about what it needs from the researcher and from its own community. The same applies to research with entities other than places.

Being systematic is what separates research from guessing. TI raises validity through:

- focus, clarity, and generativity of the research question;
- research concepts and constructs made clear and specific;
- triangulation of data sources, participants, and methods (in other words, the more sources and voices, the more we learn);
- a list of key areas of questioning when interviewing participants;
- coding checks for intercoder agreement;
- member checking (respondent feedback);
- an audit trail that includes a research journal;
- use of participant or informant quotations in the final story-summary;
- accurate interview transcription;
- identifying and monitoring potential researcher biases;
- coherent linking of all parts of the study (e.g., lit review with interview questions);
- thick, context-aware descriptive writing;
- dream monitoring;
- researcher cultural situatedness;
- negative evidence and rival interpretations of the data dealt with;
- usefulness of the knowledge produced;
- transformation of participants and researcher and reader.

Generalizability vs. Resonance

Qualitative research tends not to be considered generalizable beyond the persons participating in the study. In other words, the findings apply mainly to them. However, the terrapsychological inquirer is interested in whether the findings also resonate with viewers and readers. As every novelist and filmmaker knows, the particular, unique, and situated often illuminates the universal. Resonance is strengthened by including diverse voices and perspectives.

Reliability as repeatability makes sense if the goal is to ensure that a molecule or a beam of light behaves the same in different settings. Alas, life as actually experienced is far more complex, limiting the utility of the replication standard. For example, psychotherapy is sometimes criticized "scientifically" because a client who sees different therapists is soon confronted by different emotional issues to work out. This is not the lack of an objective cure in therapy, it is exactly what should happen. Different therapists trigger different sides of ourselves. The relational matrix constellated by each collaboration is unique. How could it be otherwise, except perhaps for machines?

TI redefines reliability as the extent to which observations by different researchers combine to form a coherent, intelligible picture of the place, objects, insects, animals, weather, etc. under study. *Generative reliability* is the degree to which the study's clarity, meaningfulness, thoughtfulness, and attention to detail allow other researchers to use it as a productive point of departure. A good study begets other good studies.

Reliability also rises when different researchers find similar themes in play. Michael Haber's finding that a primary theme of Santa Cruz is "Flow" aligns with my earlier informal study of the town's ongoing imagery of rapid movement and mobility (Chalquist, 2009).

When the objection surfaces that TI, like other forms of qualitative research, does not meet standards of positivist or postpositivist rigor, our responses have included these:

- Standards employed for the study of simple objects that do not talk back cannot be applicable to research focused on experience and interpretation.
- TI stands much closer to research as understood in the humanities, where criteria include quality of scholarship, expressiveness, and relevance to life, than to an inapplicable natural science model. It is worth considering that this model, though useful, has revealed to us the nature of less than 4 percent of the composition of the cosmos. The rest is made of dark – something or other, we don't really know. A school of medicine, education, or psychotherapy with a 4 percent success rate could not sustain itself.
- Empirical-positivist standards do not guarantee accuracy in research. Of twenty-one studies published in the journal *Nature and Science* between 2010 and 2015 and repeated to evaluate them, only thirteen obtained results replicating those originally found (Camerer et al., 2018). That degree of inaccuracy is a result fairly well replicated when evaluating flawed social science research (Stokstad, 2018).

It turns out, then, that Procrustes, mutilating agent of exact measurement, has friends: Cronus, the Titan who ate his own children, and Astraea, also a Titan, obsessed with purity and precision and placed in the sky as the constellation Virgo. At their best, these busy titanic gods exemplify the kind of attention to precision needed when conducting research. At their devouring worst, however, they turn judgmental. Their "objective" standards are fantasy structures which have forgotten their own sources in human imagination. So fierce is the shame arising from doubtful research findings that the Max Planck Institute for Human Development founded a Loss-of-Confidence Project so cowed psychologists could "come out" about their science imperfection fears and receive support. The problem is not their research but how it is received.

It's worth remembering that although Maslow's findings on self-actualizers achieved renown, criticisms of the rigor of his research did not. By all means let us pursue rigor, but not to the point of misery. Iacchus and Baubo, Hermes and Eshu, and Aunt Nancy and Ame-no-Uzume stand ready as folkloric exemplars for keeping handy a spirit of humor and play. Besides, the proof of the pudding is in the eating, where we can actually taste it. What changed because of the study?

Significance of the Findings

The question of significance is often known as the "so what?" of the research. What good was it? What did it accomplish?

> While there are several reasons to study the terrapsychology of the San Lorenzo River and look for clues and possible solutions to help this region heal, the most important goal is to serve as a basis for further research and planning. By bringing to light new (and old) ways of thinking about terra-damage and environmental degradation, better and more creative solutions may be found. Without understanding that the fundamental issues facing the river and the community stem from limitations in human thought processes and value systems, solutions are shortsighted or we focus on temporary fixes that never address the bigger societal issues.
>
> *(Haber, 2019, pp. 10–11)*

> It seems clear that humans – especially those humans who live in industrialized societies and whose lifestyle of unchecked production and consumerism seems to be impacting the biosphere most significantly – need to change our relationship to the world … In fact, it may be that, through these challenges, we are being called to a fundamental shift in consciousness, one in which we re-engage the world from a deeper sense of unity with, rather than mastery over, the world.
>
> *(Filocamo, 2008, p. 18)*

In psychocartographic inquiries, the finding is often a reactivated myth that fits a particular time or place. A reader unfamiliar with terrapsychology might wonder at first why identifying the presence of such myth in a particular place – Demeter in agriculturally fertile Ventura County, California for instance – would be significant. The myth's thematic power becomes evident in how much experience it organizes and gives meaning to:

> Archetypally, the Castro is the home of Dionysus, the god of winemaking, fertility, ritual madness, theatre and spiritual ecstasy. Dionysus is known as the half-mortal son of the Greek god, Zeus. Considered androgynous, attractive, and prone to vice and excess, Dionysus is representative of the death-rebirth process so often found in San Francisco.
>
> *(Olivieri, 2017, p. 92)*

The implications of this are multileveled and substantial:

> Through terrapsychological and heuristic investigations of San Francisco's queerspaces in the Castro and Mission districts, an intense overarching theme of radical juxtapositions emerges ... Speaking in myth, symbolism and metaphor, these trends have displayed themselves throughout the minutia of daily experience, from landscape and weather to culture and geography ... Queerspaces have taken on additional dimensions of community, safety, support and worship analogous to those traditionally displayed in religious spaces.
>
> *(Olivieri, 2017, p. 133)*

Myth came up for Humphrey too in her investigation of Orange County, CA:

> My own sense that as a culture, we are poised on the cusp of a shift from a colonizing to a relational ego is also expressed by much of the literature of depth and ecopsychology. Given this interest, possibilities for further research on the importance of place to psyche, and methods for working therapeutically with that connection, are practically endless ... In terms of the specific myth of Erysichthon and Mestra, I believe the story is very active culturally because of its recent emergence in scholarship and popular culture and its resonance with the larger story of the Western colonizing ego. I see much room for further research as the story works its way toward the resolution that, in terms of the larger collective, is still missing.
>
> *(Humphrey, 2012, p. 95)*

What we find, and how we find it, also reflects on our methods. Leetch (2017, p. 150) used some of her findings to study the methodology even as she used it (see Figure 6.2 below):

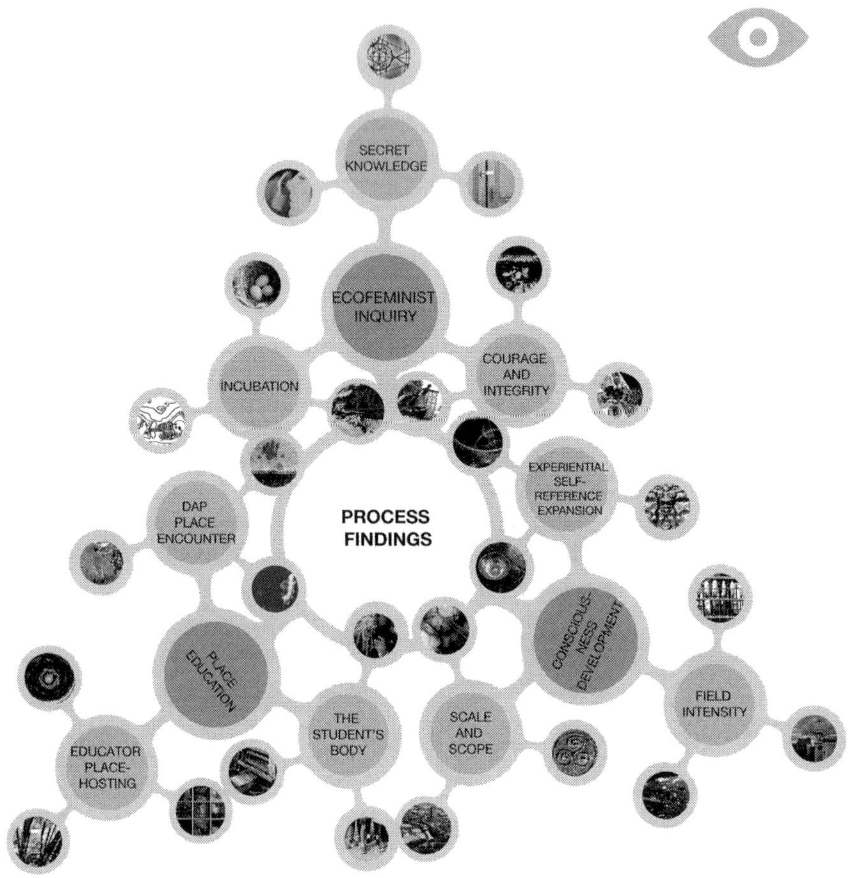

FIGURE 6.2 Finding molecule 2: Process findings.

Source: Amanda Leetch (2017, p. 160).

> These process findings focus on the applications, experience and evolution of using terrapsychology as an inquiry method. These meta-processual findings explore how TI can inform field trip facilitation, the experiential reality of ecofeminist inquiry, and the consciousness development that is prompted through the form of inquiry itself.

She adds:

> Terrapsychological Inquiry, through the cultivation of place-tuned perception, strengthens and reinforces an imaginal sensory connection to place that expands out into the field; in this fashion, the limited and egoic sense

> of self is composted, and the embeddedness of the self-system becomes the new self-referential frame.

Researchers who conduct interviews consistently report deep changes in the participants as a result of the study. As Filocamo writes of a participant who tried an outdoor exercise for reconnecting with more-than-human nature,

To begin, "Steve" provided a particularly poetic description of the environment he had "settled into":

> ... I gradually began to hear a symphony of sounds, ranging from a deep bass rumble from the earth to a high string whisper of the wind through the trees, and encompassing the intermittent woodwind and percussion sounds of chimes, small birds, mourning doves, ravens, rustling branches, and scampering squirrels. I then became aware of a complex dance of flies darting in and out of bright islands of sunshine, warming themselves for a while then darting off into the shadows in complicated patterns of some mysterious dance.
>
> *(Filocamo, 2008, p. 101)*

This opening led to an altered perception of the surround and its intense aliveness:

> The tree's intense adoration of the sun drew my attention to the rest of the vale and I realized that the entire symphony was a magnificent paean of joyous longing for the sun – the tree's groaning with the strain of reaching, the flies buzzing with its excitement, the wind sighing in the release of movement.
>
> *(Filocamo, 2008, p. 101)*

Here Filocamo anticipates and responds to a common objection:

> In reading these beautiful descriptions of movement within the environment – an environment whose bounds now seemed to reach toward the sun – some might say that Steve was "projecting" his own thoughts and images onto the environment. Steve's expression in this writing suggests an awareness attuned to poetic expression, and this "poetic ear and eye" was certainly used to express his experience with the environment. The question that emerges for me, though, is what *in the environment itself* may have sought to communicate this particular beauty through Steve's particular viewpoint and "voice"? Is Steve the only presence that has awareness in this encounter? Or could there be some other presence or

> awareness in this environment that sought to be known and expressed through Steve's poetic perspective?
>
> *(Filocamo, 2008, pp. 105–106)*

These kinds of questions arose from the other participants' accounts as well:

> Carina, Kerry, Samuel and Steve each conveyed the ways in which their one-hour visit with a particular place on the land left them feeling more connected to the place than when they had started … This deepened awareness of embodied self, combined with the intention to engage the places that they were drawn to with mindful attention, made it possible for the participants to experience the world in a way that felt more connected, deeper and richer.
>
> *(Filocamo, 2008, pp. 110–111)*

All TI researchers have also testified to deep changes in their own perceptions.

> Initially I perceived a limited construction of the self-field relationship … Through the iterative channels of this study I found that the reality is much more lush and total; everything we partake of is our consciousness constructing itself, and it will work its way through the echoes and ripples the actor makes out in the world around it. This finding would not have been uncovered by the traditional methods of inquiry.
>
> *(Leetch, 2017, p. 154)*

This change of consciousness also altered her sense of self and its powers:

> From this perspective I understand my role as a culture creator, as molecular assemblage, as interpermeated field. All of this transcends my prior perspective, supported by my attuned, sensitized partnership. I can extend out beyond the ego identity as self-reference in a way that was merely theoretical before. I am able to see how our threads have become interwoven.
>
> *(Leetch, 2017, p. 156)*

About her relationship with Petaluma, CA, Sarah Rankin noted:

> I have watched the way her river twists and turns, beating as her very heart. I have done my best to follow the lines of the stories of her most ancient inhabitants, through the ripples of peopling and events, some beneficial to her and others, damaging, threading my way through to the present day … I see her standing before me, arms outstretched, a mischievous grin

> on her sunlit face. She has taken form and when the light is just right, I see wings behind her, reflecting the light of the setting sun, as she rises in the form of the Phoenix.
>
> *(Rankin, 2007, p. 118)*

Researchers also reported new learnings arriving even after the study had formally ended. For example,

> As I work to write this process and the findings into a coherent thesis I also find myself in the position of having new and unexpected aspects of the work reveal themselves. I could organize this work 100 different ways and still not manage to convey all that the Lowell placefield had to teach me, and that is unfolding more and more every day; the perspective granted through this study permeates my being, and is part of the personal enfolding of my own being from this point forward. This is both the gift and the catch of terrapsychological research.
>
> *(Leetch, 2017, p. xvii)*

Perhaps the larger significance of using TI is in how its practices and perceptions permanently shift researcher and participants from states of relative distance from things, elements, places, creatures, and people into fuller intimacies bringing a new sense of responsibility and care for our life together here in an animate world.

For Discussion

1 In the inquiry you contemplate, how much rigor is needed? Will you have to demonstrate the validity and reliability of your methods, or can you be more relaxed about it?
2 What do you make of a research methodology you can modify as you work? Does the prospect scare you? Please you? Something else?
3 What are some ways to staying open to new findings after the inquiry formally ends?

References

Anderson, R., & Braud, W. (2011). *Transforming self and others through research: Transpersonal research methods and skills for the human sciences and humanities.* New York, NY: SUNY Press.

Camerer, C., Dreber, A., Holzmeister, F., Ho, T., Huber, J., Johannesson, M., … Wu, H. (2018). Evaluating the replicability of social science experiments in nature and science between 2010 and 2015. Nature.com. Retrieved from www.nature.com/articles/s41562-018-0399-z

Chalquist, C. (2009). *The tears of Llorona: A Californian odyssey of place, myth, and homecoming*. El Cerrito, CA: World Soul Books.

Ciceral, A. (1982). Interviews, surveys, and the problem of ecological validity. *American Sociologist 17*(1): 11–20.

Denzin, N., & Lincoln, Y. (2017). *The Sage handbook of qualitative research*. London, New Delhi, and Thousand Oaks, CA: Sage.

Filocamo, K. (2008). The alluring universe: Exploring an erotic relationship with the world (unpublished master's thesis). John F. Kennedy University, Pleasant Hill, CA.

Haber, M. (2019). Unattended trauma of the San Lorenzo River: A terrapsychological inquiry (unpublished dissertation). California Institute of Integral Studies, San Francisco, CA.

Humphrey, K. (2012). Anima loci, greening self: Reconnecting with place by meeting the mythic soul of Orange County (unpublished master's thesis). Pacifica Graduate Institute, Carpinteria, CA.

Leetch, A. (2017). Weaving meaning: Terrapsychological Inquiry and the historic industrial placefield of Lowell, Massachusetts (unpublished master's thesis). Prescott College, Prescott, AZ.

Olivieri, C. (2017). Your church, my bar! A terrapsychological inquiry of the relationship between queerspace and queer spirituality in San Francisco, California (unpublished dissertation). California Institute of Integral Studies, San Francisco, CA.

Rankin, S. (2007). A terrapsychological study of the psyche of Petaluma as found in the stories of the land and as mirrored by my own psyche (unpublished master's thesis). Sonoma State University, Rohnert Park, CA.

Rogers, C. (1995). *On becoming a person: A therapist's view of psychotherapy*. New York, NY: Mariner Books.

Stokstad, E. (2018). This research group seeks to expose weaknesses in science – and they'll step on some toes if they have to. *Science*. Retrieved from www.sciencemag.org/news/2018/09/research-group-seeks-expose-weaknesses-science-and-they-ll-step-some-toes-if-they-have

Watkins, M., & Shulman, H. (2010). *Toward psychologies of liberation*. New York, NY: Palgrave Macmillan.

7

SHARING THE RESULTS

The normal outcome of a terrapsychological inquiry is a report or summary that tells the story of the topic, its investigation, the participants, and the researcher's experiences, including surprises, and the findings. In academia, this means a class paper, a master's project or thesis, a presentation, or a dissertation ("doctoral thesis" outside the United States). It can also mean workshops, slideshows, poems, paintings, collages, dances, songs, ceremonies, films, plays, novels, and scripts (someone in Dubai contacted me a while back about a script plot involving a terrapsychologist) … the possibilities are as large as we can imagine.

Although this chapter more or less follows the usual order of dissertation sections, the work need not be confined to such a format. In fact, an important activity at this stage of the inquiry is to engage the topic in imagination to ask it how it wants to express itself. We can also ask the topic for dream hints about this. Alchemically, this stage of the work corresponds to the operations of *proiectio*, the radiant display of the newly blended philosopher's stone of wisdom and healing, and *multiplicatio*, in which the stone's emanations give rise to more stones and the creative efforts needed to bring them into being.

The final summary or production of a TI is the *transmutative exposition (expo)*: the narrative telling the metastory of the research background, methods, and outcomes. For some, the expo will be a master's thesis or dissertation; for others, a report, essay, creative exhibition or performance, festival, stage production, film, or novel.

Whatever form it takes, the expo should touch on the following.

DOI: 10.4324/9781003462965-8

Structuring Your Writing

In the academic world, a brief abstract (about 150–250 words) introduces a research document. It should contain the following:

1 The hook: Get the reader's interest with an evocative first sentence. (As you might guess, "the hook" is not academic terminology. But it is what I advise my students to do.)
2 Purpose/objective of the research: Describe its overall intention.
3 Problem statement: Where you summarize the topic.
4 Approach/methods: Where you briefly mention TI.
5 Results/findings: What you learned from doing the project.
6 Implications: Psychological, social, and ecological; the significance of the study.

Even if you are not doing academic work, this remains a useful exercise in concisely stating what your work has been about. Most students are taught to write the abstract last, but I suggest writing an initial version and working on it throughout the study.

Introduction

The introduction section of the expo begins by acquainting the reader with your topic. What did you study, and why? What's the background? Share a little about why the topic spoke to you, but do keep the focus on the topic rather than on you.

State your research question(s), then name the methodology (TI). Give a description of it.

Briefly summarize the research you carried out. You will discuss it more later.

Summarize the significance and contributions of the research. You may wish to include how your inquiry develops TI.

For non-academics, consider turning the introduction into the origin story of your research. The Quest is an archetype that seldom fails to excite when described imaginatively and from the heart. How did it all begin? Where did it go? What was the point of the grand adventure? Tell the tale, and flesh it out with evocative imagery.

Literature Review

Begin working on the literature review as soon as you have sources to put into it. The review is more than an annotated bibliography. Here you show that you know the work relevant to your own, usually from a variety of fields. "Relevant to your own" means directly applicable to your research question. Anything more and the review grows too large and diffuse.

Consider the review to be your tribute to your intellectual ancestors, each of whom you critically appreciate on your way through. Lay out a clear path of sensible topic sections and subsections and inform the reader up front of your rationale for it.

Some students mistake a literature review for a bibliography. Your review should both appraise and put the voices of the sources into conversation with each other:

> While at one point Talbot indicates that consciousness and matter are part of an interactive continuum (p. 42), at another point in his writing Talbot states, "The entire physical universe itself is nothing more than patterns of neuronal energy firing off inside our head" (p. 37). What I wanted to find were views that presented the co-existence and co-creation of matter (or matter/energy) and consciousness. I began to find that perspective in a work by Brian Swimme.
>
> *(Filocamo, 2008, p. 29)*

If you are not writing an academic document, consider a brief, informal review of the relevant literature to place your inquiry in the context of what has been looked into previously.

Suggestion: do not get cute with section titles, or for that matter the chapter titles of anything. Being clever is fine, to a point, but titles like "I Could Not Carrot Less" or "Here Today, Lawn Tomorrow" fail to tell the reader anything about what appears in those sections or chapters.

Method

State the purpose of the study. Why are you conducting it? This statement should align with the research question(s), which you may now restate. Provide your rationale for using TI for your topic. Why is TI a good fit? (Technically speaking, TI is a methodology, not just a method, but it goes in this section anyway.)

Say what you did as a primary research activity: analyzed texts, made trips, built a new practice model, created a theory, carried out interviews, put on a theatrical production, etc.

Describe the participants and how you obtained them. If you are working academically, check in with your school's research policies about participant names: usually they are kept out of the study for reasons of confidentiality, but exceptions have been made when participants petitioned to be named openly. A copy of the questions you intend to start with should go into an appendix along with any release/consent forms, the list of participants' rights, interview transcripts, and whatever else your school requires.

Describe how you collected and analyzed the data. If you used codes, provide a rationale for which ones. Also, specify the criteria by which you picked out the relevant themes from the data.

Lay out the study's delimitations: the areas related to your topic that you chose not to pursue.

Position yourself as a researcher so the reader can see the background and biases you bring to the study:

> I am a white, currently able-bodied, neurodivergent, queer, cis-gender woman. I spent most of my twenties living below the poverty line, and I now live in relative economic stability, enjoying the privileges that come with that, including the immense gift of being a full-time student researcher and activist ... Additional details about my positionality, with regards to personal life experience, Family Systems and somatic aspects can be found in Appendix I.
>
> *(Leetch, 2017, p. xxvii)*

The Study

The programs I teach in emphasize the importance of research *process*. Here is where you tell the story of what you did and how you did it. In some locianalysis work, an additional background chapter appears right before this one to tell the reader about the place and its characteristics: geology, history, original human inhabitants, ecological challenges, flora, fauna, climate, weather, and so on.

The quotation-reinforced steps described in Chapter 4 should give an idea of the kind of detail to include in this section or chapter. Bear in mind that quite a lot of terrapsychological activity takes place nonverbally: wind currents, traffic patterns, body states, dreams, moods, etc., so describe these when needed.

Results

Describe the data analysis and the resulting themes. Consider using graphics, charts, and photographs to make the information easy to assimilate. Remember to provide a rationale for any codes and for how you discovered themes. Because TI researchers are often intuitively good at detecting a theme, they tend to forget to tell the reader exactly *how* they did it: what the criteria were for detection. Don't let your intuition take over here and skip steps: be specific. Lead the reader by the hand.

Provide the summary of findings.

Conclusion

Say how the findings are significant.

What surprised you? How did you change as a result of the research?

What directions would you recommend for further research on this topic?

Storytelling Your Findings

On the one hand, many are the ways to present your work, especially if you are not academically constrained. On the other hand, a doctoral student of biochemistry studying at a mainstream university included in her dissertation defense presentation a group dance with fellow students and goats, all filmed outside. (She passed.) Some standards are loosening.

> I plan to use images, maps, and data tables to help convey my message (the importance of protecting, preserving and honoring our aquatic systems, more specifically the San Lorenzo River watershed area in Santa Cruz County, an important part of my community) while presenting my findings in an articulate and compelling way to both my dissertation committee and to the local community.
>
> *(Haber, 2019, p. 48)*

Haber brings in the intention of moving from presentation to community action:

> I am hoping to find other ways to spread the message, possibly through development of a non-profit organization focused on restoring, exploring and understanding aquatic systems and their importance to our psychological and somatic health. An activist at heart, I also hope to build coalitions of fellow supporters who can carry this message of marine or aquatic system conservation from an indigenous perspective into communities throughout the world.
>
> *(Haber, 2019, p. 48)*

Maggie Hippman created a short film, *Salt* (2019), from her thesis: "A meditation on the ways in which the psychology of a people is entangled with the particulars of the landscape they inhabit, centered on Salt Lake City, Utah" (2019).

Whatever tools or means you decide on for presenting your work to a wider world (and you should present it, especially if you bring to voice what cannot speak on its own behalf), consider unfolding it in the form of a story or series of stories. Why? At age one, a baby can pretend to put a doll to bed. What does it mean that we spend half our waking life in fantasy mode via daydreaming and a third of our entire life asleep dreaming stories? It means that human beings are two-legged creators and transporters of tales. We are *Homo narratus*, with fictions that allow us to anticipate before we act and to reflect after we act.

Our best facts mean nothing at all without storied frameworks that give them meaning and context. Changing the story changes what facts mean. Actions result not from facts but from what we tell ourselves the facts really mean. New facts offered without new stories are usually discounted. Stories allow people to explore meanings and draw conclusions without being preached at. Our examples lead to their conclusions. Nobody is made wrong, yet actions and attitudes change.

Anecdotal stories can reveal and disarm the hearer's silent objections by showing how the teller worked through them. Such stories offer more guidance than fixed rules that cannot handle conflict or paradox. Persuasion and argument push, and people resist being pushed. Stories pull you in. They spread long after the effort required to cajole and manipulate has dissipated. A hearer beaten down with logic is less reliable ultimately than one who makes your story their own.

Stories about what's relevant to listeners inspire trust. Honest personal stories can make a connection before anything else can happen. They let you demonstrate, not just talk about, your trustworthiness and deep involvement with the topic. A story character can present a different, attitude- and action-changing point of view more effectively than simply making an argument for it. It's hard to empathize with an argument or take the side of a set of numbers.

Stories can reach across cultural and political divides, opening common ground where the conservative and the radical, the materialist and the spiritualist, and the dreamer and the cynic can meet. They also allow unexpected, nonlinear solutions not calculable with charts of data. New stories can bring fresh perspectives that shrink problems without having to rationalistically analyze them to death. Causal analyses that fail to account for what people make of the causes doom themselves to irrelevant fact-chasing. They miss the need for new forward-looking visions that can motivate new attitudes and actions.

Stories are big-T True because, unlike the small-t truths of statistics and surveys, they capture the great existential Truths of our existence. They show what is too complex to be charted. Imaginatively living through future scenarios can give you more visceral, emotional, and intuitive information than emotionally distant cognitive strategic planning. (The audiences imagined by singer-songwriter Johnny Cash did not align with the target demographics cranked out by his record company. He quit and went on to win a lot of Grammys. The record company failed and was sold off to a competitor.)

Big picture stories rely less on pedantically detailed planning than on connecting what people want to do to what they can create together. It's one thing to get paid to hammer a nail, but another to know that nail helps build a city. Big picture stories give purpose to frustration and struggle. A single story can exert enormous impact. *Uncle Tom's Cabin* galvanized Union efforts during the American Civil War. The *Kalevala*, an epic woven of folktales, solidified the independence of Finland. *Roots* was the most-watched film of its day.

When President Kennedy stated, "We choose to go to the moon!" the naive thought him blinded by science fiction; they were ignorant of how symbols and aspirations – not facts and figures – drive us, especially in a "mythless" culture divided into huge voids of meaning. To act differently, people must think and feel differently, and those require new stories that prompt and inspire.

Inspiration is key. Martin Luther King Jr. did not say, "I am a victim." He said, "I have been to the mountaintop." You can last three hours without shelter, three days without water, and three weeks without food, but you can't make yourself go one hour without a fantasy.

Prisoners fantasize. Poor children growing up in a dump also play there. People about to die imagine what death – supposed nonexistence – will be like. We imagine, therefore we are, and vice versa. Perhaps we evolved, or our stories evolved us, not just for our own complexification but ultimately for theirs. When Camelot fell, the kings and nobles, schemers and heroes died on the field of battle. The tale survived.

Communicating the Nonverbal

According to received psychoanalytic wisdom, we become speechless when we are triggered by a trauma inflicted before we had words. Something is said or done that touched the old wound, and our power of vocalization goes temporarily silent. It can also go silent when an ecological complex or other edgy aspect of our topic transcends our ability to express what it means to us, how it lands in us. No wonder: the encounter with what is wordless makes us so at times. All terrapsychological inquirers run into this at some point. Filocamo describes what he encountered while writing about his inquiry with Tree:

> A huge and frustrating challenge for me was finding ways to communicate the presence that I sensed in Tree while visiting "her." I wrote on February 13, 2008 that "I am stymied, wondering how I can communicate moments like these, where I experience contact with Tree and wonder at the presence that seems to exist within the physicality. A mystery that I cannot yet communicate, that I can barely know." I experienced this

> limitation of understanding and language numerous times while writing, using phrases such as "I don't know how to describe what happened, or how it changed" (Nov. 28, 2007), "It's challenging for me to find words to describe the sensations that stirred in that part of my body" (Dec. 23, 2007), and, "Again, not something I can describe ... nor is it something I can prove" (January 8, 2008).
>
> *(Filocamo, 2008, p. 96)*

It's important that he kept on with writing. He also returned to his research journal:

> Interestingly, it was during the writing of this journal entry that I at one point sensed tingling along my back and then sensed Tree's presence behind me ... As this experience unfolded, questions arose as to the nature of this experience: "I sense the presence as more human-like, as if hands were holding me, supporting me. Is this Tree, or Tree's 'essence,' that I am humanizing? Or another experience entirely? When I first noticed the sensation, how did I 'know' it was Tree?" (February 13, 2008). Because of the felt-sense nature of this experience within my body, I found it difficult to describe the experience in words generated by my conceptual mind.
>
> *(Filocamo, 2008, p. 96)*

These states of wordlessness are temporary. Sometimes simply acknowledging them as deepenings of the relationship to the topic is enough. Silences are where what we study gets into us. When they persist, switching to nonverbal methods like music, art, or movement can help move the work forward. When I get stuck in wordlessness for longer than I deem productive, I go for a walk or put on stirring music and dance for a while.

> On January 1, 2008, as I wrote about being overcome by Tree's immensity, I noted, "As I write this now, I feel ... wonder, wide-eyed excitement and joy." And on March 18, 2008, as I was describing the beauty of Tree's canopy high above me, I wrote, "I write this today mindful of the magnificence of the form; it inspires a subtle sense of awe in me as I imagine it." It was as if I could feel as well as imagine Tree's magnificence of form as I wrote.
>
> *(Filocamo, 2008, p. 96)*

> That non-human material contains its own intentions was confirmed for me by a dream I had while finishing up this draft. In it I was carefully carting a vibrant little green stone all around town as per its specific instructions. So I suppose that is what I've been doing – trying ardently to listen

> to the voice in matter in its myriad forms; watching as it spoke through my own experience.
>
> *(Hippman, 2017, p. 3)*

Amanda Leetch devised a collaborative multimedia approach:

> The TI data I collected through the other methods described in this chapter was synthesized through a self-designed arts-based research method: *terrain weaving*. *Terrain weaving* is an impressionistic working of themes and insights gathered through hosting the placefield encounter. It transmutes encounter into symbol using various types, textures and colors of yarn, roving, ribbon, as well as different weaving techniques, to represent the communications of the field as a visual, tactile narrative: a map of an experience of place.
>
> *(Leetch, 2017, p. 109)*

She compares this to coding texts, with each fiber a color code complexified by the weave "to communicate the dynamic processual engagement this research required." Colors and fibers stood for recurrent motifs (Leetch, 2017, p. 109). She made twelve weavings for the inquiry.

> Every few weeks, when it felt right, I would look back on my research notes, journal reflections, pictures, videos, artworkings and any other material or textual elements that have been gathered during the research period. I would meditate on the data for at least 20 minutes, allowing spontaneous associations to bubble to the surface … I would then journal my meditative reflection, which was usually a vivid visual experience, and impressionistically weave these reflections onto a 5″ diameter metal frame, coding themes as colors, weights, fibers and stitches, fibers adopting a symbolic meaning, once used, carried through the production of all the weavings. I also wrote weaving reflections after each weaving session.
>
> *(Leetch, 2017, p. 111)*

As she worked, she regularly checked in with participants and with her resonance panel of research advisers (Leetch, 2017, p. 120) and tended the image (Figure 7.1) that emerged:

> Every week, I reflected on the data gathered, meditated on these themes, and wove the reflections from my meditation. I then wrote a synopsis of the weaving, and a brief meta-reflection of the weaving process itself. I catalogued which fibers corresponded to which meanings and used them to represent recurring themes. There was a three-week period where I did not collect place data as I was struggling with place-consent and self-care

FIGURE 7.1 Visioning, transcending, returning. This piece communicates the creative, transformative, and regenerative potentials that emerge from the patterns of Lowell when those patterns are uncoupled from the anthropocentric historical narrative.

Source: Amanda Leetch (2017).

> procedures … These terrain weavings both uncover and reinforce the emergent placefield findings.
>
> *(Leetch, 2017, pp. 128–129)*

She then conducted a weaving with four members of her resonance panel,

> representing a combined 85.33 years of experience with the Lowell placefield. I engaged place-educators in their own place processing. I took video of the experience, and collected demographic data and artist statements. I then coded their artist statements, weavings and insights to my other data findings.
>
> *(Leetch, 2017, p. 129)*

She also included chalk drawings with children, leaf sculptures, social media, and 1,678 photographs sorted for themes.

> I made art almost daily with children in the field of all ages, taking the form of projects resonant with placefield motifs, public art installations, chalking the breezeway with body maps and a popup museum to showcase the emergent lessons of place. All of these are ways that place constantly communicated to and through me that form the underlying basis for my analysis.
>
> *(Leetch, 2017, p. 131)*

Finding sound to be key to how the Lowell spirit of place communicated, she recorded waterfalls, wasteways, birds, and other relevant auditory sources from the field. She also made video recordings.

Whether you are willing to undertake work of this magnitude or confine yourself instead to something presentationally modest, you will see for yourself how your account of your work transmutes your audience's feelings about the topic and its importance. Terrapsychological storytelling provides strong leverage for altering (and altaring) how people relate to themselves, each other, and the animate world below, beneath, above, and within us.

After the Study

> Extracting myself from the field created a sense of loss and isolation, and the absence of this place connection has required grieving and adjustment. I am also now painfully aware of how field-ignorant I am in the place I live.
>
> *(Leetch, 2017, p. 158)*

Because terrapsychological research is so intensive, involving participation on every level, finishing can bring shifting moods. And post-inquiry surprises. Although I began developing my version of terrapsychology through my dissertation, I spent, all told, eleven years exploring the presence of place throughout California. This resulted not only in the Animate California Trilogy but also in a final dream in which Queen Califia, a recurrent dream personification, approached me in an office as all the lights went out and people left for the day. It was closing time. She gave me one strong hug, and I woke up thinking, *That's it?* I wasn't sure what I expected. Surely not the tide of good things that flowed in afterward from San Diego, Ventura, Los Angeles, San Francisco, and other Californian places.

Feeling somewhat sluggish, bloated, and ungrounded, Kevin Filocamo wrote movingly about post-visit effects:

> What I want to focus on is how the "presence of Tree" seemed to accompany me past the visit. For instance, as I wrote about my visit on Feb. 13, 2008, I suddenly felt as if Tree were behind me: "Energetically, I feel tingling along my shoulders and the back of my neck. I suddenly sense Tree, as if it were standing behind me, holding my shoulders, supporting me from behind. It is the strongest sense of Tree I've had today." Note that this visit, February 13, 2008, was the visit in which I struggled so much with doubts about myself and the process.
>
> *(Filocamo, 2008, p. 94)*

He also mentions another person's observation that when he spoke and wrote about Tree, she could feel the entity's presence, as though he had now internalized it and she could meet Tree through him.

The inquiry deepened his empathy for other forms of life:

> Finally, these experiences with Tree may have made me more attuned to the aliveness of other beings, and my desire to respect their aliveness. My final journal entry reflects this possibility. A moth was trapped in my room. Rather than ignore its plight or kill it, I decided to try to release it outside ... Carrying the question of "Who are you?" with me, and asking it of the beings that I encounter – both human and non-human – may continue to deepen this sense of curiosity, compassion, regard, and possibly love that I experienced with the moth, and with Tree.
>
> *(Filocamo, 2008, pp. 95–96)*

Nearly always, the "what I should have done/learned/been aware of" inner critic has things to say after the study ends. Lessons learned. Stating them can be valuable for researchers who come later.

> If given the chance to do this research again, I would have found out what species Tree belonged to earlier in the process, allowing me more time to work with the factual material in partnership with the subjective experiential data ... However, gathering facts about Tree was not the main focus of this research, so I didn't work with this information as completely as I could have. Still, I am grateful for what I have learned about Tree and its place in the history of San Francisco's Golden Gate Park, and as I have said, I find that this information – "tucked away" in my mind – continues to impact my experiences with Tree today.
>
> *(Filocamo, 2008, p. 127)*

I always ask students: What now? Sometimes that takes time to surface. At other times, it becomes apparent as the study closes:

> I hope others will use this research to argue for real change and the possibility of restoration of the river area ... removal of unnecessary levees and dams, alternate flood control methods, native habitat restoration, ecological studies to support indigenous species of flora and fauna, and plans to create a natural reserve, where people can come to enjoy the river's beauty.
>
> *(Haber, 2019, p. 17)*

Haber then speculates about what the results might be:

> Drawing a connection between health of the land and health of the inhabitants of that land might help to broaden the scope of awareness, action, and advocacy to embrace and include the river area. This change in focus could also provoke change in people when the focus shifts from identification of problems to actionable deeds for the betterment of the community. The river was once a thriving ecosystem in the middle of a prosperous and growing community. Reinventing the river as the focal point for the downtown community would refocus human activity in connection with nature.
>
> *(Haber, 2019, p. 20)*

If you possess literary gifts, you may continue to write about where the research led you, as in this exquisite passage from Maggie Hippman:

> On dark days the lake is nearly erased, tucked safely beneath the brown blanket of numb air. But on days made in diamond clarity, in the wake of a winter storm, the sky almost rings with crispness. On those days, the Great Salt Lake functions as a prism, refracting the entire spectrum of experience in its glassy surface, waiting for the right light, the right eyes to dip into that white seam between worlds where nothing is broken.
>
> *(Haber, 2019, p. 11)*

Another important question is: How has the work changed me?

> All I can say is that, for distinct moments during most of the visits that I had with Tree, I sensed what I can only describe as a "presence" from Tree or from the environment that was not mine but was relating directly with me, to the best of my knowledge. And I am not alone; as I have reported here, others have experienced a sense of presence with the nonhuman entities and environments that they have engaged (or that have engaged them). These questions remain, and they are important questions

> to continue to consider with openness, humility, and receptivity as we explore our place in, and our relationship to, the world around us.
>
> *(Filocamo, 2008, p. 130)*

Many researchers find that they must sacrifice oversimplified ways of knowing for more comprehensive frameworks:

> You are bound in the storied threads of a false narrative history. You can unravel the story, untangle yourself and emplace the threads into a much broader tapestry, but one so broad it is impossible to ever see the whole thing at once. You lose the simplicity of a linear narrative, but you are liberated into an infinitely reconfigurable relationship between the threads.
>
> *(Leetch, 2017, p. xxvi)*

The new frameworks can provide points of departure for further investigation:

> Terrapsychological Inquiry, within the context of its definition, provides an invitation for us to dream up a new myth. TI calls us to create a new paradigm, one that "involves the collective creation of a truly planetary psychology" and contains a "meaningful vision of where we belong in the world" (Chalquist, 2010, p. 53). Accepting this invitation in conjunction with the heuristic creative synthesis, Queer Archetypal Lifespan Development Theory (QALDT) has comes into early evolution.
>
> *(Olivieri, 2017, p. 133)*

For Olivieri, the customary linearity of developmental stages of psychology is itself queered by the inquiry:

> QALDT, for me, has been the primary focus of future research stemming from this inquiry. Utilizing Terrapsychological Inquiry as the "how to" of developmental psychospiritual growth and change, this infant theory seeks to provide support for the new myth as a facet of Queer Spirituality and as a container in which the Queer Archetype can be held. In addition, this theory seeks to expand upon the emergent themes of this inquiry as indicators of developmental milestones, thus becoming functions of *queerness itself*.
>
> *(Olivieri, 2017, p. 133)*

With terrapsychological work, we gain the realization that some of what we felt as purely personal sources of loss, sadness, anger, or other challenging conflicts actually reflected states of the more-than-human beyond us. Do we hurt less to realize this? Sometimes; not always. But we are not then victims anymore: we are witnesses of dramas and encounters that transcend us.

> Instead of getting rid of the pain the plagued me I've ended up walking more deeply into it, dropping any illusion that it is something I can control. The sadness has not gone away – far from it – but I have begun to see it as its own landscape with breath-taking vistas in the most unexpected pauses. It is the way the undercurrent of existence seems to speak to me. The process seems to be something like the making of a pearl.
>
> *(Hippman, 2017, p. 5)*

As climate change accelerates, we all face pearldom. Ecoresilience will not remain an interesting add-on but instead become a vital survival practice for every human community. Damien Arabagali, who is a Huli from Papua New Guinea and author of several books on the changes wrought by modernist industries on traditional societies like his, warns:

> Is the Earth sick? Yes. Our ancestors prophesied that we would see the Earth turn sick. When the *kunai* grass in the swamps dries up. When we dig gardens where the pine trees used to grow. When the wild *pandanus* trees disappear. When the birds fly away … We are heading for a period when this land will say, "I can't produce anymore." Our land has been reused and reused. It can no longer reproduce. "I have had enough," says the Earth.
>
> *(Arabagali, 2004, pp. 217–218)*

To preserve what remains will require the equivalent of growing a new sense: the ability to listen to nature. To tune in to locale, climate, weather, insect, plant, animal, stone, river, sea, and everything that hints about how to adapt to what is already upon us.

As we undertake this task with no foreseeable end, may the spirit of wonder remain with us. Even in travail, Earth keeps its knack for astonishing us. Ecologists speak of carrying capacity; perhaps we should also speak of caring capacity as we practice the sense of empathy we see modeled all around us: in the foods that feed us, the animals that help us, the networks of soil fungi that look after entire bioregions. Our own caring capacity blended with unchained imagination will prove invaluable for our personal and collective rebalancing.

Mary Austin is known primarily as a writer. She was also intensely tuned into nature and place, plants and animals, and soil and sky. The Native American image of the Earth Horizon, a meeting of upper and lower, all in natural array, spoke to her. What she wrote in her autobiography resonates with many who take up the burden and joy of terrapsychological research, listening when the world speaks from without and within together:

> I have not been entirely happy in my adjustments. I have suffered in my life, in my means, and in my reciprocal relations; but I have this pride and

> congratulation, that I have not missed the significance of the spectacle I have been privileged to witness. I have not only had the pleasure of associating with those who have known what it means, but I have had glimpses of its meaning. I have known, to some extent, what the Earth Horizon has been thinking about.
>
> *(Austin, 2007, p. 368)*

For Discussion

1. What are your ideas about how to share the results of your inquiry? Which media might you choose?
2. What issues arise when you consider coming to voice like this? How will you face and deal with them? (It is not only on your own behalf that you speak.)
3. What will you do at the end of your writing, presentation, ceremony, or whatever you plan to do to give the participants some vital nugget to take along with them?

References

Arabagali, D. (2004). They trampled on our taboos. In D. Rothenberg & M. Ulvaeus (Eds.), *The world and the wild: Expanding conservation beyond its American roots*. Tucson, AZ: University of Arizona Press.

Austin, M. (2007). *Earth horizon*. Santa Fe, NM: Southwest Heritage.

Chalquist, C. (Ed.) (2010). *Rebearths: Conversations with a world ensouled*. Walnut Creek, CA: World Soul Books.

Filocamo, K. (2008). The alluring universe: Exploring an erotic relationship with the world (unpublished master's thesis). John F. Kennedy University, Pleasant Hill, CA.

Haber, M. (2019). Unattended trauma of the San Lorenzo River: A terrapsychological inquiry (unpublished dissertation). California Institute of Integral Studies, San Francisco, CA.

Hippman, M. (2017). The psychology of salt (unpublished master's thesis). Environmental Humanities Program, University of Utah, Salt Lake City, Utah.

Hippman, M. (2019). *Salt*. Retrieved from www.youtube.com/watch?v=XN_sjMpTc-8

Leetch, A. (2017). Weaving meaning: Terrapsychological Inquiry and the historic industrial placefield of Lowell, Massachusetts (unpublished master's thesis). Prescott College, Prescott, AZ.

Olivieri, C. (2017). Your church, my bar! A terrapsychological inquiry of the relationship between Queerspace and queer spirituality in San Francisco, California (unpublished dissertation). California Institute of Integral Studies, San Francisco, CA.

Talbot, M. (1993). *Mysticism and the new physics*. New York, NY: Arkana/Penguin.

8

TERRAPSYCHOLOGIZING FOR LIFE

Some of us involved in terrapsychology's growth and refinement have used it not only as a path of deep inquiry but as an ecospiritual wisdom path as well: a way of being in a world reenchanted by what we have learned about its vital presences so alive around and within us. I have been asked to write about this more than once, but I didn't much, partly because I wanted to reflect more first on what spirituality and wisdom in general meant to me and how terrapsychology informed them..

What follows, then, is a look at some of the questions of living and being which walking this terrapsychological way has brought up in me. "Research" here widens beyond specific projects into living in a state of perpetual deep inquiry.

I will start by considering the potentially vexing terms "spirituality" and "wisdom" from a standpoint informed by terrapsychology but reaching beyond it.

Spirituality and Wisdom Held Terrapsychologically

Most Western psychology and social science researchers shun spirituality, preferring to enact it at second hand instead through elaborate methodology rituals, ritualized conferences, deuteronomic literature reviews, disciplinary sects, text exegesis, data collection commandments, rigid proceduralism, and interdisciplinary conflict. We should have learned by now that remaining unconscious of something as potent as the capacity for spirituality cannot banish it but will strengthen it while allowing it to operate out of view. For some, then, systematic inquiry functions as an unacknowledged religion whose invisible pantheon includes the likes of devouring Cronus,

DOI: 10.4324/9781003462965-9

troublemaking Eris, warlike Mars, Apollo the distant reasoner, Hephaestus the mechanist, and of course the infamous Procrustes.

In part, the shunning of spirituality is a reflexive response to millennia of religious authority attempting to monopolize knowledge and sacred experience while defining piety as uncritical subservience toward one or more gods. In some versions of monotheism, the one God is a male-gendered supernatural being who alternates between unexpected parental affection and mass murder for disobedience. Combining that ideology with the wars, pogroms, and persecutions carried out by the religious, we can see why throwing out anything to do with spirituality would be appealing, especially where disciplined inquiry is concerned. The historical irony is that scientism owes its hierarchical literal-mindedness to the gradual emergence of science from hierarchical and literal-minded religious thinking.

Two decades of reflection combined with education and terrapsychological work has given me different spiritual bathwater to swim in. Spirit is not supernatural and has nothing to do with human authority, creed, or dogma. Taking a cue from languages in which "spirit" refers etymologically to wind or breath, I appreciate the lore, found within all cultures, describing the things of the world, Earth itself, and even the cosmos as animate and sentient (in their own way), active partners in a great conversation so many of us no longer hear, let alone respond to. Behind the forms and flux, something addresses us, enlivens the whole, produces synchronicities, and goes by names like Mystery and Big Mind. Spirituality is the capacity for conversing with it rather than believing or disbelieving in it. Wisdom includes being open to its transformative influence.

Spirit is a presence – perhaps a presence of all presences – we feel pouring into us during our encounters with what is numinous, what fills us with awe and wonder. Behind those feelings moves an intelligence beyond our own. The question of whether spirit also transcends the cosmos is a metaphysical one we need not entertain here.

Often, when I go walking, from long practice I note tangible presences: the soil or pavement underfoot, the cries of birds, fragrant sage, a distant roar of traffic, the colors of the sky, and pools of water here and there. These register on my senses as entities, and in my mind, feelings, and heart-rooted imagination, as partners in ongoing nonverbal exchange. I suffer a loss one day, and a mourning dove flutters down onto a nearby fence and sings to me: we are in the same conversation, one in which the place itself participates. Beyond these presences, I feel seen, addressed, kept living, kept breathing not only by place and Earth but by Something I sense but cannot see.

The world is the medium of sacred communication. In spite of all the harm the shadowy undersides of the world's religions continue to inflict on humanity, these traditions also carry acknowledgements of the sanctity of the natural world: Judaism's image of the divine feminine Shekinah dwelling among us, Christianity's Book of Nature tradition of reading the world's symbolic language like a holy text, Islam's recognition of signs of the divine in nature, and Buddhism's teaching that all beings possess the Buddha mind. Leaders within these and other faiths have also made public declarations that safeguarding the natural world is a sacred responsibility.

From a terrapsychological standpoint, the communicative presences around and within us are not gods or spirits operating groves or hillsides like machinery, but inherent in these things, as when people living near a river for millennia describe it as a goddess. They don't mean that a supernatural deity animates the river, but that the river is itself sacred, responsive, alive. Perhaps something similar is true of the universe. On Earth, Gaia Theory has been misunderstood to mean a being like Gaia or Tellus working behind weather or seasons, but whatever its strengths or limits as a theory of planetwide ecological self-regulation, its name allows the mythology to creep in long enough to suggest a living presence beyond energy flows and atmospheric feedback loops.

In a sense, these kinds of insights and relationships reflect an ancient stream of ecospirituality in which all our ancestors swam at one time or another. Ecospirituality, the norm or template for our species, was in former times inseparable from a wisdom path, nor did it necessarily collide with what today we think of as scientific investigation.

How else might one use terrapsychological methods and insights as an ecospiritual path?

Tools for an Ecospiritual Wisdom Path

Although needs vary, a basic outline of what is needed for a viable ecospiritual path could include a name, deepening practices, a basic cosmology, a set of values and ethical commitments, acts of service, meaningful rituals (including seasonal observances), times for reflection, a quest for life purpose, rituals for health and wellness, and various forms of spiritual healing. What is not needed is an overemphasis on belief, a freezing of imagination into preauthorized categories, idealization of or domination by authority figures, patriarchy, exceptionalism, or a single and supposedly inerrant truth for everybody to follow regardless of need or temperament.

In the past, I've referred to my own path as Terragnosis, but then an ibogaine company in Canada found the word, which I have used online for several years, slapped an "inc." on it, and appropriated it as their own name. I found this out just as the newest terrapsychology edited volume had gone to print. For my chapter, which examined Terragnosis as an updated Hermeticism, I asked the publisher to change the word to "Tellusgnosis," which is actually a bit more accurate: Terra has tended to mean the actual land of Earth, whereas Tellus was understood by ancient Roman tale-tellers as its indwelling goddess. So the name of the practice became Tellusgnosis (Chalquist & Barnwell, 2023).

Practices mentioned in Chapters 3, 4, and other parts of this book should be useful for an ecospiritual path. For example, time spent on an ultimate concern as a researchable question for personal inquiry; being chosen by whatever arises; formulating and reformulating questions urgent for walking one's path. Tracking what the body does with all this. Recording dreams as a psychospiritual practice. Being alert to which mythic plots and archetypal motifs show up just now in one's life, and what gifts and messages they bring. Getting to know one's locale deeply through sophisticated innocence and amplification of motifs. Instead of a research journal, an ecospiritual journey account. Place-hosting that includes service to communities. Practices refashioned into rituals.

Likewise, Terrapsychological Inquiry's (TI's) values and commitments (Chapter 2) turned into areas of ethical concentrations and cares. Research wellness practices made use of on the path.

For life purpose and cosmology, the following speculations might resonate:

Geologically understood, California, named for a fictional Black queen who embarked on risky adventures, is quite young and restless. The coast used to start somewhere in Nevada. Over millions of years, plate tectonics scooped up island arcs to form our edgy state "west of the West" and to crack it with rumbling earthquake faults; the San Andreas gets its name from the saint who was martyred by being pulled apart. We watch for incoming waves and balance on shifting surfaces. Little wonder we're such an impulsive, quirky, and innovative bunch.

Haunted by metaphors of angels and demons, Los Angeles serves as the mythic messenger of California, with Hollywood one of many examples. San Francisco, with its Dionysian deaths and rebirths and dramas; witch-like San Diego; the alchemical Great Central Valley topped by the philosopher's stone of Mt. Shasta: these and other animate sites make up parts of the Golden State's terrapsychological personality. The state itself recalls Minerva, whose face adorns the Great Seal of California, named after Athena-like Queen Calafia from the land of Spanish fiction.

California in turn is the westward-facing Athena of the United States of America, part of a continent named America. Etymologies can reveal underlying terrapsychological hints and truths: "America" means "great work" or "master craftsman," and this land hosts an almost incalculable variety of productive ecosystems. North, South, or Central, there is alchemical work to be done here.

Our continents are part of – geopsychosocial organs of – Earth, our homeworld haven within the presence of Sol system, each of its worlds a subpersonality of its own. And so on and outward: the stellar nursery in the Arm of Orion, itself part of the galaxy named after Hera's breast milk (with thematically similar meanings in other systems of mythology), our galaxy part of a Local Group within the Virgo Supercluster.... We spiral around our sun not only through dark space, but through a cosmos of presences nested within one another.

Each of these places or layers can be imagined a kind of imaginal altar. Each has its own style of presence. To change location is to change sacred ground. From an ecospiritual perspective, we converse with divine presences every day, every moment, with our feet, our location, and every breath we draw. Every path we take is inevitably a spiritual path: we need only grow our sensitivity to it as we move through the span of the years we are given.

Some of these presences are local. Others, however, are universal.

Sentient Natural Forces?

Mythic figures like Athena represent one cultural face of a universal archetype: in her case, Wisdom, as found in the polis (today, the metropolis). Every place we can locate hosts some such mythic presence that at its core harbors archetypal qualities. But if archetypes are universal, what are the implications for our relationship with them in terms of an ecospiritual wisdom path?

What if each archetypal deity, sprite, spirit, daemon, and familiar also reflects some intelligent aspect or quality of the natural world? Not just locally, as with place, but everywhere? Perhaps Sophia is the within of everything, the subjective dimension of the cosmos. Across pantheons, her wise sisters go by names like Athena, Minerva, Star Woman, Fatima, Andraste, Brigid, Nuwa, Sekhmet, Yemaya, and Amaterasu. They personify the scope and power of trans-human Wisdom filling the universe.

What about love? Perhaps Aphrodite and her erotic sisters bring the attractive force that binds hearts and hadrons, particles and anti-particles, seducing them into giving up their passionate energies to hold everything together. And why not just call the fruitfulness of Earth (otherwise known as Arda, Terra, Tellus, Ala, and Gaia) by holy names like Demeter, Sita, Flora, Pomona, or Pachamama, with a contemporary understanding of them not as otherworldly mega-people somewhere *behind* the crops and plants, but as Fertility or Growth itself a sentient abundance everywhere, imaged, animate, and fully capable of response?

When scientists set up a perfect vacuum with all matter and energy expelled, they watch the quantum flux no experiment can get rid of because it is the background of everything. Out of that flux radiate particles and antiparticles that find each other, rush together, give up their energies to each other, and disappear back into the quantum foam. This continual quantum coupling is what we call "reality."

Looking back, we glimpse in many mythic traditions the figure of the beautiful erotic love goddess born from sea foam, like Aphrodite rising from the waves. What discipline-spanning truth is at work here? Perhaps that the cosmos is permeated by beauty. A mythic way of holding what science tells us about universal structure is that the attraction drawing matter together, from subatomic particles to galactic groups embedded in scaffolds of dark matter and energy, is aphroditic. The *cosmos* – the very word is linked to "cosmetology" – is composed of and held together by the all-pervading power of love.

Philosophers of all cultures have wrestled through time with questions about the nature and origin of beauty and love. My favorite answer was offered by a friend from long ago who seemed the very incarnation of Aphrodite's charms. I asked her, "Why are things beautiful?" With a sexy wink she replied without hesitation, "To invite us to joyfully approach them." Beauty as a standing invitation to get closer in appreciation.

In an aphroditic cosmos held as such, myth and science stand together, not bicker as supposed opposites. Just look at our creation story. What is the Big Bang but a scientifically supported replay of the Cosmic Egg motif found in the lore of ancient Egypt and China? It looks like that story could be up for change. In M Theory's image of vast interdimensional membranes touching to spark the birth of our daughter universe, we glimpse another common motif, that of the fertile Cosmic Parents.

In 2015, for the first time ever, scientists photographed a photon in motion as both particle and wave. A rainbow spectrum of colors washes across the scene like a ripping fabric. Have we glimpsed the magic voyager's cloak of Hermes, the swift god of transformation never quite where you expect him to be, as impossible to pin down as quicksilver, an Uncertainty Principle in winged sandals? In many mythologies, Love and Beauty animate and hold the cosmos, but Trickster creates it and rules the quantum world, with its charms, quarks, and spooky action at a distance.

Of course, these are all old god images. As collective consciousness moves on, the traditional forms, stories, and rituals of the gods grow tired and collapse, prompting the short-sighted to believe the magic gone forever and the divine safely reduced to neurobiology while bewildered true believers cling to and literalize the fading images.

But then the mythic star rises once again. The time of renewal dawns, IF we can provide what the ancient Greeks called *xenia* – hospitality – to What addresses us in plants, animals, symptoms, synchronicities, places, nature, and dreams. In this way, we help these images of the divine to evolve. "The most that we can do," wrote Jung, who also explored transformed god images, "is dream the myth onward by giving it a modern dress" (1981, 160). Taking his cue from the Gnostics, those past masters of updating myth by reinterpreting it in depth, Jung used one of their words, "archetype," to refer to the gods not as superhuman people hiding behind clouds and inside volcanoes, but as psychical entities born in fantasy. Gilgamesh and Thor are heroes-within; Osiris and Dionysus depict our interior deaths and rebirths.

By deliteralizing the gods into their constitutive metaphors, Jung gave us direct access to them through the medium of psychological experience.

Ecospirituality in the light of terrapsychology takes the further step of reimagining the gods as sentient natural forces and spheres of communicative presence. As the era of the Big Machine worldview of Modernity runs out of steam and draws to a close, we boldly look for mythic structures not just within ourselves, as Jung did, but also around us, including in what science continues to reveal about who and where we are. For example, Jung often used the spiral archetype as an emblem of individuation, the evolution of consciousness. But spirals twirl all around us: swirls of water, spiraling plant shoots, and the majesty of rotating spiral galaxies. In their luminous dance, we see the stately cycles of story, myth, and archetype inviting a closer look.

There has been much talk of reenchanting the world and the cosmos, but the enchantment never left them: it is *we* who stopped appreciating their attractive beauty by refusing to go on being seduced. We failed to see that orbital cameras snapping photographs of our still-beautiful planet wave at us from above as Gaia's new hand mirrors.

Instead of asking how to reenchant things, then, perhaps we can ask: What sorts of up-to-date altars of appreciation would be favored by divine presences returning this time not as deities to worship, and not as purely psychological entities, but as the immanent powers of animate matter, Earth, and cosmos?

Of course, a path of appreciation is often richer and deeper when shared. Might converging ecospiritual paths constitute a kind of religion? A playful religion beyond belief?

A Fictional Religion

In the past, religions have for the most part hardened into hierarchical, patriarchal, and authoritarian structures that cling to a medieval worldview while emphasizing belief and obedience, which is why millions have turned away from religion and spirituality altogether. As a meme I saw recently in social media put it: Why am I not religious? Maybe because I prefer to live in the twenty-first century instead of the seventh. Yet an arid atheism also feels unsatisfying, especially for living in a reenchanted world where formerly mute objects show up as lively presences. A world in which things speak, each in its own way.

Another point of departure is the massive Western overemphasis on belief, an obsession that reaches across religion, science, politics, finance, philosophy, and many other realms of human life. Belief is variously defined but usually amounts to a conviction that something is true or existent whether or not evidence supports this conclusion. A proto-Indo-European root of the word means "desire." A conviction driven by desire: something many of the world's sages have warned us against time and again.

The more anxious we are, the harder we tend to push for something to believe in *absolutely*, which is a different psychology from everyday beliefs like: I believe the floor will remain long enough for me to walk across. Repeating a thought experiment conceived by Ibn Sina centuries earlier, Rene Descartes, raised by his grandmother, sent away to college at age eleven, and always a wanderer with fragile health, took comfort in the certainty of his own thoughts. The Protestant Revolution placed belief in the very center of being a Christian. Science hardened into scientism and positivism. Belief when clung to serves as a defense against agonizing uncertainty.

Once we have learned to live with uncertainty, the need for absolute belief diminishes. People of this more relaxed mindset – what Carl Rogers called "a loosening of constructs" (1995, 137) from rigidity to free-flowing experience – tend to gravitate away from religious or scientific authority structures and toward paths kindled by inspiration and adventure. Faced with arguments over what is necessarily or eternally true, they tend to shrug and go their own way. They see science as a set of shifting tentative hypotheses and documents like the Bible as collections of wisdom stories, albeit with plenty of trauma mixed in.

As is emphasized throughout this book and especially in Chapter 7, storytelling is basic to how we know ourselves, each other, and the world around and within us. Facts, opinions, and attitudes mean nothing without storied frameworks to make sense of them. In my consulting practice, I refer to "keystone stories": those by which we navigate through life, including those that inform our worldviews.

I call my primary occupation and field of endeavor "loreology" because by combining what I've learned from TI with several other fields, I help individuals and organizations trace the lore that powers these influential stories (some unconscious), evaluate their results and consequences, and either move beyond them, integrating whatever lessons they have brought, or reimagine and retell them to create openings for more spacious kinds of work, play, love, and vocation. A loreologist is a mentor with resources for exploring the limits and possibilities of the personal and collective lore we navigate by to deepen, expand, or outgrow it and the guiding stories it founds (2023). Loreologing turns the unhelpful literalisms of the mythic and archetypal motifs in our keystone stories back into lore to reenchant our way forward. (Loreology also gives a name to what I have done for my entire adult work life, whether as terrapsychologist, psychotherapist, professor, ecopsychologist, or depth psychologist.)

The new story we dream up for individual or collective life paths is our *loreway*: *an imaginative body of fictionally framed narrative and personal practice that fills out a mythic-feeling story arc and provides life guidance via ideals, a sense of play, fun, and meaning to participate in.* More briefly, a loreway consists of *archetypal tales told for guidance and inspiration.* Not a mythology, religion, or a legendarium, fixed on the past. Not a franchise, fixed on money. Not a philosophy to be believed, but an enactment to believe in.

One implication of this for an ecospiritual path (individual) or religion (collective) is that their lore is held as enlivening fiction. Normally, a distinction is drawn between fiction and myth, with the latter believed in as factual by some. In Finland, many sites, businesses, and special occasions are named after the fictional characters and locales of the *Kalevala*, the Finnish national epic; nobody believes them to be factually real. Loreology defines fiction as an emotionally resonant story dreamed forth via imagination. Recall the Hermetic tradition of valuing disciplined imagination as a source of deep knowing (Chapter 1). As evolutions of this tradition, alchemy as a wisdom path, Islamic gnosis, Romantic philosophy, depth psychology, spiritual ecology, and terrapsychology all draw on the power of imagining.

So to raise one last question as we wind up these speculative fantasies: What might a post-patriarchal religion look like that involved no absolute belief, no authority hierarchies, and no sacred book or creed but instead a loosening of constructs to the point of taking its own stories as inspiring fictions to be guided by rather than totalistic truths?

In my fix-it novel/story collection *Tales of Terrania Rising*, just such a religion springs forth a few decades from now.

Imagine that humanity is on a Long Adventure toward greater consciousness and maturity. This Adventure is an aspect of the ongoing creativity of the cosmos and its guiding Powers, sentient natural forces who play archetypal roles in what happens, here and elsewhere, but do not interfere directly. A goal of this Adventure, and a marker of its successful negotiation, is Terrania: the just, equitable, delightful, and Earth-honoring civilization we can see bits of today. It's up to us to build it from the ground up, not from the top down, because empires never last.

Obviously, we have a lot to face as a species on our way forward. The Resource Wars are one name future historians have given to a time beginning about now when nations and smaller groups fight over dwindling supplies of water, food, rare earths, and important metals like copper. These Wars are an event in a longer period called the Darker Ages.

A wandering philosopher responds to all this turbulence by writing down a set of cosmic and earthly operating principles called the Ten Lamps. The first is, "The nature of the cosmos is unfolding creative diversity, an infinite variety of affiliating voices, entities, and presences." Many of the Lamps sound terrapsychological. The Lamp of Universal Sympathies, for example:

"We are inwardly linked to the intelligence of Earth, the cosmos, the presence of place, and one another in relations of mutual reciprocity."

When the Ten Lamps go viral, seekers of hope in a hard time, and of sacred community beyond the belief structures of traditional religion, begin cobbling together their own homeground faith, which they name Lamplight. This faith includes the ecospiritual values, ethics, and practices mentioned above, the Ten Lamps, and a special emphasis on Lamp 10: "Humanity can create a just, equitable, delightful, and Earth-appreciating civilization worthy of our labors and struggles, but only if we relearn how to dream together."

In the terminology of loreology, Lamplight is a loreway: a fictional collective path not of literal and monolithic Truth, but of fun, play, ideals, and meanings to experiment with. One of its festivals is the use of Earth Day not to sell and buy things (a self-contradiction truly planetary in scope), but as a day of reflection on the quality of our relationships with everything and everyone sharing this world with us.

Lamplight is not the first fictional religion. The Jedi Church offers teachings, ceremonies, and even ordination. Earthseed, a religion invented by science fiction author Octavia Butler, has inspired a movement for ethical and diverse intertwinings of biology and technology, especially in the context of longevity. Many use Star Trek as a religion, as I saw when attending a convention in Los Angeles many years ago; the same for Star Wars. A key difference from how these and other religions based on fictional lore originate is that Lamplight is not part of a franchise.

Here, then, at the end of this inquiry, we meet examples of how terrapsychology has inspired ecospiritual wisdom paths as well as a fictional religion. Is this research? Yes, if by "research" we include the dimension of the sacred as mediated by story, imagination, and hope. In the end, the real difference is not between fiction and reality but between fiction and the falsehood of taking fiction – whether a myth, a truth, or a theory – as unerringly factual.

Of course, even in fiction we find important truths. Not factual ones, perhaps, although occasional facts serve the story, as when Cli Fi (Climate Fiction) weaves plot and character and event around the science of climate chaos. Fiction as a body of art and performance, image and imagining illuminates truths we live by, which is why one can often find more useful psychology in Shakespeare or Morrison than in a dry, literal-minded psychology text.

And when the elves whisper in the ears of Tolkien, the dragons speak to Ursula K. Le Guin, and mythic characters like Philemon and Salome address Jung's personal shortcomings from within his own fantasies and dreams, how long can we maintain that fiction is just what we make up? Does not the imaginal, for time out of mind a bridge of symbols linking us to ourselves and to the world and everyone in it, possess its own alluring sparkle of reality?

References

Chalquist, C. (2023). What is a loreologist? Chalquist.com. https://www.chalquist.com/post/what-is-a-loreologist

Chalquist, C., & Barnwell, G. (Eds.) (2023). *Terrapsychology: Further inquiry into self, place, and planet.* London & New York: Routledge.

Jung, C. (1981). *The archetypes and the collective unconscious.* CW Vol. 9, part 1. Princeton: Princeton University Press.

Rogers, C. (1995). *On becoming a person: A therapist's view of psychotherapy.* New York: HarperOne.

GLOSSARY

applied folklore Exploring how plots, images, or themes from myth, folktale, fairy tale, or legend recur in a contemporary event and thereby illuminate some aspect of our relations with nature or matter. Formerly known as archetypal mythology and formerly confined to myths.

archetype For terrapsychology, a basic, universal theme or pattern found in both the natural world and in human affairs. Such a pattern shows up as an existential quality: Life, Death, Resurrection, Great Mother, Earthrise, etc.

dialogical alchemy Interaction with objects or natural elements as aspects of our own psychology – and ours of theirs.

ecological complex Thematic knots or junctures where human and ecological wounding combine. Example: inner splitting in several areas of one's life while living near an international border built to sever families and keep immigrants out. Trauma to nature tends to show up psychologically in our own nature.

ecological transference (ecotransference) The process by which an activated aspect of the world triggers us emotionally and even physically. Example: a sudden leveling of emotion corresponding unconsciously with a fertile meadow paved over into a parking lot. Another example: a surge of creative writing while sitting next to a healthily flowing stream. The connection need not be conscious. Ecotransference is an experiential aspect of *intersubjective animism* (defined below).

ecopsychology The study of how human psychological health depends on ecological health.

ecoreactivity The strength with which an aspect of the world triggers us. Example: some places are more ecoreactive than others and therefore more apt to foster a stronger *ecological transference*.

ecotherapy An application of ecopsychology in which various practices consciously reconnect us with the natural world for the healing of both. "Ecotherapy" performed without giving something back to the natural source of healing is nature exploitation.

enchantivism The many ways we make lasting change by telling reenchanting stories about our relations with ourselves, each other, or our ailing but still-beautiful planet; sharing our reflections and inviting others' reflections on the relevance of these stories; and then letting the stories impel creative and thoughtful responses to how things are. The stories can be narratives, displays of imagery, humor, and even dance and ritual.

eradigm A large-scale and perhaps planet-wide worldview that holds an archetypal theme at its core and shapes human experience. The Big Machine eradigm, for example, which coincides with the rise of industrialism and science, sees reality as a vast mechanism stocked with parts that can be isolated for study. By contrast, the Earthrise eradigm emphasizes global concerns and participatory and ecological networks.

heartsteading Setting up a small research group designed for mutual support, collaborative problem-solving, and reflective listening and dialog. Heartsteads can be set up anywhere. They might also be used for reclaiming community strengths, decolonization, storytelling, preservation of crafts and skills ("reskilling"), and self-education. Heartsteads can serve as ecoresilient hubs of healing, resource-gathering, mourning, remembrance, cultural creation, and problem-solving for communities devastated by political, financial, or ecological disaster.

hermeneutic Interpretive, as when a text, event, or dream symbol is explored for meanings beyond what is apparent on the surface. In research, also known as "theoretical." TI can be used for hermeneutic/theoretical work without recourse to fieldwork or interviews if required by the primary focus of the study and its research question.

intersubjective animism (interanimism) The palpable if ultimately mysterious resonance linking "external" objects, elements, and events with "internal" states. Interanimism is a name for how the world gets into us intimately, and how what we normally take to be personal feelings or moods or dreams etc. reflect our environment. "Intersubjective" because we imagine this conversation as unfolding between subjectivities rather than a human subjectivity encountering inanimate things.

locianalysis Studying the stories and ecological complexes gathering upon a specific site. Terrapsychology started out as locianalysis, the study of place presence alive within human personal and cultural life.

lorecasting Fanciful interpretation of the meaning of natural events like epidemics, floods, and earthquakes as though they were gestures or messages. Examples: jellyfish clogging ocean-warming power-plant intakes and tornados on World Environment Day as terrestrial protests of human destructiveness.

personification The psyche's propensity for representing nonhuman realities and presences as characters, e.g., a city, river, or mountain appearing in a dream as a person.

placefield The psychological terrain of a locianalytic study. The terrapsychological counterpart to the interactive field between analyst and analysand (or therapist and client) or between group members.

placefield motifs The recurring themes shared by people and places alike. These motifs are to a place what character patterns and long-standing structures are to a human personality. In Escondido, California, for example, a place once called the Devil's Corner and sold in the 1800s as a rancho for $666.66, the motifs of *hiddenness* and *visibility* alternate across the decades and throughout the city in many different manifestations. A motif like visibility takes on fresh meaning through ongoing incidents of conjunctivitis, missing glasses, and broken mirrors as experienced by the researcher (*see* ecological transference).

placehosting Concluding the inquiry by giving something meaningful back to the research site and its presences and inhabitants. The inquiry initiates a careful, multileveled, and transdisciplinary tending of the ignored or silenced "voice" of place to foster an ecological empathy between us and our surroundings. Placehosting deepens the encounter by shifting from analysis into an imaginative, open-hearted, and creative-communal mode of personal response brought back to the locale and the community.

psychocartography Charting myths and archetypes inhabiting particular places.

sensitized innocence A state of heightened consciousness that moves back and forth between what one knows of the topic and a freshness of mind and body able to receive whatever plays across one's senses, moods, thoughts, associations, and dreams.

terragnosis Taken together, reverent practices that appreciate the spiritual of aspects of the natural world. A kind of ecospirituality that emphasizes nature's intelligence and presence as they show up in our "interior" life.

terrapsychology A growing field of studies, ideas, and practices for reimagining and restorying how deeply and intimately our psychological life is involved with our surroundings, whether human or other than human. More informally, tending how the world gets into the heart and how the heart reflects the world. Terrapsychological Inquiry is the field's research approach. Earthdreaming is terrapsychology's experiential side.

terrestry Ancestry studies that take the presence of place into account while searching for the metaphors alive in one's lineage. Example: detecting a pattern of fire-setting across generations of a family now living in Hawaii, home of the fire goddess Pele.

thematic analysis Sifting research data to find themes in accord with a clearly stated rationale. Themes are recurrent and highly symbolic patterns of experience that link inner and outer, psychological and ecological, literal and symbolic, and manifest and latent.

transmutative exposition ("expo") The response narrative that caps a Terrapsychological Inquiry. The exposition should include the study's background, methodology, methods, delimitations, researcher positionality, and findings and may take the form of a master's thesis, dissertation, or other creation.

APPENDIX I

Common Research Obstacles

Here are some common traps encountered while conducting research:

- Hoarding too much data; also known as *separatio* anxiety. More data do not prove your points; quality data do. Keep what is relevant and dump the rest.
- Sample size envy. If you're interviewing more than three people, have a rationale for why. Go deep, not necessarily broad. More rigorous than thou (obsessive-compulsive). If you allow yourself to get caught up in worries about being accurate or rigorous enough, you'll never finish the study. Find ways to lighten up.
- An unfocused research question. If the question is too vague or broad, the study will be. Work with your research colleagues, allies, or committee to concentrate the question into what really engages you about the work ahead.
- Preoccupation with generalizability. Remember the truth of novels and films: the more specific and narrow the focus, the more vivid the results – and the greater the resonance with audiences everywhere.
- Lack of self-care. Working with more-than-human forces and elements can place an enormous emotional burden on the researcher. Never work alone. Seek out supporters who understand the burden.
- Fixation on method. Remember, it's not about the type or number of methods/methodologies, it's how thoughtfully you apply what you use.
- Ignoring what's disconfirming. If what you find is contrary to what you expect, change your expectations and welcome in the new data.

- Reification. Beware of the psychological habit of turning living, flowing processes into things: motivation, identity, self-esteem, anima, archetype, and other supposed objects or nouns.
- Literalization. A method or methodology that forgets to be a flexible system of symbols and metaphors tends to degenerate into a power ideology.
- Failing to distinguish patterns that matter from those that don't. "Everything is connected," but so what? Hone your research question to focus on connections that matter and are supported by the data.
- Too confessional/cathartic. The topic is not about you. It's about itself.

APPENDIX II

Place Assessment Checklist

> I've spent a life trying to get better at understanding the place I live in. Yet no matter how far I go out in that direction, in the end I'm steered back to the center of human community with a different perspective, perhaps some foolishness hopefully mixed with a drop of wisdom. Stories about places have been told as long as we can remember because they embody an ethic that respects the full range of nature.
>
> *(Cochran, personal communication, November 7, 2018)*

Initial Aim

- To get a sense of the place's living character or soul, a sentience beyond its elements, for locianalytic work.
- To decipher the combination of stories and local images illuminating the place as a nonhuman person. We learn to see a place's features symbolically.

Areas of Focus as Aspects of a Place's Inner Self

- Bioregion (watershed)
- Geology
- Climate
- Ecology (strengths, weaknesses, diversity of life)
- Water (sources, flow, quality, quantity)
- Plants (native, invasive, crops)
- Animals (same)
- Soils: tilth, structure, and texture

Infrastructure

- Key industries and their impact on the environment, water utilities, energy, sewage management, and garbage disposal, traffic patterns, transportation pathways (the place's arteries), age and type of local architecture (its skeleton), preferred structures for power/information/entertainment transmission (its nerves), federal presence, military.
- Cultural/communal component from the place's founding to the present: original people, colonizers, ethnic groups, social justice issues, art and culture, political climate, population demographics, crime, fashion trends, typical community events, local folklore and legends, public figures, stories about the place's founding.

Ecotransference Manifestations

- Dreams: incubated, series
- Persistent fantasies and associations
- Moods: shifts, swings, persistent
- Body states
- Changes in relationships
- Personal complexes resonating to ecological complexes
- Ecological complexes: syndromes of repeating motifs, images, historical reenactments, symbolic wounds: the "neurosis" of a place. What is needed for these symptoms and syndromes to soften back into stories? What is the deep true character of this place, the presence that makes it unique?

Tools

- Sophisticated innocence: vigilant openness to what moves around and within.
- Bioregional maps expanded to include local myths, moods, and dreams ("psychocartography").
- Journal for recording observations, outstanding features, moods, dreams, etc.
- Photography/video.
- Dialogical Alchemy: listening in on objects and matter for images they reveal.
- Research allies or committee to monitor inquiry from outside the field.
- Symbolic sensitivity ("Deepening" or "Terrapsychologizing"):
- Mythological comparisons: "Who (archetypally) is here?"
- Interpretations/amplifications (ongoing).
- Search and sift for recurring patterns that fill in the place's character.
- Ecotransference analysis to see how the place gets into one's psyche.

Outcomes

- A holistic picture of a place as a totality exceeding the sum of its aspects.
- A multidimensional understanding of how that totality reaches into its inhabitants.
- A new awareness of how the "language" of place permeates descriptions of it.
- A deep transformation of relationship: from place-as-object to place-as-person.
- Freedom from unconscious ecohistorical reenactments of the place's complexes.
- A capacity for tuning in to the "inside story" of what a place was, is, and needs.
- A wiser basis for action on behalf of those needs, matching deeds to local style.
- A new sense of responsibility, protectiveness, and care for what happens there.
- A new sense of belonging, relatedness, and friendship with the animate world.

APPENDIX III

Creating Heartsteads

In 2007, the book *Terrapsychology* introduced the word "heartsteading" to mean "dwelling deeply in places through knowledge and love that strengthen over time in continual interactions between the human and the nonhuman" (Chalquist, 2007, p. 52). Doing so would require reweaving the sacred fabric of place, spirit, society, self, and heart, preferably with help from wise elders and guiding mentors capable of opening awareness through dialog. In the case of research, the elders show up as a thesis or dissertation committee or research advisers guiding the inquiry.

A *heartstead* is a small group designed for dreaming up practices of reenchantment – with ourselves, each other, place, nature, Earth – and its implementation. It begins in communion, dedication, imagination, and dream. It can be used for mutual support, collaborative problem-solving, resource-gathering, reflective listening and dialog, reclaiming of interpersonal strengths, deep storytelling, practical research, recovery from mainstream attitudes that do not serve, preservation and relearning of traditional crafts and skills, and ongoing education of self and group. Heartsteads can be ad-hoc or long-lasting, with inquiry participants carrying forward the work.

Why the "heart" in heartsteading? Psychologically understood, the heart is an imaginal core, a seat of affects that involve us in the world's doings. The heart's wisdom partakes of an embodiment and solidity that brain alone cannot aspire to. Heart knowledge is holistic, centered, and inclusive of head knowledge. To know from the heart is to know fully; to speak from the heart is to be sincere and open. To reflect and act from the heart issues a developmental challenge to soul-disconnecting economics, politics, cults, and sciences that would dominate life rather than grow up enough to participate in it.

Unlike the homestead, the heartstead can be set up anywhere to form a circle of people visioning together in inquiries that imagine and take steps toward just, sustainable, and abundant forms of community. The mood of participants can move back and forth between lighthearted fun and serious work.

Setting Up Your Heartstead

As a first step, start a list with the title, "I want to set up a heartstead because" and describe the topic, goals, and methods of your inquiry. Be as specific as you can.

Take the idea of your list to bed for a few nights and ask your unconscious mind (which is tuned into the mind of place, nature, and Earth) for dreams about it. Write down whatever images visit you; if you like art, find colorful ways to collage or craft them.

Start discussing your ideas with carefully selected research participants you're thinking about including in your heartstead.

Announce your intention to hold meetings and determine what frequency and length would be comfortable. Talk about where and when. Decide on whether you will facilitate the first meeting, alone or with someone else, and whether the facilitator will be a rotating role. Conform to the standard guidelines for confidentiality in research.

Holding the First Meeting

Secure a suitably quiet conversation-stimulating location for a first meeting, a place where you will not be interrupted. Consider serving water, coffee, or tea and making the event a potluck. You might also want to bring people in remotely; if so, remember to set up electronic access (test it) and to include sufficient lighting.

Invite the people you've spoken with and send them an agenda. Keep it modest: introduce yourself, speak a bit about the inquiry's goals and methods, and agree on conversational guidelines. Request that upon entering the meeting space, all cellphones are turned off. Include a time limit; at least an hour and a half is recommended for the initial meeting. If it feels appropriate, suggest that attendees also bring natural objects that encourage reflection, conversation, and imagination: "Bring something that enchants you."

Send around a reminder a few days before the meeting. Show your enthusiasm. Determine whether you will record the meeting; if you do, get written permission from all participants.

At the first meeting, start by setting up a group altar for whatever objects are brought. Experiment with low background music or nature sounds that aren't distracting. Eating and chatting before the formal start often breaks the ice.

Open the space by making a formulaic action – "Let's begin" or "We're in session"; ringing a chime; etc. – and invite participants to sit in silence for a moment to become fully present and embodied. Thank everyone for coming, hand out copies of the agenda, and begin.

Consider adding an icebreaker or other playful exercise. In fact, think about each meeting including an activity led by a different member each time. Adding objects to an altar, problem-solving, reading a poem, drawing together, collage work: the options for engagement are endless. Make sure they align with your research goals and data-gathering aims.

Ask group members to keep an eye out for a name, symbol, or image that arises from the group mind to name or mark the heartstead. Think of that as your imaginal logo or guiding spirit. (Sometimes in response to a dream request, the image or name appears outside, in the daytime world. That works too.)

At the end, once you have next steps to carry out between meetings, check in with everyone about how they feel it went. Thank them for helping the inquiry move forward. Make notes about how you feel the meeting went, what the next steps are, and what you'd like to experiment with. When you turn in on the day of the first meeting, ask for dreams in response to it.

Conversational Guidelines

It's important at the outset to agree on what constitutes meaningful and appropriate forms of exchange and what does not. Doing so creates a safe and nurturing space for participants, gets their agreement on its structuring, creates firm and reasonable boundaries, and promotes deep visionary work. Guidelines are best framed positively and clearly. You might wish to print them decoratively and post them for each meeting. Here is a sample:

- We agree to be fully present and on time for each meeting barring the occasional unforeseen delay.
- Digital devices will be off unless someone is on call.
- We agree to speak heartfully, honestly, and to the point.
- We agree to listen without interruption or speaking for other members.
- We agree to be courteous and respectful in speech and manner.
- We agree to own our feelings without blaming other people for them.
- We agree to be open to feedback from other heartstead members.
- We agree to keep private what's spoken in the group.
- We agree to carry out what we commit to.

Depending on the type of inquiry conducted, heartsteading usually requires emotional maturity and adequate communication skills. Facilitators should keep an eye out for the behavioral signs that someone might not be a good fit for the group: needing to be the center of attention, dominating conversations, frequent absenteeism or tardiness, a habit of making dogmatic assertions, withdrawing into sulky resentment, habitual defensiveness, frequent judgmentalism (including labeling or diagnosing others), hurtful sarcasm or bluntness, blaming and accusing when feeling threatened, frequently going off topic and thereby derailing the conversation. Reinforce helpful interactions in the group.

Additionally, facilitators should be involved in self-reflective practices (e.g., journaling, psychotherapy, dream analysis, meditation) and meet regularly with each other and with peers outside the group to receive ongoing feedback and support. By doing this, they also model how to replace isolated positions with open networks, rule-bound attitudes with flexible ideas, and conflictual interactions with clear relationships. If you facilitate the heartstead by yourself, check in regularly with your research allies.

Evolving Your Heartstead

After a few meetings, you'll have started to get used to each other, begun to deepen your group process. A guiding image or motif might have visited you as well and offered itself as an emblem of your heartstead. See whether any of the following suggestions fit your research goals, adapting whichever make sense to use:

- Do fun things!
- Meet somewhere you can decorate to be an enchanting ritual space.
- Meet outside on occasion as well so the natural world can participate in the conversation. Share stories about some nature encounter that changed you.
- To work collaboratively, try putting together a compelling question you all want answered, a cause you all embrace, or an occupation all of you wish to create. Try listening to dreams.
- Play with the idea that your group is a new form of culture. What sort of society do you wish it to be? What are its guiding norms, values, favorite activities, costumes, holidays?
- For task work, the following model can be useful: decide on the central task or goal, go off and each do homework on it to educate yourselves about it, meet to discuss and present what you found out, create next steps (what, who, and by when), assess how they worked, and continually pool and document your knowledge. Repeat this cycle of learning-reflecting-doing-assessing.
- For an occupational focus, problem-solving activities might include these: role-model difficult work situations; receive feedback on a resume; ask for assistance with networking; practice giving a presentation; inquire

into what makes a good leader; create an outreach campaign for skill sets within your group; discuss what sort of work would give group members joy and a sense of purpose.

- Like families, groups that meet over time coagulate not only a group mind but also a set of archetypal roles within it, with one member a Dreamer holding most of the dreams, one a Thinker or Scientist, one a Feeler, one a Bottom-Liner, an Archivist who holds group memory, a Trickster who shakes things up, etc. Spend some time getting clear on the roles in your group, and feel free to play with them humorously, even inviting members to switch on occasion and see what happens.
- Try a "becoming familiar with this place" meeting or two by learning about the location's history, climate, weather patterns, flora, fauna, energy sources, ecological weaknesses and strengths, native lore, Indigenous culture, geology, and geography. (See Appendix II.)
- Do dream work together. Night dreams bring some dreamers rich imagery and detail from our elemental psychic connection to lands, animals, places, and elements. Such dreams may be spoken aloud in small groups, reflected on carefully for what they say about our relationship to the world, and knitted together (by one member acting as Recorder) into one extended episode of social dreaming. In this way, members can see how the group unconscious perceives things.
- Sometimes you might want a meeting to focus on emotional support. Members who need to can tell their medicine story: anecdotes that highlight aspects of our history, actions, thoughts, or feelings silenced or disallowed by dominant or official stories. The Heartstead Medicine Story brings up traumas living at the intersection of I, We, Past, Present, Future, and Here: having watched as a child while a favorite meadow was paved over; worries about one's own children living in a crime-ridden neighborhood; nightmares about mass extinction; being laid off work ... The idea is not to get stuck in a self-defeating victim role but to have one's sufferings witnessed and held by an understanding, supportive, and caring group. Medicine stories are received with respect and empathy, not with suggestions (unless asked for) about fixes or solutions. For a finish, include the Future dimension of how you wish the story to end.
- Plan celebrations together to mark important achievements and rites of passage.
- Recruit diverse members. Diversity powers the abundance of the natural world: the more of it, the more resilience and the richer the interactions between living beings and between them and their surroundings. Consciously reach out to people of different abilities and backgrounds. Diverse participants will also help your heartstead avoid falling into insulated groupthink.

The heartstead can provide a container of inquiry, temporary or ongoing, in which dualisms that split people from place, nature, and each other can be melted down into new recipes for just, sustainable, and self-replicating culture, brewed by mixing the wisdom of group participants with the wisdom of the deep psyche as it connects with that of the Earth.

This wisdom is to be pooled and passed on through multiple channels. Another way of saying this is that heartsteads should be designed to encourage groups of humans to imagine and grow into an ethical responsible relationship to each other and the natural world as a basis for an authentically evolved civilization.

Reference

Chalquist, C. (2007). *Terrapsychology: Reengaging the soul of place.* New Orleans, LA: Spring Journal Books.

APPENDIX IV

Exploring Deep Ancestry

The word "family" started out with a much wider meaning than that of housing parents and children under one roof (for which the Romans used the word *domus*). The Roman *famulus* also included everyone who served the household. Throughout history, the psychology of family has included extended kin, trusted members of an estate, close neighbors, nearby villagers, and ancestors.

Our immediate families are living emotional systems linking family members across time. From a terrapsychological standpoint, our appreciation of family dynamics serves self-understanding on the one hand and our fit in larger systems – cultural, national, and, ultimately, planetary – on the other. Another way of saying this is how Linda Buzzell explains it: the family system is a smaller version of an ecosystem (Buzzell, personal communication, 2007). Family psychology shades over into cultural psychology and into ecopsychology and terrapsychology.

The Family System

Back in the 1950s, social workers and psychotherapists noticed something peculiar. Addicts who were their clients progressed steadily in therapy and recovery, but when they returned to their families of origin, they began to drink and use again. Furthermore, when the therapists interviewed the families, they saw unconscious enabling behaviors subtly encouraging the addicts to go on being addicts. Yet family members honestly wanted their addicted loved ones to recover. What was going on?

Some of these therapists got the idea of shifting their view from inside people and their unconscious motivations to inside the family as a psychological organism. This group psyche feared being destabilized by rapid change. For decades it had patterned its interactions around the symptom, encapsulating it much as a tree grew cambium around a permanent wound. Furthermore, the sick family member unknowingly acted as a lightning rod for stresses found elsewhere in the family, stresses it lacked tools for tackling. To preserve itself, the family unconsciously pushed back against recovery, and the addict relapsed.

This taught therapists to see the family as a whole, recognizing that a problem in one person actually signaled a family problem. Thereby was born Family Systems therapy, which since the mid-1950s has evolved into several major branches in many countries. Family Systems helps counterbalance Western psychology's modernist/capitalist belief in separate, self-contained individuals.

Unlike a heap of rocks, a true *system* self-organizes, uses feedback to learn, and exhibits emergent properties: novel actions that emanate from the organism as a whole. The actions are often nonlinear, meaning that relatively small influences can lead to disproportionately large outcomes, as when a breeze here and warm current there combine with other local influences to produce a storm front not predicted by analyses seeking straight-line causes and effects. In systems-theory terms, such analyses are too simplistic to deal with complex organisms.

When we look at the family as a complex system, important features come into view. Families that embrace change and new experience flourish; those that remain isolated wither. Overt rules of family communication lead to clear expectations; covert rules – the kind nobody is allowed to comment on – spread secrecy and power struggles and silent legacies of intergenerational shame and wounding. Intrusive enmeshed relations between parents and children bring up dependent, needy children, but clear boundaries foster self-esteem and independence. Sick families scapegoat; healthy ones support ailing family members while reorganizing how they relate to one another in order to make the symptoms unnecessary. Family members in fragile emotional coalitions triangle in others, whether to blame them for the conflict or to elicit emotional rescuing, or both; healthy family members openly and respectfully discuss conflictual interactions and resolve them.

The hardest time for families is usually when vertical stressors like unresolved wounding from the past or from previous generations (unspoken wounding never goes away: it only goes underground for a time) collides with horizontal stressors toward which the family advances as it ages: births of children, children entering school, young adults leaving the nest, marriage, family members moving in or out, deaths of family members, job loss, and other changes wrought by time and circumstance. These constitute developmental challenges or rites of passages for the family as a whole.

Each stage of development brings an implicit question: *How can the family adapt itself to negotiate this rite of passage?* Families that don't leave their members feeling dismembered. Families that do gain comfort and strength even in hard times. All these dynamics provide fertile soil for growing a terrapsychological inquiry.

From a Family Systems perspective, a symptom represents a signal that something in how the family communicates with itself has gone awry. Repetitive interactions (arguments, stormings-out, pleas for sympathy, even illnesses) cluster around these sore spots like scratches around an itch. Scratching inflames it. But hunting for and trying on the message in the symptom, the metaphor in the problem, brings it into the open for the entire family to play with – as when a medically unnecessary crutch used by the IP (Identified Patient: the family scapegoat) is reframed as a metaphor by the therapist: "I want to hear how the rest of you limp. Where do you limp, Mom? Who supports you? What about you, Dad?"

As family therapist Virginia Satir observes, symptoms mean that someone's growth into maturity is being curtailed (Satir, Banmen, Gerber, & Gomori, 2006). They have surrendered some authenticity (usually unconsciously) to keep the family going, like the teen I saw in therapy who sabotaged her path to college because she feared that her angry parents would divorce. The overall task for the family at such a time is to create new kinds of safety, stability, and balance while allowing the symptom to go away. As long as it serves a purpose, it will remain.

Another way families deal with stress and change is by subliminally assigning roles to family members. These assignments come from the unconscious of the family as a whole. To some degree, we accept these roles even when they pinch; subtle reinforcement by the family encourages us to stay in them. More common family roles include the Hero or Savior, the superrational Computer who likes to solve problems, the Rebel or Outcast who often grows up to move far from the family, the Second Parent who is a child but gives orders to other children, the Go-Between who tries to get fighting parties to make up, the Trickster or Clown who stirs the pot and makes people laugh, the Bully who frightens with bouts of rage, and the Martyr who uses illness (real or fake) as a source of manipulative power.

These roles often overlap, especially in small families, and there are others. What passes for "sibling rivalry" is often a case of role collision, as when my birth mother (Rebel) waged a lifelong fight with her brother (Hero). This illustrates where roles become problematic: when they grow rigid. Family therapists will sometimes encourage family members to temporarily switch roles to experiment with flexibility and build empathy.

Some of us think we can depart the family forever. We remain distant and out of touch. The real question, psychologically, is whether the family has departed us. To a family therapist, the Outsider or Exile is often the most loyal family member. They bring a degree of novelty, separation, and experimentation into an otherwise frozen family system. For their kin they hold and express the need for independence and individuation. The cost, however, is often a steep and lingering one: a knee-jerk unwillingness to connect intimately in relationships for fear of being hemmed in and engulfed.

These dynamics do not confine themselves to the family. Entire nations have shored themselves up and ignored their own unaddressed fragilities by scapegoating groups of people. During a layoff at work many years ago, I watched the Rescuers go around the division comforting fearful coworkers while managers cowered in their offices waiting for the fatal phone call from Human Resources telling them to pack and leave. Old roles can be useful.

Notice that the roles described above sound rather like archetypes (Chapter 3). Roles have an archetypal root; Hero, Trickster, Rebel, and Parent are obvious examples. When the role fits one's personal archetype and the personal myth containing it, one grows up in a congruence of inner with familial. But when the role collides with the innermost self archetypally – when, for example, a born Trickster is expected to be a family Hero – then getting on with one's family could require a great deal of accumulated inauthenticity that will need working on later.

Such a collision does bring its blessings, however. I am not, by nature, the extraverted Hero my family encouraged me to become, but that particular family pressure prepared me for the kind of teaching and presenting I find most congenial. It was a matter of taking what had been put upon me and turning it into a tool that could satisfy my natural inclinations. (I also do well in emergencies.)

Tracing family roles in archetypes might develop a terrapsychology of archetypal Family Systems. Archetypally charged family roles can work as sites of tension for what we will consider next: intergenerational legacies.

Handed-Down Legacies

One of my graduate students well along in school admitted to having dropped out of college more than once just before graduating. Afraid she would do it again, she attributed this tendency to "self-sabotage," which didn't explain much. So I asked her some questions about her family. It turned out that her grandmother and other women in the family line had made similar choices, dropping educational and professional opportunities in order to look after ill family members, raise children, or parent abandoned younger siblings.

By exploring her mother line, this student realized that, emotionally, graduating would feel like betraying all those women who had given up their dreams to ensure the well-being of the family. That no such obligations burdened her life – no ill relatives, no siblings to raise – only showed the power of this kind of emotional legacy handed down unconsciously by those who came before.

What we feel as personal, then, can be intergenerational. Exploring, naming, and reflecting on it allows us to take up a present-day stand toward these complicated loyalties and legacies. My student did this, and she graduated. Her decision was to honor in less self-sacrificing ways the women in her family and what they had given up without suspecting the emotional debt their choices would leave behind to be accounted for.

In many families, we also see legacies of shame: for example, the Black ancestors my White birth family never spoke of. C. G. Jung wrote of the need to respond to the questions his ancestors left unanswered (Jung, 1989). For some of us, that includes facing injustices never made right.

In some cases – perhaps all? – a *family archetype* reaches down through the generations, bringing with it a family mythology, often unconscious but active and potent. My birth and adoptive families are historically packed with aggressive Rebels: discontented marines, misguided Confederate soldiers, Gauls who burned Rome to the ground, Vikings in dreadful longships … My forebears include the likes of Mary Tudor and Napoleon Bonaparte. They stand behind me whether I want them to or not. Their legacy of violence confronts me with questions: *How does one become a peaceful warrior? How do I take my place among them without reenacting their destructive aggression? How do I respond to the legacies of injustice they left?* There is no single answer to such questions, but one response for me has been to teach alternatives to empire thinking by highlighting the importance of Earth community.

When family emotional legacies remain invisible, they express themselves with disturbing concreteness, not only in coalitions, rivalries, vendettas, and repetitive arguments but in disputes about possessions: who gets the car, for example, or the house, or the money after the owner dies. Fights over wills and trusts reenact unaddressed splits that can reach back for generations. Family legacies also include the beneficial inheritance of stories: old loves and rivalries, who moved where and why, persistent strengths and talents, valuable life lessons learned at great cost. How important for our sense of roots and identity to collect and interpret as many of these stories as we can before they vanish forever?

Ancestral Relations to Place

When we go back far enough into our ancestry, we find groups of relations for whom no separation existed between consciousness and the surround. The notion of a purely internal psychological disturbance did not exist, which is why healers focused on restoring the conflicted person's relationship to the natural world and to place. It was not (as some have argued) that individuality had not been invented yet; rather, individuality was always seen in the context of other beings, whether human or otherwise.

Up until 2300 BCE, no real wars were fought, just tribe-level skirmishes mostly for territorial defense and for points of honor. All that changed when Sargon I became the first true emperor in world history. The Age of Empires that followed (and that we are still in) was set up much earlier, when monocrop agriculture led to permanent settlements defended by bands of armed settlers, but after Sargon, soldiers under officers fought on scales never before seen. The trauma inflicted by what was now increasingly total warfare destroyed entire communities and, in some cases, their ancestral lands as well and has rippled down the generations largely unseen.

Most of us march to the emotionally subliminal but persistent music of this trauma of warfare, displacement, slavery, or massacre; it shows up in symptoms, nightmares, and relationship troubles diagnosed as psychological when in fact it originated as psychosocial. An obvious example is narcissism, which serves as a kind of personal aristocracy. The traits of narcissism and those of uncaring nobility make a match.

What this means for us terrapsychologically is that our inaudible wounds invite us to explore how our ancestors lived in the places where they originated and relocated, then make the symbolic move of seeking parallels down the generations. Here are some examples:

- Migration: How does this show up as a theme acted out in my family history? In my own life? Now that I'm aware of this theme, how might I explore it and come to terms with it? Same questions for:
- Captivity and/or displacement;
- Otherworldly disparagement of the world (e.g., nature treated as a mere backdrop, a transitory way station);
- Deep love of some aspects of nature or place;
- Migration patterns (like the question mark described above in my own ancestral map);
- Topography: preference for living near seas, in valleys, on mountains, in deserts, etc.;
- Involvement with sacred sites, prompting the question: Which places are sacred to me now?
- Ancestry and metaphor

Some years back, when I had regained contact with my birth families and wanted to continue tracing my roots, I used two genetic testing services so I could compare results. I also consulted family members whose role was that of Family Archivist: they who keep informal but effective track of the history and genealogy. Most families have one.

Sometimes this history is hidden, especially for people whose ancestors were slaves or otherwise forcibly displaced. Genetic testing can help fill in gaps but brings concerns about privacy. However, I have often been impressed by how much a persistent investigator can unearth from mere traces. Alex Haley (2007) began his journey to know his roots with little more than a few garbled African words handed down by the women of his family. Dreams can also bring ancestral images when asked to.

Having received my test results, I held a map of the travels of my ancestors northward 40,000 years ago from Mother Africa, where we *Homo sapiens* all come from. The path they took inscribed upon the land a gigantic question mark. *Where do we go from here?* We can read persistent ancestral themes just as we can read the motifs of dreams and the archetypes and myths that haunt us and our families. We can read ancestry symbolically.

When I met my birth father, he asked me about the kinds of trouble I had gotten into as a boy. He nodded when I mentioned setting some lockers at my high school alight after being bullied there and fighting back: "It runs in the family." Not only had he burned or blown up his own path through childhood before becoming a marine, where they taught him to do it professionally, but we both came from like-minded ancestors who torched what they disagreed with, including ancient Rome. Fire is a family motif. It can ravage and destroy, but also warm, cleanse, and illuminate. The task is to treat it with care. Were I to write a motto for my birth father's side of my family, it would be the admonition *Hold Your Fire*. My adoptive father's family name includes a Swedish word for "twig" or "small branch": fuel for fire.

My birth mother's family name means "sea warrior": the water element throughout, with many sailors in the family. Coast people. Scottish Lowlanders: people of the depths. My adoptive mother's side were Germans mixed with Highlander Mackenzies; their names reflect the presence of Aphrodite, whose alluring glow ran like a thread through generations of struggle – often lost – with puritanical Christian prohibitions against delights of the flesh. Aphrodite, born in sea foam, shimmers with the water element. A task left to me by my fractious families, then, is to reunite water and fire on many levels of my life, thought, and work.

Ancestral themes we fail to read symbolically return to life as reenactments, as when we discover one day that our wanderings and exiles reflect those of our forebears – and that, as in Post-Traumatic Slave Syndrome (Degruy, 2017) in Black families, their sufferings are now ours to come to terms with. They represent unfinished stories we must learn from and learn how to creatively conclude. What is crucial is not to take them as entirely personal, as though therapy or self-help could put an end to the questions they raise. Their story, setting, and action are bigger than we are, even when they land in our lap asking for a personal sequel.

As you collect images from the near and distant family past, treat them like images to collage into the pattern of your life. What goes where? What relates to what? What fragments call for more attention? Which legacies are worth elaborating? Which seek an end? If you can, use what you know to construct a map of the travels of your ancestors. What shapes in the journey can you pick out? How did the various branches of your family relate to nature, place, and planet? Where will you go from here?

While you're at it, try your hand – or encourage research participants to try theirs – at an ancestral introduction of the kind people native to their place announce when they arrive somewhere new and announce themselves. Here is one of mine:

> Greetings!
>
> I was born in San Diego, ancestral home of the Kumeyaay tribe, in California, first spotted by European explorers on July 6th, my birthday. California was named by colonizers who had read about Queen Calafia, a powerful fictional character in Garci Rodríguez de Montalvo's novel *The Exploits of Esplandian*. I am one small figure in California's ongoing dreaming, a dreaming that is part of Earth's.
>
> My name is Craig Steven Chalquist. "Craig" means "outcropping of stone" and, in Scotland, often denotes a fortress. "Steven" means "crowned." "Chalquist" is Americanized Swedish for "Kallqvist," which means a cold twig, stick, or small branch. That side of the family farmed and gardened and was not a terribly expressive bunch except for their tempers.
>
> I went to college near Rancho Camulos, and my school "Kingsman" colors were royal purple and gold. Lightning-wrapped dragons chased me in childhood nightmares. Removed from one family at birth and raised by another, advised by a wise male teacher who really saw who I was (what a blessing), I was finally reunited with my birth father, who had given me names that mean "lake" and "battle to the death" before I was taken away from him.
>
> My adoptive family goes back through Kallqvists and Highlander Mackenzies and Kleinkaufs into Sweden, Scotland, and Germany. My birth families hie from Pylands and Trowbridges and Murdochs and Leggs: Celtic on the one side (Wales, Ireland, France, Spain, Italy, England, and especially Scotland) and Germanic on the other (Germany, Sweden, Norway, Switzerland). These two foundational wings of my ancestry, each so heavy with military presence, first combined during the Saxon invasion of England, or Angleland as it was known then, a cross-fertilization around the time of mythical Camelot. The theme of opposites that must be reconciled runs like a silver thread throughout my life.
>
> My ancestors include James Pyland of the Virginia Colony, who was kicked out of the House of Burgesses for disagreeing with the majority; the Pillings who came to Yorkshire with the storming Normans; Mary, Queen of Scots; and Clan Murdoch of Galloway, whose bow-wielding soldiers

helped Robert the Bruce liberate Scotland from English colonizers. The Murdoch crest displays sharpened arrows and declares, "Under Favorable Auspices." The Pyland motto reads, "By Virtue and Strength."

My Welsh and Pictish foremothers and forefathers held out against the long night of the Roman Empire, and my Gaulic foremothers and forefathers burned down Rome. My Viking ancestors swarmed from longships to loot monasteries in revenge for what the missionaries did to Scandinavia. "Liberty" is a sacred word in my vocabulary. It comes from *liber*, or "free," which derives from the word "beloved."

Looking still farther back, I nod to the prehistoric artists who painted the magic images in the caves at Lascaux. DNA testing confirms that I am their direct descendant.

My African ancestors trekked out of eastern Africa 40,000 years ago. Their travel route over the world traces an enormous question mark. They too were part of Earth's dreamings.

I know my ancestry. I remember the gods and stories of my ancestors, I know my myth, and I know my place. I know these things because I have recovered what was taken from me when I was declared dead at birth, my roots and history shut away until I grew old enough to break open all the locks.

This is who I am. All ancestry is ultimately metaphor awaiting new life, new realization, in the calling we come in with.

Who are you?

Cultural Complexes

> One of the problems of Jungian psychology, at least until recently, was its propensity to move from analysis of individuals to analysis of archetypes at play in the world without developing its own perspective on the missing layer of culture. All the early depth psychologists had something to say about one's culture of origin, but they tended to reductively oversimplify, as though American or Japanese or Indian social forces could be understood in terms of breastfeeding customs, toilet training, or the archetypal Mother or Father. Clearly, this left much to be desired.

In 1937, psychoanalyst Karen Horney gave some examples of the cultural influence on neurotic drives in her book *The Neurotic Personality of Our Time*.

> When we have recognized that neurotic persons in our culture are impelled by the same underlying conflicts, and that in a diminished degree the normal person is also subject to them, we are confronted again with the question that was raised at the beginning: what are the conditions in

> our culture which are responsible for the fact that neuroses center around these particular conflicts I have described, and not others?
>
> *(Horney, 1994, p. 282)*

Instead of reducing collective psychology to personal, she pushed her thesis in the other direction by observing that syndromes of distress in individuals could receive reinforcement by patterns of cultural pathology. An obvious American example is the Narcissistic Personality Disorder, reinforced on every side by a culture that glorifies fame, publicity, and "winning."

Going even farther, psychoanalyst Erich Fromm (1990) asked: Is it possible for an entire society to be insane? If an individual were lost in consumerism, plagued by constant wars, and dedicated to love of death rather than a thwarted love of life, as much of the industrialized West now is, would we not diagnose a serious problem? Fromm (1990, p. 79) described what he called the *social character*: that aspect of personality which reflects collective psychology. "I love to shop" may be felt as a personal desire, but Fromm saw it as an aspect of the social character – the psychic agent of society – deposited in individuals by self-perpetuating market and industrial forces intent on expansion. Fromm called for self-examination of the social character combined with full development of our consciousness-rooted human powers of loving, working, and being as a psychological adult.

Filling a gap in Jungian psychology, Thomas Singer and Samuel Kimbles (2004) edited the anthology *Cultural Complexes* to reintroduce an idea coined by Joseph Henderson to delineate a new area of study: that of complexes alive in groups, in what Henderson referred to as the cultural unconscious. A complex is an emotionally charged group of ideas and images clustering around an archetypal core. Similar to what others refer to as a neurosis, it exerts a compulsive pull on mood, behavior, and lifestyle until made conscious and worked with. Think of it as an unhealed wound.

Cultures have unhealed wounds too. The individuals sharing the ideas and images connected to these wounds are not conscious of being wounded. So they act out. In the resulting emotional reactivity, repetitive and often self-destructive attitudes and actions, rigidly self-validating points of view, oversimplification of complicated issues, resistance to change, and flagrant self-righteousness, we see the signs of a cultural complex in full operation.

Ordinarily, the cultural complex remains mild. Who has not heard jokes about Japanese exclusivity, French snobbery, Canadian passivity, German fussiness, Italian passion, British cynicism, Chinese stoicism, American innocence, and Filipino fatalism? But when stress and trauma build, especially when political, the cultural complex rigidifies, as any system of defense does when subject to strain.

Looking critically at my own culture, we might discern a Hero/Victim complex simmering in the American psyche. When tensions rise, we pick leaders who try to police (conquer) the world as though it were the Wild West in need of taming. When those whom we would subjugate fight back, we turn into loudly complaining victims in search of retaliation: at the national level, usually through lawsuits, trade wars, or military assault rationalized as self-defense. Our infamous youthfulness, loudness, recklessness, brutality, us-vs-them splitting, craving to consume, and grandiose entitlement are all folkloric markers of the immature Hero in need of initiation into adulthood. Otherwise the Hero always brings the Monster, and sometimes is one. The last thing we need, then, is still more glorification of Heroism. Rather, it would help us to send the Hero home and post-heroically grow up to rejoin the world community as responsible members of it instead of clinging to the poise of the lone gunman sauntering into town just long enough to shoot up the saloon, grab the cash, bed the landlady, and ride on to the next misadventure.

Analysis of cultural neuroses or complexes gives us an extra dimension for self-exploration. What unhealthy societal trends live in my psyche? And that of my family? What strengths accompany them? Which to keep, and which to outgrow? Getting to know people from outside one's culture of origin, studying critical accounts of its history, and traveling to other lands increase the ability to stand back somewhat and self-assess through the perspectives of people who grew up differently.

Liberation Psychology

Before his execution in El Salvador in 1989, psychologist Ignacio Martín-Baró conducted research on the psychological impact of oppression. After his death, his papers reappeared in the book *Toward a Liberation Psychology* (1996) – and launched a new field.

Psychology, he observed, had bought into and spread the industrial-competitive ideology of a lone ego subject to fixed developmental stages culminating in separation from one's family and community. The search for universal traits of personality echoed the standardization and uniformity of oppressive colonization regimes like culturally blind IQ tests and involuntary boarding schools. What would psychology be like if it prized Indigenous ways of being, local dialog, personal reflection, authentic community, and social justice? What if it conducted research with people instead of on them?

At its core, liberation psychology pairs *individuation* with cultural and political *emancipation* within the ignored but important interdependency of psyche, culture, and nature (Martín-Baró, 1996). To appreciate this complex web requires appreciating the evolving diversity of views, values, and lifestyles that help weave it. Especially those rejected by elites in control of mainstream cultural life.

Being of service to people cast aside or left behind by the dominant culture means *accompanying* them: not rescuing, diagnosing, or otherwise "helping," but witnessing and walking with them as they struggle to come forward and survive (Watkins, 2019). Depth psychology welcomes the internally exiled aspects of self back into conversation; liberation psychology hears the voices of the outwardly exiled as well. Terrapsychology links these dynamics to where they unfold and with which aspects of the natural world they involve.

Clearly, this requires challenging dominant power hierarchies, especially when they enable censorship, hunger, poverty, and repression. Responses of challenge include becoming conscious of normative cultural privileges (being White means being arrested less often; being male means earning more money on average; being heterosexual means hugging and kissing in public without fear of assault), prizing local culture and language, highlighting and opposing ecological and other systemic forms of injustice, creating safe spaces for honest dialog and inner decolonization, and welcoming emancipatory-themed images, art, literature, music, dance, storytelling, and ritual that reveal alternative possibilities of living.

Instead of exalting the solitary rational ego, liberation psychology envisions subjectivities in community. Because forms of inner oppression, including defense, forced forgetting, projection, denial, splitting, sadistic inner critics, shadow, and narcissistic entitlement, echo and perhaps even originate in forms of outer oppression that characterize colonial domination, liberation psychology treats these "inner" conflicts as oppressive internalizations in need of deconstruction and working through. The goal is personal and cultural regeneration as new liberatory and creative possibilities are tried out.

The resulting consciousness is characterized by flexible ego boundaries, delight in multiple perspectives, openness to voices from the margins of culture and consciousness, attention to dream, image, thought, feeling, intuition, and sensation, critical awareness of the shadows of mainstream ideologies and monological perspectives, comfort with dialogical forms of discourse, and eagerness to visualize "utopic" (terrapsychology would say: "terranian") forms of community.

To prize those culture-of-origin norms, customs, and values we resonate with while subjecting the rest to critical scrutiny, standing back from them to assess which to discard and which to keep: that remains a key task of becoming more conscious as a local member of a global family, a task Terrapsychological Inquiry can accompany.

References

Degruy, J. (2017). *Post-traumatic slave syndrome: America's legacy of enduring injury and healing*. Portland, OR: Joy DeGruy Publications.

Fromm, E. (1990). *The sane society*. New York, NY: Holt.

Haley, A. (2007). *Roots: The saga of an American family*. New York, NY: Vanguard Press.

Horney, K. (1994). *The neurotic personality of our time*. New York, NY: W. W. Norton.

Jung, C. (1989). *Memories, dreams, reflections*. Edited by A. Jaffe. New York, NY: Vintage.

Martín-Baró, I. (1996). *Writings for a liberation psychology*. Cambridge, MA: Harvard University Press.

Satir, V., Banmen, J., Gerber, J., & Gomori, M. (2006). *Satir model: Family therapy and beyond*. Mountain View, CA: Science and Behavior Books.

Singer, T., & Kimbles, S. (Eds.) (2004). *The cultural complex: Contemporary Jungian perspectives on psyche and society*. London and New York, NY: Routledge.

Watkins, M. (2019). *Mutual accompaniment and the creation of the commons*. New Haven, CT: Yale University Press.

INDEX

Note: *Italic* page numbers refer to figures.

Made in the USA
Monee, IL
13 September 2026

62980180R00118